THE U.S. NAVY
SEALS

THE U.S. NAVY SEALS

SEA, AIR, AND LAND SPECIALISTS

DAVID JORDAN
FOREWORD BY DICK COUCH, EX-SEAL TEAM ONE

THUNDER BAY
P·R·E·S·S

San Diego, California

Thunder Bay Press

An imprint of the Advantage Publishers Group

5880 Oberlin Drive, San Diego, CA 92121–4794

www.thunderbaybooks.com

Editorial and design by
Amber Books Ltd
Bradley's Close
74–77 White Lion Street
London N1 9PF
United Kingdom
www.amberbooks.co.uk.

ISBN 1-59223-060-1

Library of Congress Cataloging-in-Publication Data available upon request.

1 2 3 4 5 07 06 05 04 03

Project Editor: Charles Catton
Design: Brian Rust
Picture Research: Natasha Jones

The views expressed in this book are those of the author alone, and should not be regarded as representing the views of the Joint Services Command and Staff College (U.K.) or those of the British Ministry of Defence.

Printed and bound in Italy

Contents

FOREWORD

It is never easy to write about a closed culture like the U.S. Navy SEALs. They are a parochial organization and theirs is a very private world. Much of what they do is classified. But in their short history, barely 60 years since the first Navy frogmen of World War II and 40 years since the formation of the first designated SEAL teams, they have compiled a rich battle history. With the end of superpower confrontation and the advent of terrorism, the SEALs have emerged as one of the premier special operations units in the United States military.

Some things have not changed since the early days. When the U.S. Navy formalized their training for Navy frogmen in the mid-1940s, they took a page from the training of British commandos—begin with a brutal and punishing physical regime. Those who survive can be trained to do some very dangerous and difficult things. This "train the best, discard the rest" philosophy exists today in modern SEAL training. But what took a matter of months in the early days now takes years. Navy SEALs are the best-trained special operations force in the world. With respect to the British Special Air Service and Special Boat Service, they are a maritime force without peer.

Under the best of conditions, it takes between two-and-a-half to three years to train a Navy SEAL. Only about one-in-five young men screened for this training will become a Navy SEAL and operationally qualified for overseas deployment. At this point in his career, a young SEAL is considered an apprentice warrior and affectionately known as a "new guy" in the teams. After his first deployment, he is a "one-tour wonder," now a journeyman in the trade. They are a mature force. The average age of an operational SEAL platoon is 28 years old. Those of us who served in the SEAL teams during Vietnam marvel at the talent, training and capabilities of modern-day SEALs. These men are indeed a breed apart.

David Jordan has written an excellent book—factual, straightforward and balanced. It is an unbiased account of these warriors from their formative days through their evolution into one of the premier direct-action forces in the world. Mr. Jordan also captures the individual stories and combat actions of several noted SEALs, and does so with equanimity and impartiality. Perhaps it is not unusual for someone outside the community to document the history of these talented warriors and their distinctive culture. I'm afraid those of us who were in the teams have clouded judgement; we see things through the prism of our own operational experience and measure the history of the SEALs from the narrow perspective of a particular era. This work is a must for any library on military special operations.

Nicely done, Mr. Jordan.

Dick Couch
Ex-SEAL Team One

CHAPTER ONE

THE EARLY YEARS

The U.S. Navy SEALs were born in the cauldron of the Pacific War, when the Underwater Demolition Teams were formed to help the Marines land on hostile shores with the minimum of casualties.

Left: U.S. Marines storm ashore to reconquer one of the Pacific islands. The UDTs were formed to reduce the high Marine casualty rate.

Right: On December 7, 1941 the Japanese launched a devastating attack on the U.S. Navy base at Pearl Harbor. Navy divers involved in the rescue and recovery operations at Pearl helped to form the basis for the first U.S. Navy Special Warfare Units.

When the majority of people hear the word "seal" being used, they most frequently think of that mammal which is held in strange affection throughout the world—furry, cute, and usually to be found in the catalogs of soft toy manufacturers. They do not think of something far from cuddly—the U.S. Navy SEAL. He is a very different beast, at home in (or on) the sea, in the air, or on the land—hence SEAL (SEa–Air–Land). The U.S. Navy SEALs are among the finest fighting troops anywhere in the world. They undergo a rigorous selection course that has seen whole classes of would-be SEALs eliminated from the program. They receive intensive and highly realistic training that enables them to operate with equal facility in boats, on land, or parachuting into their target area. They are well armed, very aggressive when the need arises, and incredibly resilient. The SEALs and their predecessors, the Underwater Demolition Teams (UDTs), have served with distinction since World War II. While much of what the SEALs do and have done is still shrouded in the secrecy associated with special forces, there is enough information available to create a picture of what these professional and courageous men do, as the United States' "tip of the spear."

The Beginning: Myth and Reality

Popular legend holds that the story of how naval special warfare originated is quite straightforward and runs along the following lines. After the devastating blow sustained in the Japanese attack against Pearl Harbor, the United States waged war on Japan with particular determination. By 1943, the tide had turned against the Japanese. The Battle of Midway had left the Japanese aircraft carrier fleet devastated and the U.S. armed forces had enjoyed other successes, including Guadalcanal and the Battle of the Coral Sea. At the Allied meeting held in Casablanca during January 1943, it was agreed that the defeat of Germany would be the prime objective, ahead of defeating Japan. However, offensive operations in the Pacific were to increase in intensity as well. By the late spring of 1943, planning was well in hand for an amphibious assault on Japanese-held territory sometime in November. The location for the operation was not an easy choice. Initially it was intended that the Marshall Islands should be the first objective but a lack of intelligence information about the defenses was not helpful. Furthermore, the relative proximity of Truk—a well armed Japanese stronghold—meant that the risk of a robust Japanese response could not be ruled out. Finally, although American forces were much stronger than they had been in December 1941, landing ships were in short supply and many of the vessels supporting the invasion were likely to be obsolescent. These factors persuaded the planners that they needed to launch the first assault against a target that could be taken with the resources available at the time. Focus moved from the Marshall Islands to another island group: the Gilberts.

At a conference in Hawaii in September 1943, the outline plans were brought together and Operation GALVANIC was approved: the first amphibious operation in the island-hopping campaign would be Tarawa atoll, in the Gilbert island group. The Gilberts had been British-controlled before the war and this meant that the planning teams had access

By 1943, the tide had turned against the Japanese. The Battle of Midway had left the Japanese aircraft carrier fleet devastated and the U.S. armed forces had enjoyed other successes, including Guadalcanal and the Battle of the Coral Sea.

Left: Marines wade ashore at Tarawa in the Gilbert Islands in November 1943. The hazards posed by the coral reefs surrounding the landing beaches were not fully appreciated, and created serious difficulties for the invasion force. This led to an increased emphasis upon beach reconnaissance and obstacle clearing. Since the Marines are coming ashore in tightly bunched groups and with their weapons not at the ready, the picture dates from well after the first landing on Tarawa, which was heavily opposed.

to a large amount of information about the islands from British and Commonwealth expatriates; however, the maps and charts of the area were outdated and unreliable. While aerial photography, reconnaissance by submarines, and the up-to-date knowledge of the "foreign legion" of British, New Zealand, and Australian expatriates could help overcome many of the problems associated with the outdated material, there was one area that could not be dealt with so easily: the tides. It is, of course, axiomatic that tidal conditions are an important consideration in the planning of an amphibious assault but this was particularly true for the Tarawa assault. The first part of the atoll to be attacked was Betio Island and this was surrounded by a coral reef extending some 800–1200 yards (758–1092 meters). While the first waves of attacking troops would be using amtracs (amphibious tractors)— which, by dint of having tracks, could drive across the reef if it was exposed—the succeeding waves would be using what were known as "Higgins boats," or, in the jargon, Landing Craft, Vehicle Personnel (LCVP). These were shallow-draft vessels, drawing only 3 or 4 feet (91.5 cm–1.2 meters) of water when loaded. If the tides were unfavorable, there would be a serious risk of the LCVPs grounding, leaving their troops with the choices of wading to the beach under fire or transferring to amtracs. While the amtracs were armored and a preferable alternative to wading through the surf, the time taken to offload the men

Below: Landing craft head for the shore. The cramped conditions aboard the landing craft are notable. In heavy seas, this made the landing craft an extremely unpleasant environment for those who had not found their sea legs. It also meant that the troops were tightly packed targets for enemy machine gunners once the ramp went down.

Left: An LVT 4 (Landing Vehicle Tracked) or "Amtrac" (short for "armored tractor.") These amphibious vehicles were extremely useful in both the Pacific and the European theaters.

from the Higgins boats to the armored tractors would impose undesirable delay on the arrival of the Marines.

This was a crucial matter but the planning team was unable to obtain all the information they required. Some of the expatriate advisors thought that while the tides might be a cause for some concern, there would still be enough water to permit the LCVPs to clear the reef. One of the "foreign legion," Major Frank Holland, disagreed vehemently. He had lived in the Gilberts for 15 years and had studied the tides closely. He argued that the planned date for the assault (November 20, 1943) was the worst one possible, since the tide at that time of the month would give no more than 3 feet (91.5 cm) of clearance over the reef. If his calculations were correct, this would guarantee that the Higgins boats would ground, with all the problems that entailed. But Holland was a lone voice. And as he was in the minority the planners decided that they would, in all probability, not face the difficulties Holland predicted. Being in a minority of one does not make a man wrong, however, and Holland's worst fears were to be realized when the assault went in on the morning of November 20, 1943.

As early as 0530 hours, it was discovered that a strong southerly current had carried the troopships out of position and within range of Japanese shore batteries. Some sporadic shelling from the enemy positions ended when the ships moved away toward their correct location but it was a poor omen for the landing. A heavy swell delayed the landing craft and H-hour—the time when the first troops were to land—had to be put back. When the first wave finally went in at 0900 hours, the Japanese were startled to see that the attacking craft did not ground on the reef but simply climbed over the coral and carried on toward the shore. However, while the amtracs had no problems with the reef, the same was not true for the Higgins boats. The sea was so low that in places large areas

Below: The extent of the on-shore defenses can be appreciated from this view of part of Tarawa. The need for demolitions experts to break through the fortifications was clearly demonstrated in the landings here, and helped lead to the creation of the UDTs.

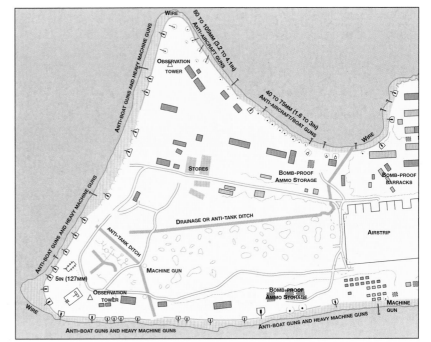

of coral were exposed; in those areas where the water was still covering the reef, it appeared that a depth of 3 feet (91.5 cm) would be the maximum that could be expected. With a terrible inevitability, the LCVPs grounded and the men on board were forced to wade ashore in the face of heavy Japanese resistance. The tanks carried aboard the landing craft had to be let off on the reef's lagoon edge and some of these disappeared into shell holes, drowning their unfortunate crews. At the end of the first day, the determination of the Marines meant that they were ashore, although the foothold was tenuous. By the end of the fourth day, though, Tarawa had fallen. The casualties were immense. Nearly a third of the Marines landing were killed or wounded on D-Day itself and at one point on November 20, the Marines had sent a signal saying simply "issue in doubt." By the end of the fighting, more than 3,000 Marines were dead and wounded out of 16,800.

The first American amphibious operation of the war had nearly been thrown back into the sea. Senior officers knew that Tarawa was not unique but the start of a series of such operations in the Pacific. It was also clear that while the war against Germany would be different from that against Japan, it would not be without the need for amphibious operations—not least to return Allied troops to the European continent from their bases in Great Britain—and that specialized troops would be needed to make those amphibious operations possible.

The story of the founding of the UDTs has its roots in the early days of World War II. In fact, it may be said that the origins of the U.S. Navy's special warfare units can be traced

THE FOUNDING LEGEND

Returning to Pearl Harbor after the battle, the amphibious fleet commander, Admiral Richmond Kelly Turner, and his staff set about writing the after-action report on Tarawa. Two of Turner's officers, Captains Tom Hill and Jack Taylor asked for a conference on beach demolitions. Hill and Taylor were developing ideas, though they were still at an early stage. The officers realized that an attempt to breach the coral reef with explosives might have been the answer to the problems faced by the LCVPs if a specialist demolition team had been available. Turner was impressed with the idea and approved their proposals for creating specialized teams to conduct beach reconnaissance, to destroy obstacles, and to guide the amphibious forces ashore. This, so the legend tells us, began the process which gave us the US Navy's elite SEALs.

Sadly for the historian trying to paint a clear, logical picture, the story is much more complicated than this. While Tarawa has a vital part to play in understanding why naval special forces are required, it does not in itself provide the neat lineage to the SEALs that some earlier commentators have suggested.

to a time before the United States was even participating in that conflict. We need to begin in about 1939, rather than in the middle of the war. This will allow us to see how beach reconnaissance specialists, underwater demolition experts, and men practiced in the arts of war were necessary to ensure that amphibious forces could reach the shore. This necessity led to the creation of a number of specialist units, some of which were active well before 1943.

A Prehistory of the SEALs

World War II did not begin well for the democratic nations. After the collapse of Poland in September 1939, Britain and France waited to see what Hitler would do next. The answer was not very much. For nearly eight months, the opposing powers sat facing in each other in what became known as the "Phoney War." Then, in May 1940, the Germans invaded France and the Low Countries. Within weeks, the British had been forced to evacuate their army from the continent and faced the threat of invasion. Fortunately, Britain's situation as an island, coupled with its strong navy, meant that invading the

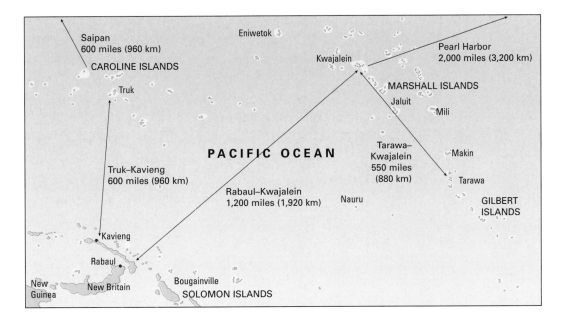

Left: The extent of American operations during 1943 can readily be appreciated from this map. Although the majority of the islands shown are small, the fighting associated with every one of them was intense and bloody.

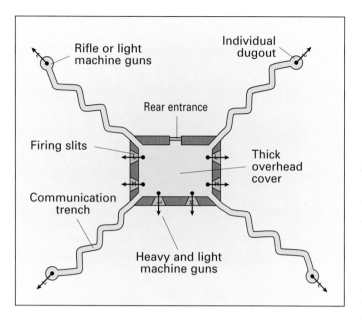

- Rifle or light machine guns
- Individual dugout
- Rear entrance
- Firing slits
- Thick overhead cover
- Communication trench
- Heavy and light machine guns

Above: A diagram showing the layout of a typical Japanese defensive position. The Japanese were adept at making use of such bunkers, and proved very difficult to dislodge. Special tactics had to be used involving combat engineers, bazookas and flame–throwers to deal with these positions—this made any advance slow as each bunker had to be cleared in turn.

Right: UDT members work on clearing a coral reef to enable landing craft to approach the shore. The dress of the UDTs is notable for its lack of sophistication: standard helmets, a few face-masks and swim shorts make for an interesting contrast with the gear worn by today's combat swimmer.

country would be difficult. The failure of the Luftwaffe to overcome the Royal Air Force in the Battle of Britain meant that invasion was postponed. British military effort changed to "hitting back" at Germany through bombing raids and fighting the Axis powers (Italy having joined Germany in May 1940) in the North African deserts.

On a quiet Sunday morning one year later, the Japanese attacked Pearl Harbor. The United States was now at war with Japan. Two days later, Hitler declared war on the U.S., instantly ensuring that his hopes of winning the war would almost certainly be dashed. At the time, though, it did not seem that the defeat of Germany or Japan was inevitable. Given the successes of both Axis nations in the early part of 1942, it was some time before victory could safely be contemplated in either Washington or London. However this did not prevent consideration of how the war could—and ultimately would—be won.

The very nature of the war combined with the sheer scale and scope of the Pacific meant that amphibious operations would be important. Japan is an island nation and if the war concluded with the invasion and defeat of that country, it would demand at least one invasion from the sea. And this did not take into account the need to retake the territory conquered by the Japanese in the first months of the war. In Europe, the only way onto the occupied mainland would be through an amphibious operation. While it would take a long time to build the forces necessary for both the Pacific and the European theaters, it was quite clear that amphibious operations would take place.

With this consideration in mind, senior officers in both Britain and the United States reached the obvious conclusion that they would need to obtain intelligence information about the disposition of the enemy forces in the landing area. Further to this, it was not hard to guess that the enemy would be eager to make a landing as difficult as they could by obstructing possible landing areas. As a result, both the British and the Americans created special units to undertake the necessary missions that would provide intelligence about the proposed landing area and to clear the beach of obstructions before the landing craft carrying the invasion force arrived. The British were ahead of the Americans in this field for the simple reason that they had been fighting Germany for two years by the time the United States was dragged into the war. Although there was little likelihood of the British being able to launch an invasion to liberate Europe unassisted, they took the view that they had to plan for such an operation. Also, in a desire to hit back at the Germans, the British created specialist forces that could conduct both raiding operations and beach reconnaissance. These units included the Special Air Service (SAS) and its maritime component the Special Boat Service (SBS—not to be confused with the current force of

Below: The difficulties posed by enemy pill-boxes can be imagined from this photograph. There is no cover for attacking troops, while the defenders have good arcs of fire for their weapons. Either a good shot with a bazooka through the embrasure would be required, or combat engineers would need to outflank the bunker and place charges to destroy it.

Below: A demolition team prepares to set off for work. The man in the center carries an M1 Carbine slung across his back. The men are all wearing uniform, suggesting that the photograph dates from early in UDT history. After the value of free swimming was demonstrated, the men abandoned their uniform for swim-trunks, face-masks and occasionally swim fins.

the same name); the Army Commandos and smaller bodies such as the Combined Operations Pilotage Parties (COPPs); and Royal Marine Boom Patrol Detachment (RMBPD). The latter two were misleadingly named, since they were both designed to conduct raids and undertake reconnaissance. Although the British had not obtained a vast amount of experience in special operations, particularly not in beach reconnaissance, they had gained enough to be able to pass on useful hints to their American counterparts. That assumed, of course, that the U.S. armed forces could agree as to which of them had responsibility for conducting beach reconnaissance and demolition operations; indeed, there was some argument as to whether the Army and Navy actually needed to have a dispute about this at all.

There was a good reason for this. A perfectly sound case could be made for suggesting that combat demolition could be handled within the framework of the Army's engineers. The Army had shown interest in using landing craft since the late 1930s. Therefore, the question as to whether they ought to be concerned about having teams able to deal with beach obstacles and to report back to the landing force planners on the conditions on key beaches was not as odd as it might at first appear to the casual observer. While the debate over which service should provide the troops dragged on, both the services made a start.

The Army established training in the various skills of combat engineering needed in a seaborne invasion while the U.S. Navy made a start by contributing to a joint service unit called the Scouts and Raiders. The name of the organization is supposed to have originated from the fact that their training establishment was to be called the "Amphibious Scout School." Just in time, someone realized that the acronym for the school would cause hilarity, so the "and Raiders" part of the name was swiftly added. Whatever the true provenance of their name, the Scouts and Raiders were a very small body indeed in the context of the war. At their creation in mid-1942, there were just ten of them, including a former football player called Phil H. Bucklew, who was to become a legendary figure in naval special warfare. There would soon be a need for them, since the Allies were planning to land in North Africa, intending to bring the war in the desert there to a conclusion.

Above: A pall of smoke marks the handiwork of a demolition team. The UDTs cleared numerous obstacles and disposed of enemy ordnance throughout the Pacific. The barren nature of the terrain is notable.

Operation Torch

Operation Torch involved two landing forces. One was to come ashore near to Algiers while the other was to land in what was then called French Morocco, where it would defeat the Vichy French forces collaborating with the Germans. On the night of November 8, 1942, the first demolition task for the Scouts and Raiders began as a team set out to cut a

On November 10, the raiding party tried again and discovered that the conditions were even worse than it had been for their first attempt. They pressed on…

cable that prevented shipping from moving up the Wadi Sebou. The team set out in a small landing craft in difficult conditions. The sea was running a heavy swell and the rain was falling quite heavily. When the team's boat reached the harbor entrance, someone ashore saw them. One of the defenders fired a red flare into the air to signal that there were intruders and the garrison opened fire on the raiding party. Since they had lost the element of surprise, they took the eminently sensible view that they should turn around and try again later. As the little boat struggled out to sea the team was treated to an artillery duel

Right: Navy engineers at Utah Beach in June 1944 experiment with a captured German-built "Goliath"—a small tracked vehicle that could be used to carry demolition charges to their target when enemy fire made it impossible for engineers to approach. Such vehicles were far preferable to using the old "Bangalore torpedo" made up of sections of explosive-filled tube, and which had to be pushed into place by engineers braving enemy fire.

ERNEST J. KING

On May 6, 1943, Admiral Ernest J. King, the Chief of Naval Operations and Commander in Chief, US Fleet, issued orders for the formation of clearance units. This was partly to meet an urgent operational need for teams who would be able to deal with underwater obstacles facing the invasion of Sicily planned for July. The first Naval Combat Demolition Unit (NCDU) was made up of 13 volunteers who had just completed training at the Demolition and Dynamiting School in Virginia. The volunteers were sent on to the amphibious training center in Maryland where they were joined by another 8 enlisted men and 8 officers headed by Lieutenant Fred Wise, who had come from one of the Naval Construction Battalions (the famed SeaBees). The 22 men were given a crash course in demolishing underwater obstacles and then set off for Sicily. On July 10, the invasion took place- and the NCDU was not required. They finally put their training into practice blowing up roadblocks along the waterfront thoroughfares and clearing obstacles that were hindering the unloading of the later echelons of the invasion force.

between a warship that was acting in support of them and the French coastal artillery. The team was recovered but they were well aware of the urgency of their task: until the cable was cut the destroyer *Dallas* would be unable to transport its cargo of U.S. Rangers to their objective, the nearby airfield.

On November 10, the raiding party tried again and discovered that the conditions were even worse than it had been for their first attempt. They pressed on, passing along the river undetected until at last they found the cable they were after. The team discovered that there were in fact two cables—a large cable holding the boom and a much narrower wire above. The raiders were not troubled by this and set about cutting the first cable, which they did. The boom parted and the supporting boats began to drift down the river. As the second wire was cut—probably an alarm, the team later concluded—shore-based artillery took the raiders under fire and they decided that they had better leave the scene. The enemy fire pursued them to the harbor jetties where the team discovered that the surf was even worse than on their arrival. The raiders' landing craft was tossed around violently. There were times when it seemed that they must surely be swamped but the raiding team returned safely to their ship. Before dawn, the *Dallas* steamed up the Wadi Sebou, exchanged fire with the shore guns, and landed the Rangers. This marked the beginning of the naval special operations story. It was to be followed by many others acts of daring in waters of both Europe and the Pacific.

It was clear that Hitler intended to sow the French beaches with huge obstacles that could seriously damage, or perhaps even sink, a landing craft... There was only one solution— removal of the obstacles by hand.

While the Scouts and Raiders showed promise in their support of Operation Torch, this did not mean that they would be the only forces conducting demolition and reconnaissance operations. Indeed, it appeared that their other role of guiding the amphibious forces to the correct beach was of such importance that burdening them with other tasks might be unwise. By January 1943, U.S. Army engineers at Fort Pierce, in Florida, were developing the equipment and techniques necessary to clear underwater obstacles. More intelligence information about German beach defenses in France had emerged, which highlighted the need for this. It was clear that Hitler intended to sow the French beaches with huge obstacles that could seriously damage, or perhaps even sink, a landing craft. Initial consideration of using machinery or long-range gunfire, or perhaps even air attack all foundered on a fundamental problem: such methods could not guarantee the clearance of enough of the obstacles. There was only one solution—removal of the obstacles by hand.

The Sicily Landings

The Scouts and Raiders were at the forefront of the action again in Operation HUSKY, the landings on Sicily. At about 0100 hours, a small team led by Phil Bucklew headed for the shore so that they could guide in the landing craft carrying the men of General Patton's Seventh Army. Bucklew's team identified the correct beach and then made a fast run past in their motorboat trying to identify landmarks. Once the end of the beach had been located, one of the team was set down with a flashlight to mark the location before the team sped to the other end of the beach and repeated the process. Bucklew then withdrew a short distance so that he could place himself in a central position on the approach to the beach, enabling

DRAPER L. KAUFFMAN'S CLOSE ESCAPE

The British naval establishment where Kauffman began his Royal Navy training was subjected to a German bombing raid and one of the bombs failed to detonate. A team of army experts went out to defuze it, but as they did so, the bomb went off and killed them. The next morning, a call went out for volunteers for bomb disposal and Kauffman was near the front of the line. Kauffman proved skilled enough to stay alive, although he had a near escape on January 2, 1941. As he was working on a parachute mine, he heard the fuze begin to buzz. It was time to leave. Kauffman had gone 40 yards (36.5 meters) when the mine exploded, throwing him through the air and leaving him slightly dazed. In the laconic style that often characterizes British Royal Navy signals, Kauffman's commanding officer noted that Kauffman had run the equivalent of an 8-second 109-yard (100-meter) dash, and that "it is possible that his extreme sense of urgency enabled him to do so."

him to act as a clear guide to the landing craft. At this point, the Germans sensed that something was amiss and illuminated the scene with searchlights. To add to Bucklew's discomfort, they then opened up with a 3.45in (88mm) gun, albeit with a pleasing lack of accuracy. Bucklew put this distraction out of his mind as much as he could and began to guide the boats into the beach. As he did so, he realized that one of the defending machine-gun posts was firing right over one of the flank signals. Bucklew later discovered that the sergeant with the light had decided that the safest place for him was right under the barrel of the enemy machine-gun, where the Germans could not see him. The sergeant received a Silver Star, while Bucklew was awarded the Navy Cross for carrying out his mission with

Above: Amtracs surge ashore. These amphibians could cross coral reefs thanks to their tracks.

Below: 8000lbs of UDT explosives clear a channel for Higgins boats during the assault on Peleliu.

such steadiness while the Germans were trying to blow him out of the water. Two months later, after guiding the landing at Salerno, he added the Silver Star to what would end up as an impressive collection of gallantry medals.

While Lieutenant Wise and his men were in action on Sicily, another part of the Naval Combat Demolition Unit (NCDU) plan was enacted. A signal was sent to Lt Commander Draper L. Kauffman, the head of the U.S. Navy Bomb Disposal School, ordering him to Washington. Kauffman reported to the Pentagon to be told that he would take command of the effort to produce naval demolition units. The choice of Kauffman

Above: UDT demolition operations under way off Okinawa on March 29, 1945. The battle for the island was to be a long and bloody affair.

was inspired, since he had acquired a wealth of experience with explosives albeit in a distinctly unusual way. Kauffman had attempted to follow his father (Admiral James L. Kauffman) into the U.S. Navy. Although he had graduated from Naval Academy in 1933, his eyesight was poor enough to deny him a commission. After failing a second eye test, Kauffman took a position in merchant shipping and stayed there until 1939. His job took him to Britain, France, and Germany. While in the latter country, Kauffman managed to attend speeches by Adolf Hitler. While he did not understand German, Kauffman was convinced from the style of the oratory that Hitler was likely to cause serious trouble. His expectations realized by the invasion of Poland, Kauffman signed up as a volunteer ambulance driver and was in the direct line of the German advance when they invaded France in May 1940. Kauffman won a Croix de Guerre for rescuing the wounded under fire but the collapse of France meant that he was soon a prisoner of the Germans. The Germans did not wish to make diplomatic relations with the United States any worse than they already were and freed Kauffman. He made his way to Portugal from where he caught a ship to Brazil. He then went up to Boston and immediately caught another ship, this time taking him to Scotland, where he managed to talk himself into a commission in the Royal Naval Volunteer Reserve.

Kauffman survived the German Blitz and returned to the United States in May 1941, where he was awarded his commission and assigned to the Navy's bomb disposal school. He was also awarded a Navy Cross for bomb disposal work at Pearl Harbor and was then given the task of establishing the NCDUs.

Training and Operations

Kauffman's first task was to establish a training regime—and it was a tough one. The infamous "Hell Week" undergone by current SEAL trainees stems directly from Draper Kauffman's program: day after day of incredibly hard work; running through the surf; carrying inflatable boats; paddling the boats; carrying the boats again; paddling them again, and again, and again. Oddly, little consideration was given to swimming skills, since it was presumed that the men would come ashore in the inflatable boats. To add to the "fun" instructors hurled hand grenades at the trainees (although they took care to ensure that they landed far enough away not to injure the unfortunate recruits). Hell Week usually eliminated 40 percent of the class. Despite this, Kauffman soon had enough men to

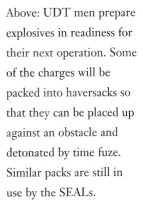

Above: UDT men prepare explosives in readiness for their next operation. Some of the charges will be packed into haversacks so that they can be placed up against an obstacle and detonated by time fuze. Similar packs are still in use by the SEALs.

Left: An aerial view of the Iwo Jima landings in February 1945. The wakes of the multitude of landing craft are clearly visible, while the extent of the smoke from the bombardment is notable. The leading landing craft will carry men from the UDTs and scouts to guide the landing craft in to the correct beaches.

Left: The hostile terrain of Iwo Jima confronts the U.S. Marines, with Mount Suribachi in the background. The battle for Iwo was remarkable for its sheer ferocity. Once again, the UDTs played a vital yet largely unheralded part in the preparations for the assault.

Ensign Lewis F. Luehrs and Chief Bill Acheson then made another small but significant development in naval special warfare. The two men had already decided that if the coral were too thick, they would swim to the reef and take a closer look. They had come prepared. Luehrs and Acheson removed their fatigues to reveal that they were wearing swimming trunks.

form NCDUs, only for the events at Tarawa to alter the format of his teams. Admiral Turner's deliberations on the invasion led to his decision that the NCDUs needed to be larger and to have the facility to reconnoiter enemy beaches as well as to clear them of obstacles. He recommended that the NCDUs be reorganized into much larger Underwater Demolition Teams (UDTs). UDT 1 was assigned to Commander Edward D. Brewster's supervision, while Lieutenant Thomas C. Crist was given command of UDT 2. The two UDTs drew men from Kauffman's training school along with volunteers from the other services. Training took place in the pleasant setting of Hawaii but the men were well aware of the fact that they would soon be called on for combat work.

Their first test came with the invasion of Kwajalein Island in January 1944. Admiral Turner's original plan had been to use UDT 1 on a night-time reconnaissance of the beaches, but aerial photographs showed that the Japanese were building a defensive wall on the favored beaches. This meant that the landing force would have to consider going over a reef very similar to the one that had caused such problems at Tarawa. Turner therefore decided that he would use his UDT to carry out two daylight-reconnaissance missions, supported by the vast array of firepower that the invasion fleet possessed. At 1000 hours on January 31, two battleships and several destroyers began to bombard the island as four landing craft approached the reef. The weight of the bombardment meant that there was little incoming fire from enemy positions against the landing craft and they were able to approach reasonably safely. As the leading boat reached the reef, the coxswain became concerned about the coral heads. Two of the UDT team, Ensign Lewis F. Luehrs and Chief

Below: A frogman is recovered at speed during postwar exercises. The technique was remarkably simple, and remains in use today: men in an inflatable boat hold out a rope circle through which the swimmer places his arm. He is then pulled into the inflatable. The procedure means that the recovery boat need not stop, making itself vulnerable to enemy fire as it sits in the water waiting to get the man aboard.

Bill Acheson, then made another small but significant development in naval special warfare. The two men had already decided that if the coral were too thick, they would swim to the reef and take a closer look. They had come prepared. Luehrs and Acheson removed their fatigues to reveal that they were wearing swimming trunks. They jumped over the side and swam toward the beach. In so doing, they were able to obtain an excellent idea of the nature of the coral reef and the state of the Japanese defenses. After about three-quarters of an hour, the two men returned to the landing craft and were rushed to the flagship, USS *Monrovia*. They reported to Admiral Turner and recommended that amtracs be used for the assault instead of boats.

Other reports revealed that the naval bombardment had not breached the anti-tank wall on the western landing beach. Turner ordered his battleships in closer to shore to engage it, as well as a massive air attack. This helped make several breaches in the wall and guaranteed that the invading forces would be able to call on tank support. The landing force went in the next day and after four days the island fell. The UDTs were not called on to conduct any underwater demolitions in support of the invasion but did blast channels through the reef to allow larger landing ships and supply vessels to deposit their cargo. On several occasions, the UDTs also assisted the army when the troops encountered Japanese pillboxes. While the army kept the defenders pinned down, the UDTs would conduct a flanking movement on the bunker, packing haversacks loaded with explosive against the walls of the enemy position. They would then run back to a safe distance and detonate their

Above: A UDT swimmer disembarks from an inflatable boat. The lack of a face-mask is evident, and the swimmer is not wearing any breathing apparatus. He will, therefore, swim on or just below the surface as he approaches his target. The large knife on his belt is the only weapon available to him—but he will be looking to avoid contact with the enemy, as he is carrying out a reconnaissance mission and will not wish to advertise his presence to the opposition in any way.

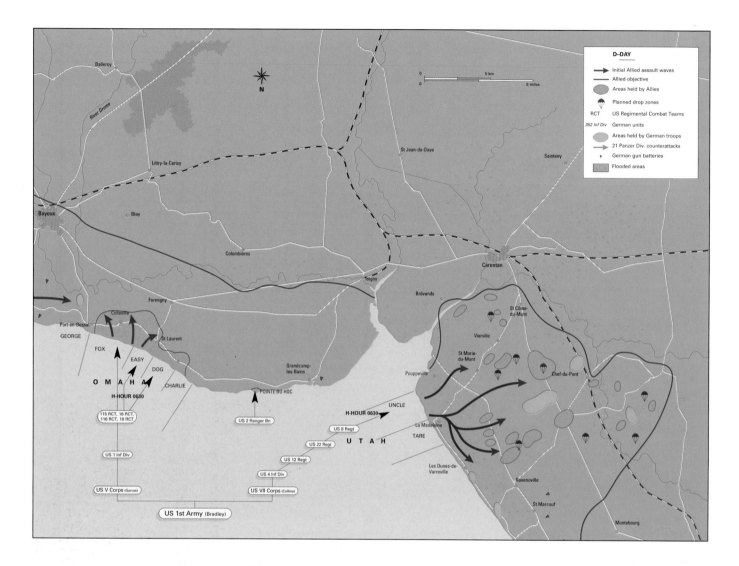

D-DAY

- Initial Allied assault waves
- Allied objective
- Areas held by Allies
- Planned drop zones
- RCT US Regimental Combat Teams
- *352 Inf Div* German units
- Areas held by German troops
- 21 Panzer Div. counterattacks
- German gun batteries
- Flooded areas

Above: The American invasion beaches in Normandy on June 6, 1944. While progress at Utah beach was relatively easy, the landing at Omaha was in jeopardy until beach obstacles were cleared by a mixture of navy engineers and infantrymen using explosives and Bangalore torpedoes to blast through the German defenses.

handiwork. By the end of the operation to seize the island, it was clear that the UDTs would play an important part in the island-hopping campaign in the Pacific. The same was true of the teams of specialists in Europe, who were preparing for the invasion of France.

The Germans had not been idle in preparing defenses to meet the Allied invaders, and the NCDU men grappled with the question of how they would breach some of the formidable beach obstacles, particularly a huge iron and steel construction known as the "Belgian Gate." The NCDUs needed to be able to blow the obstacle down without sending massive amounts of shrapnel flying through the air to endanger both the demolition parties and any nearby troops. The solution to the problem was discovered by Lieutenant (Junior Grade) Carl P. Hagensen. He filled waterproof canvas bags with C-2 plastic explosive and then fitted the pack with a cord at one end and a hook at the other. This enabled it to be attached precisely to an obstacle. Tests on a mock-up of a Belgian Gate demonstrated that the pack worked perfectly. Sixteen such packs were fitted to the critical points of the Belgian Gate and then detonated. The Gate fell flat, just as required. The next problem was one of manpower. Six men were obviously not going to be enough and in the weeks before D-Day every available man at Fort Pierce was sent to Britain. By the end of May, sixteen teams, each thirteen-men strong, had been trained to enable them to breach the eight gaps in the obstacles planned for Omaha Beach and the eight for Utah Beach.

OVERLORD

While the UDTs were training for their operations in the Pacific, six men from the 11th NCDU were sent to Britain in November 1943 to prepare for the invasion. A few weeks later, the Scouts and Raiders appeared, including Phil Bucklew, and began to conduct reconnaissance missions. Bucklew and his men took depth soundings of the planned invasion beaches. On one occasion Bucklew crawled ashore, filled a bucket with sand, and took it back to England to allow experts to test its load-bearing capacity so they could judge how well the sand on the landing beaches would be able to take the weight of tanks and other heavy vehicles.

Early in the morning of June 6, 1944, Operation Overlord began. Phil Bucklew was one of the early participants, bobbing around in a small boat as he led the troops in toward the landing zone on Omaha Beach. Once again, Bucklew led the invasion force in (earning a Gold Star in lieu of a second Navy Cross in the process) but their troubles had only just begun. The current had ensured that several of the gap assault teams had drifted off course and landed in the wrong place. Some of them found that they were the first men on the beach, instead of the tanks and infantry, and were cut down by defensive fire as they attempted to land. While the other teams set about destroying obstacles, some of the blasts had to be delayed as frightened soldiers attempted to take cover behind the sturdy beach defenses. The demolition men solved this problem by setting the fuses and telling the sheltering GIs that their cover would blow up in two minutes. This did the trick and the obstacles were removed. Other difficulties came from the loss of explosives and the NCDU men were forced to salvage German mines and add their explosive power to the C-2 that they had available. By the end of the day, 52 percent of the NCDU men had been killed or wounded. It was the worst day in the history of naval special warfare. Despite the high cost, they had done their job well.

Below: A UDT has a cigarette. The valves for his life vest are notable in this picture, as is the lack of personal equipment other than the ubiquitous diving knife.

The End in the Pacific

Back at the NCDU training camp at Fort Pierce, Draper Kauffman was becoming frustrated at the lack of action. He "pulled strings" and was assigned to command UDT 5, which—slightly ironically—was first posted to the new training base on the Hawaiian island of Maui. Kauffman discovered that the results of the Kwajalein operation had led to some changes in the operating procedures for the UDTs. The new training camp placed heavy emphasis on the use of swimmers rather than boats. Whereas the NCDUs at Fort Pierce had always worn life jackets when swimming, those at Maui would not. The logic behind this change was that the life jackets would hamper the swimmers when they needed maximum mobility. Also, unlike the training at Fort Pierce, the swimmers would make use of facemasks.

As Kauffman adjusted to these alterations, he was summoned to meet Admiral Turner. Turner briefed Kauffman on the assignment for UDT 5, which was to support the invasion of Saipan. Kauffman was shocked to realize that his men would have to swim for a mile to reach their objectives; just as he was recovering from this surprise, Admiral Turner revealed that they would conduct their reconnaissance in daylight. He promised fire support from the fleet, knowing that this had proved effective at Kwajalein. Kauffman came to terms with the Admiral's plan but worried that the men would find swimming in under fire disconcerting even if it was friendly. He managed to persuade Turner to lend him some cruisers and destroyers and UDT 5 began practicing swims ashore under the protective fire from friendly forces.

On May 30, 1944, UDTs 5, 6, and 7 left Hawaii to join the invasion of Saipan. Although Kauffman feared that the teams would suffer heavy losses as they carried out their reconnaissance work, he was delighted to be proved wrong. Kauffman was in the lead boat, marking the channels for the tanks as they surged ashore. The success of the operation was not in doubt. From May 1944, when Saipan was taken, to the end of the war, the UDTs provided an invaluable service to the invasion forces as they approached the Japanese homeland. At Iwo Jima, the UDTs successfully carried out their task. Tragically, they were embarked on a ship that was hit by a Japanese bomber and eighteen members of UDT 15 were killed. While the team was recovering from this, they were forced to prepare for the next step in the war, the assault on Okinawa.

Below: The Okinawa landings were difficult, particularly for the UDTs, who had to deal with the problems caused by the cold waters surrounding the island. They cleared over 1000 beach obstacles to enable the landings to take place.

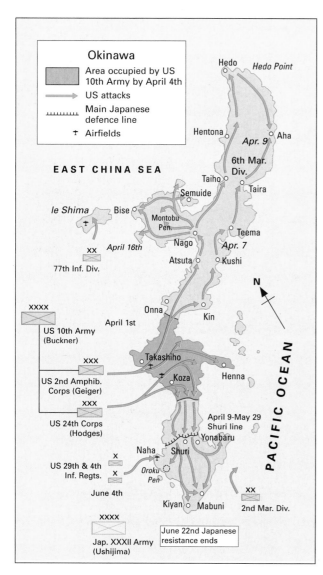

Okinawa

Okinawa was a difficult operation for several reasons and not just the fact that the Japanese would defend the island with considerable ferocity. The waters around the island were cold. The term "cold" is perhaps misleading, since the temperature was usually around 70° Fahrenheit (21° Celsius). However, at temperatures below 75° F (24° C), staying in the water leads to loss of warmth and energy, diminishing the capacity to operate efficiently. The UDT men discovered that if they were in the water for any length of time they would suffer from cramps and lose the use of their hands.

Nevertheless, the teams set about their tasks, of which the most important was to clear a huge number of simple but deadly obstacles. The Japanese had driven hundreds of sharpened wooden stakes into the beach, attaching small explosive charges to many of them. Kauffman, by now acting Captain in charge of

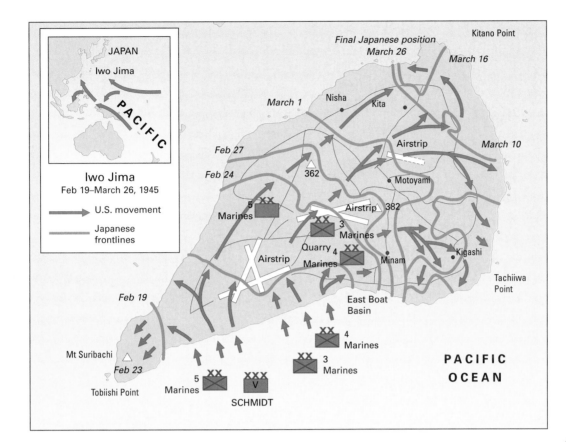

JAPAN
Iwo Jima

PACIFIC

Iwo Jima
Feb 19–March 26, 1945

→ U.S. movement

Japanese
frontlines

Kitano Point

Final Japanese position
March 26

March 16

March 1   Nisha   Kita

Feb 27   Airstrip   March 10

Feb 24   362   Motoyami

5 Marines

Airstrip   382

XX
3 Marines

Quarry   4 XX
Airstrip   Marines   Minam   Kigashi

Feb 19   East Boat
Basin   Tachiiwa
Point

XX
4 Marines

Mt Suribachi   XX
Feb 23   3 Marines   PACIFIC
OCEAN

5 XX
Tobiishi Point   Marines   XXX
V

SCHMIDT

Left: Despite its small size, Iwo Jima posed a formidable objective for the invasion forces, as the Japanese defenders put up a vigorous fight, usually to the death. By the time the fighting ended, 6821 U.S. Marines had been killed, and over 20,000 wounded, while 27 Medals of Honor were won. All but a handful of the island's 21,000 defenders died.

Below: A U.S. Marine in 1943. The work of the UDTs undoubtedly saved hundreds of Marine lives in the Pacific War.

the overall demolition effort, sent in UDT 11 and UDT 16 to clear the beaches. More than 160 men were sent out, but when the time came for the explosives to be detonated, only half the obstacles were cleared. It transpired that Team 16 had come under fire and a number of the men had swum away without placing their charges. As Orr Kelly has observed, this represented perhaps the most serious failure of any naval special warfare team. In fairness to the team, however, it should be noted that twenty of them were decorated for their actions at Okinawa. Kauffman resisted the temptation to send UDT 16 back to complete the job, tasking UDT 11 instead. They carried out their task faultlessly so that by the end of the campaign UDT 11 had cleared some 1300 yards (1189 meters) of beach and somewhere in the region of 1400 obstacles that the Japanese had hoped would prevent the Americans from coming ashore.

Kauffman's thoughts turned to the invasion of Japan. Like most, if not all of his colleagues, he feared that invading the Japanese homeland would be a costly business. He planned on the basis that resistance to the attack would be so fierce that casualties exceeding 60 percent could be anticipated. He was still worrying about these losses when taking leave in Washington in the first weeks of August 1945. But his cares soon fell away. Instead of invasion, the United States used the atomic bomb as the decisive tool against Japan and the American forces that would land in the home islands would do so as occupying forces placed there under the peace treaty that brought the war to an end. Although their role is not one that figures greatly in the narrative accounts of either the European or the Pacific campaigns, the part played by the Scouts and Raiders, NCDUs, and UDTs should not be underestimated.

Left: Marines storm ashore during the Inchon landings in the Korean War. The use of ladders to enable the men to leave the landing craft so that they can climb onto the beach wall is obvious. As with other landings, the UDTs will have been busy preparing the beaches, both through reconnaissance and demolition of obstacles that would otherwise impede the landing fleet's progress.

General Douglas MacArthur decided on a bold counter-stroke landing behind the North Korean troops at Inchon. Not all of MacArthur's subordinates were convinced that Inchon was the best location. So as well as using the UDTs to reconnoiter MacArthur's preferred site, teams were sent to look at alternative locations.

Right: UDTs carry out a reconnaissance of Wonsan beach during the Korean War after crossing a minefield which they later cleared. The UDTs carried out a number of reconnaissance missions and assaults against communications targets.

Below: A UDT takes a swig of brandy and enjoys a cigarette following immersion in the freezing waters off Korea. Although he is wearing a dry suit, the intense cold will have made his tasks more difficult as he struggles against fatigue.

Postwar

The end of the war in the Pacific had a serious effect on the naval special warfare community. Many of the officers and men returned to civilian life taking their expertise with them. The UDTs shrank to a fraction of their previous size. It became one of those branches in an armed service which is guaranteed to offer interesting work that will largely be unappreciated by senior officers and with virtually no chance of promotion. This did not prevent a number of independently minded officers and men who did not wish to spend much time in the "real" navy from conducting vital experimentation as they sought to improve the way in which the UDTs could operate in future. This included the use of underwater breathing apparatus. Also, to deal with the problem of swimming in cold water, the UDTs began to work with wet and dry suits, with UDT 1 using the latter when it was involved in operations in Arctic waters in 1947. Also during these trials, a combined UDT and marine unit operated from the submarine USS *Perch* to test out new methods of transporting the UDTs to operations.

POSTWAR CHANGES

As well as working on the use of underwater breathing apparatus during operations, UDT officers including Commanders Doug Fane and John Koehler began to think about training the UDTs to operate in a commando role. Draper Kauffman had successfully fended off an attempt to use the UDTs as additional infantry during World War II by pointing out that some of the men had no idea of how to use a rifle. Now after the war the idea was that the UDTs could and should conduct carefully defined raiding operations, attacking targets close to the beach before leaving the scene. The UDTs were also used in exercises against shipping. On one occasion they "sank" the carrier *Bon Homme Richard* with a simulated limpet mine. Despite these successes, the UDTs were at their lowest numbers with each UDT having at most 50 men. Much of the decline in numbers had come about as the result of the belief that a war was unlikely even though tension with the Soviet Union was increasing. This complacent view was shattered in June 1950, when the Korean War broke out.

UDTs in Korea

When the Korean War broke out it became clear that UDTs were needed, but not only in their original role. One of the first tasks undertaken was an outgrowth of plans to use the UDTs rather more aggressively. The U.S. Navy wished to assist the Army by targeting North Korean supply trains with naval gunfire but had the problem of not knowing when the trains were moving. The solution lay in the UDTs. Elements of UDT 3 under Lieutenant (junior grade) George Atcheson were given the task of demolishing a railroad

Below: UDT members walk along a beach as they ensure that it is clear of obstacles. The long coastline of Korea meant that beach surveys were of key importance.

bridge. The team would land at night from inflatable boats launched by the fast transport USS *Diachenko*. The insertion went well until a group of ten North Koreans appeared. Atcheson's number two, Boatswain's Mate Warren G. Foley, had gone back to the beach to call in the second inflatable boat leaving the unfortunate Lieutenant by himself. Atcheson concealed himself below the bridge, while Foley, who had heard the arrival of the Koreans, made his way back to his officer, taking with him a Thompson submachine gun. As he ran along the sea wall, the North Koreans opened fire on Foley, as did Atcheson, who could not identify the armed man running toward him. Foley was hit and fell over the sea wall. Atcheson decided that it was necessary to leave, threw several hand grenades at the Koreans, and ran for the beach. There he found a wounded Foley (the wounds caused by the Koreans and not Atcheson's pistol) and the rest of his team. They departed quickly for the *Diachenko*, which took the team back to Japan. While they were on their way back, UDT 1 under the command of Lieutenant Commander David F. Welsh arrived aboard the Transport *Horace Bass*. Along with the UDT 1 team, two platoons of the Marine 1st Amphibious Reconnaissance Company were aboard the *Bass* and the three units were combined into the Special Operation Group (SOG).

Below: A UDT demonstration at Carson Beach, South Carolina. The team crawls back to the water and safety after placing charges on the enemy's defenses.

Inchon

The reverses suffered by the UN forces in the early days of the war began to be overturned as the desperate defense of the Pusan perimeter proved successful. The Commander-in-Chief of UN forces, General Douglas MacArthur, decided on a bold counter-stroke landing behind the North Korean troops at Inchon. Not all of MacArthur's subordinates were convinced that Inchon was the best location. So as well as using the UDTs to reconnoiter MacArthur's preferred site, teams were sent to look at alternative locations for a landing. It turned out that the alternative landing sites were unsuitable, whereas the judgement of the UDTs was that Inchon would be best, despite the difficulties associated with the terrain. This was to be the last action of the SOG, which was dispersed as the Marines joined their counterparts at Pusan. In preparation for the landings, the UDTs carried out a number of reconnaissance missions and surveys, charting the harbor areas and underwater obstacles. Enemy emplacements were also located and some of the reconnaissance missions turned into close-quarter combats with the enemy as the UDTs withdrew.

With the successful completion of the Inchon landings, the UDTs were put to a new task—mine clearance. The North Koreans made considerable use of mines in an effort to disrupt the UN forces' work. By November 17, 1950, UDT 1 had been responsible for clearing mines from over 200 miles (322 kilometers) of water. Although this was the major duty for the Team during 1950, a new SOG was assembled, this time drawing on 41 Commando, Royal Marines. During the night of October 7, the combined UDT/British unit destroyed railroad bridges and tunnels at two locations. The Royal Marines were slightly unused to deploying in small rubber boats and later reverted to the use of ramped landing craft.

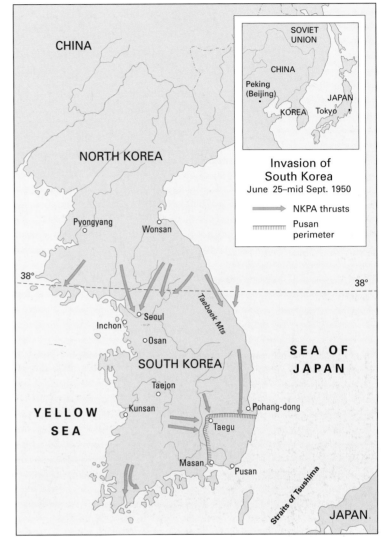

Above: The invasion of South Korea saw the North Koreans driving the defenders back to the Pusan perimeter before MacArthur's brilliant decision to land at Inchon.

THE SPECIAL OPERATIONS GROUP

The Special Operations Group (SOG) was tasked with disrupting enemy logistics, which usually meant the destruction of railroad tunnels. They launched a number of successful missions, including one where the raiding party found two North Korean guards asleep. The guards were tied up with explosive primacord, since the UDT scouts did not have any rope or string available for the task. The UDT men then called forward their colleagues, who packed the tunnel mouth with explosives. As the raiding team returned to their transport, they saw a loaded train enter the target area just in time to arrive as the tunnel blew up.

Despite this change in operations, the new multinational SOG worked well, conducting an array of raids. One of the UDT men, Lieutenant Ted Fielding, was released from his regular assignment to work with the Royal Marines and was awarded both the Navy Cross and the British Distinguished Service Cross for his work on raids.

An additional task of the UDTs was to cooperate with the CIA, dropping guerrilla parties into North Korea in a precursor to the type of operations that would be carried out in Vietnam a decade later. As the war dragged on, the UDTs settled down to a routine of mine clearing and raiding, adding one further task to their list under the auspices of Operation FISH. This duty commenced when it was decided to interfere with the food supplies of the Chinese Army that had joined the conflict in late 1950. The majority of the Chinese troops had fish as their staple diet and it was decided to use the UDTs to interdict North Korean fishing operations. This meant that the UDTs would make note of the location of any fishing nets they encountered while moving along the coast on operations. When they could, the UDTs would destroy or confiscate the nets; if they could not stop, the location could be passed on for use by other teams.

When the Korean War ended with an armistice on July 27, 1953, the UDTs had participated in 61 landings and had added the art of fighting on dry land to their growing expertise. They returned to the United States, where it was decided to re-designate each of the UDTs. UDTs 1, 3, and 5 became UDTs 11, 12, and 13 while Teams 2 and 4 were renumbered as UDTs 21 and 22. The newly numbered units then spent the rest of the 1950s carrying out a variety of reconnaissance missions—some of them around China

Below: UDTs carry out underwater training during the 1950s. The improvement in their equipment in comparison to that available in World War II is marked. Even so, the development of reliable breathing apparatus had not yet been fully realized.

Left: If this picture had been taken after 1962, the caption "SEAL meets penguins" would have been irresistible. A frogman from UDT Team 21 meets some of the locals (Adelie penguins) during Operation Deep Freeze II in January 1957.

Below: In a photograph dating from around 1955, a UDT frogman does a passable imitation of a seal. The cold water would soon reduce the effectiveness of the UDT man, despite his dry suit and superior levels of fitness.

when it appeared that amphibious operations in support of Taiwan would be required. They also kept the ships of the fleet alert by staging fake attacks in which they would plant simulated limpet mines. In some cases they walked onto ships and planted fake explosive charges while the crew wandered past them, blissfully unaware of the fact that their ship was in the process of being "sunk."

Although the UDTs were successful in these operations, this was not enough to prevent UDT 13 from being decommissioned in 1956. It appeared that in an era when war was assumed to mean nuclear war, the UDTs did not have much of a role. They were assigned to some unusual tasks in the meantime, including experiments in support of the nascent space program. UDTs endured the strange delights of centrifuges and simulated weightlessness underwater. Once the space program began, the UDTs would be employed to recover astronauts after their spacecraft had splashed down in the ocean. While all of this represented important work, the most notable change in the nature of naval special warfare was to arrive with the inauguration of the president who would launch the drive to place an American on the moon by the end of the 1960s.

Forming the SEALs

President John F. Kennedy had distinct ideas as to how warfare would be in the new decade. He anticipated that

Below: One of the rare occasions when the UDTs worked in the full glare of publicity was during the space program of the 1960s. UDTs provided the frogmen who assisted with the recovery of the astronauts once their craft had returned to earth. Once the astronauts had been helped out of the capsule, they were flown back to the recovery ship.

there would be a need for U.S. Forces to be able to conduct guerrilla-type warfare as they supported their allies in combating communist-led insurgencies around the globe. On May 25, 1961, Kennedy announced that he had directed the Secretary of Defense to expand the United States' abilities to fight non-nuclear war and, as a part of this, special forces and unconventional warfare units would be increased in size.

The commanding officer of UDT 21, Lieutenant Commander Bill Hamilton, realized that Kennedy's announcement was a validation of the ideas about using special naval forces for commando raids and the less orthodox types of operation. With other officers in UDT 21, he proposed that a naval commando force be created but one that would not be so tightly attached to the fleet. Hamilton proposed that this new force should be as at home operating at sea as it was at operating on land or in the air.

Hamilton was not alone in such thoughts. The Deputy Chief of Naval Operations, Admiral Ulysses S. G. Sharp, aware of Kennedy's thinking even before the speech was made, appreciated that it would be in the interests of the navy to adopt a capability that was

clearly highly prized by the president. Sharp's ideas were echoed by Admiral Arleigh Burke, the chief of naval operations, and it was he who authorized the formation of the "Unconventional Activities Committee." This reported at the end of May, having already used the SEAL acronym in a memorandum in April. The report agreed that unconventional units, known as the SEALs, would be created. Bill Hamilton's report had not gone unnoticed. He found himself moved to the Pentagon, given a budget of over $4 million, and told to get on with establishing the SEALs. In December 1961 the Pentagon granted formal authorization for the SEALs. In January 1962 the teams were commissioned. SEAL Team One was placed under the command of Lieutenant David Del Giudice. SEAL Team Two was temporarily under Lieutenant Roy Boehm while the team awaited the arrival of the designated commander, Lieutenant John Callaghan.

The events of January 1962 represented a turning point in naval special warfare. While the UDTs would continue to provide the same services to the fleet as they had done since World War II, the SEALs would undertake a variety of new tasks as they mastered the art of unconventional conflict. They had little time to do so. Within months of their creation their attention was turned to a country in which they would make their reputation as an elite unit: Vietnam.

Above: The introduction of the helicopter into widespread service opened new avenues for inserting and extracting frogmen. Here, a U.S. Navy Sikorsky HO3S helicopter recovers a swimmer on a training exercise in warm waters during the mid-1950s. The HO3S gave great service in Korea, and was one of the first effective military helicopters, despite its relatively limited payload.

CHAPTER TWO

VIETNAM: WAR IN THE DELTA

Vietnam was the making of the
U.S. Navy SEALs. Formed just as the war
began to escalate, they proved themselves
to be deadly enemies of the Viet Cong in
the Mekong Delta.

Left: A view of the Mekong Delta in Vietnam from the air. The vast
swamps made for a difficult operating area for the SEALs.

Above: UDT divers practice beach obstacle demolition at Roosevelt Roads in August 1965. Beach reconnaissance and clearance was of vital importance to amphibious and riverine operations throughout the conflict in Vietnam.

Since the end of World War II, Southeast Asia had been a source of much concern to the U.S. government. In 1945, the main issue was that of colonialism. The U.S. was reluctant to see the rebuilding of the French and British empires for a variety of reasons but this viewpoint was complicated by the matter of just who would replace the colonial powers. While Britain faced a number of difficulties with its imperial possessions, it was on the verge of divesting itself of India, which was the hub of its colonial might. France, however, was far less eager to begin the decolonization process. This was problematic, since the French, recovering from the devastation caused by the war, were in no position to send troops to their major regional possession, Indochina, once the Japanese had surrendered. This meant that the nationalist Viet Minh movement, headed by Ho Chi Minh, was in a good position to press their claim for independence without the immediate interference of the colonial power. On returning to Indochina the French were confronted by a nationalist uprising by the Viet Minh. The leader of the nationalists, Ho Chi Minh, enjoyed considerable popularity in the region, and was the likely leader of any independent state.

If Ho had only been a nationalist, this might have been enough to cause the United States to apply considerable political pressure to persuade the French to give up their desire to retain their colony. Ho, though, was a communist, as well as a nationalist, and this led the U.S. to the view that, in the short term at least, it was better for the French to return before handing over power to a democratic, indigenous government. Ironically, Ho did not—to begin with—see the United States as an obstacle to his desire for an independent Vietnam. Between 1945 and 1948, he made at least eight requests to Washington for the

American government to support his efforts. The State Department demurred, and after the Chinese revolution in 1949, their attitude hardened. Secretary of State Dean Acheson remarked that the question of whether Ho was as much a nationalist as a communist was irrelevant, since all Stalinists in colonial areas espoused nationalist ideals. Acheson feared that the Chinese communists might turn south in a desire to spread communism, and this simply could not be allowed. The American position in Indochina was thus rather complicated: while the U.S. wished to see French colonialism end, they did not wish to see this come to pass if it meant that Ho Chi Minh would take over. With the outbreak of the Korean War in 1950 (taken to demonstrate the communist threat in Asia), the United States sent large-scale military aid to the French, their lack of commitment to full independence for Indochina notwithstanding. This was to mark the beginning of nearly a quarter of a century of involvement, often painful, with the region.

The massive aid given to France (over $4 billion between 1950 and 1954) did little to help: the nationalists kept fighting, and in 1954 were presented with a glorious opportunity. The French dispatched a force to garrison Dien Bien Phu, which was well within the area controlled by the Viet Minh. An underestimation of the capabilities of the Viet Minh meant that the French garrison was situated in an area that was almost impossible to defend against a vaguely competent enemy. The end result was disaster and the destruction of the French forces when Dien Bien Phu fell on May 7, 1954. The French decided that they had taken as much pain from Indochina as they could, and—against American wishes—agreed to a peace

The American position in Indochina was thus rather complicated: while the U.S. wished to see French colonialism end, they did not wish to see this come to pass if it meant that Ho Chi Minh would take over.

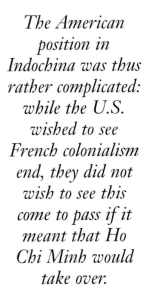

Left: UDT divers on an exercise in the early 1960s preparing to blow up part of a coral reef. In essence the primary role of the UDTs had not changed since World War II.

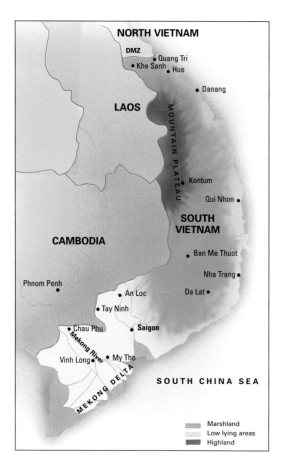

Above: The varying terrain of Vietnam is shown to advantage in this map, along with the extent of the Mekong Delta. While the SEALs operated beyond the Delta, they made their reputation in this forbidding area.

Far right: U.S. Marines come ashore near Da Nang in 1965 to be greeted by the world's press. The beach had already been reconnoitred by UDT members. Both the UDTs and SEALs had an active role supporting small-scale amphibious assaults and raids by the Marines during the war.

conference in Geneva to end the war. Two agreements came from this meeting. The first was a cease-fire, which saw all French forces withdraw south of the Seventeenth Parallel, while Viet Minh forces moved north of that line. The agreement stressed that the parallel was not to be taken as constituting a territorial or political boundary. The second agreement, the Final Declaration, provided that there would be elections in 1956. It was patently obvious that the elections would provide Ho Chi Minh with a mandate to run a unified Vietnam, and Washington did not want to see this happen. The French were pushed out of the South as the result of intense diplomatic pressure by the Americans, and were replaced with a government headed by Ngo Dinh Diem. From the beginning of Diem's rule in the South, the U.S. set out to protect his position—the Seventeenth Parallel became a boundary between the North and South Vietnam and the 1956 elections did not occur. The U.S. government, fearing that the fall of Vietnam to communism would trigger a "domino effect," bound itself ever more closely to South Vietnam.

The North Vietnamese and communists in the South reacted to these developments by continuing their guerrilla war. President Eisenhower increased American commitment to the South, sending military advisers. When John F. Kennedy succeeded Ike in 1961, he was determined that Southeast Asia would not become communist. He ordered that more advisers be sent, committing up to 10,000 troops during 1962–63. By 1963, there were, in fact, more than 16,000 U.S. personnel in the country. Then, on November 1, 1963, Diem was overthrown in a coup and murdered by the plotters. The military situation became worse and the U.S. advisers increasingly did more than just advise, often participating in combat. Three weeks after Diem's death, Kennedy was assassinated in Dallas. Vietnam was now Lyndon B. Johnson's problem. While these dramatic political events unfolded, the SEALs had gone to war.

OP 34A

Shortly after the creation of the SEALs, the commanding officer of SEAL Team One, Lieutenant David Del Giudice, and another SEAL officer went to Vietnam to reconnoiter the area and to see what support could be provided to the Vietnamese. Within a month more SEALs were preparing to deploy to the area. From March 10, 1962, more SEALs arrived in Vietnam to instruct Vietnamese troops in covert maritime operations, running a variety of training courses. SEALs and UDTs also came close to doing more than instructing. In 1961, Kennedy had given the CIA permission to assist the South Vietnamese in undertaking clandestine operations against the North. (This was one of the reasons for the need to train South Vietnamese troops in such missions.) The CIA had sought advice from the military as to how these missions could be carried out. The navy had suggested that SEALs and UDTs could conduct raids against transportation targets, most notably the North Vietnamese road and rail networks; by September 1962, this proposal had expanded to the use of high-speed boats and SEALs to conduct a whole array of commando operations against the North.

Right: UDT Team 12 members welcome the Marines to their landing beach near Da Nang. Some idea of the relatively benign environment that most landings enjoyed can be gained here, although there were several occasions when the beach reconnaissance was interrupted by sniper fire from the Viet Cong.

The U.S. government was not entirely convinced by these proposals, and compromised: while the use of high-speed boats was permitted, they were to be manned entirely by Vietnamese personnel. The SEALs and UDTs would have to wait a while longer before they became embroiled in full-scale combat. However, this did not mean that they were entirely out of the line of fire. As 1962 drew to a close, the U.S. Pacific Fleet decided that it required more information about Vietnam. As part of this, beach surveys needed to be conducted.

FIRST INVOLVEMENT

Operations by UDT men began in February 1963 near Da Nang. The beach parties found themselves coming under sniper fire on more than one occasion. No casualties were inflicted but it demonstrated that the Viet Cong were more active in the area than had been appreciated. This was brought home on March 12, when a beach party came under attack from a group of guerrillas when they were surveying the area near to Vinh Chau. The beach party extricated itself from the fray without injury. This marked the end of the reconnaissance operations, since the U.S. Navy determined that they had obtained more than enough information.

These first missions took place as the campaign against the North intensified. By 1964, U.S. involvement had increased to the level where the military began to take control of covert operations from the CIA, under the auspices of Military Assistance Command, Vietnam-Studies and Observations Group. This was something of a mouthful and the acronym of "MACV-SOG" was used more frequently. Even this was rather long, and led to the abbreviation itself being abbreviated to just "SOG." SOG's maritime element, including SEALs and UDTs, was located at Da Nang. For reasons of security, the organization was claimed to be part of the South Vietnamese coastal survey service, while the Americans were part of a Naval Advisory Detachment (NAD), giving assistance to the survey teams. In fact, the NAD was used to train South Vietnamese commandos, who would be formed into so-called "action teams." The action teams would conduct raids against small targets, ambush enemy forces, and seek to take prisoners who could then be interrogated. To support NAD's operations, Norwegian-built fast patrol vessels were purchased. These boats appeared to have the ideal name for aggressive use, since the Norwegian name for them was the "Nasty" class. (The Norwegians did not take account of the meaning of the word in English when naming the vessels. They thought that they were naming the boats after a species of fish). These boats were soon joined by the smaller boats of the "Swift" class. Both types gave the South Vietnamese commandos an armed capability against the North. The boats would carry out coastal raids themselves, using speed and surprise to enable them to attack the enemy and then escape. They would also be employed to deliver and recover raiding teams. The pace of operations by the commando teams increased as the Viet Cong carried out more and more attacks in the South. In January 1964, President Johnson authorized what were known as "34 Alpha" raids, operations which are now generally (but by no means exclusively) referred to as "OP 34A."

The first OP 34A mission took place on February 16, 1964. South Vietnamese commandos attempted to destroy enemy patrol craft and a ferry but they were unsuccessful. The following missions also failed to achieve their intended aim, adding to the frustration felt by American commanders who had been privately questioning the ability of the South Vietnamese commandos. Eventually, some success was achieved. In June, a storage

Below: A Viet Cong guerrilla, the chief opponent of the SEALs throughout the war in the Mekong Delta.

GULF OF TONKIN

On July 31, four "Nasty" boats bombarded a radar site and radio transmitter and followed this up three days later with an attack on another radar site. However, the North Vietnamese were convinced (rightly so) that the Southern commandos were being supported by the U.S. Navy. They discovered that an American destroyer, the USS *Maddox*, was operating off the North Vietnamese coast and concluded (incorrectly) that the commandos must have had support from the *Maddox*. In fact, the destroyer was conducting separate operations, eavesdropping electronically upon the North Vietnamese. The North Vietnamese decided to retaliate and on August 3, they sent fast attack craft against the *Maddox*. The North Vietnamese gunboats launched torpedoes against the destroyer, which managed to evade them, and air support was called in from the carrier *Ticonderoga*. At least one of the boats was destroyed and another seriously damaged by the air attacks. The crew of the *Maddox*, understandably at a heightened state of alert, continued their patrol. The following night, accompanied by the USS *Turner Joy*, the *Maddox* sent an urgent report that it was under attack again. In fact, it now appears that a justifiably tense crew misinterpreted radar returns, not helped by the poor climatic conditions that made the radar picture difficult to read. Whether or not the second attack actually happened, at the time, the U.S. government was convinced that it did. President Johnson ordered a series of retaliatory air attacks against North Vietnamese targets, and secured the Tonkin Gulf Resolution from Congress,

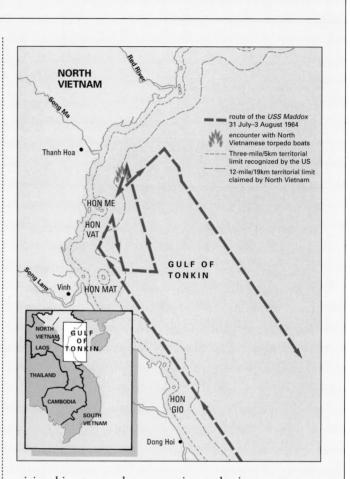

giving him tremendous executive authority to act over Vietnam. Raiding operations by the South Vietnamese continued for the rest of 1964, as the buildup of American forces began.

facility was destroyed and a bridge blown up as a precursor to a larger-scale operation. On the last day of June 1964, a team of commandos attacked a pumping house at a reservoir. They were attacked by North Vietnamese troops. Supported by fire from "Nasty" boats, the raiding party withdrew while in contact with the enemy, boarded its inflatable boats, and successfully left the area. This marked the start of a series of successful operations in which the South Vietnamese troops demonstrated the value of the training given by the SEAL and UDT members who had been assigned to instruction duties. A month later, the success of the commandos was to have a profound effect on the conduct of the Vietnam War.

Combat

On March 8, 1965, the first American ground combat units were sent to Vietnam when Marines went ashore near Da Nang, ostensibly to provide security for the airbase there (which had already suffered from Viet Cong mortar attacks). The landing was an odd affair,

UDT OPERATIONS

There were two ways in which the UDT teams could operate. In the first, they left the submarine as it sat on the ocean floor before swimming to the target beach. Once they had completed their survey they reversed the process, reentering the submarine through the swimmer escape trunk. The other method saw the submarine approach the target beach on the surface, while the UDT members sat in inflatable boats perched on the submarine's deck. At the appropriate juncture, the submarine would submerge and the boats would be left to paddle the remaining distance to the beach. The teams recovered to the submarine by the simple expedient of catching the periscope of the submerged vessel with a line. The submarine would tow the boat out to an area where it could safely surface, whereupon the swimmers and their boats would be taken onboard. If this method were not possible, the UDT team would leave its boats and rejoin the submarine through the swimmer escape hatch.

since the Marines were faced only by journalists recording the event. The newsmen did not pay much attention to the first men ashore, though. A group of men from UDT 12 had conducted a reconnaissance of the beach prior to the landing. UDT detachments were now in increasing demand for beach reconnaissance operations. UDT Detachment Charlie operated from the submarine USS *Perch*.

By the end of 1965, the UDT detachments were undertaking a range of survey missions in support of amphibious assaults in South Vietnam, as the Marines landed in force and sought to engage the enemy. The UDTs conducted their business in a highly professional fashion, their activities receiving high praise from senior officers.

Left: UDTs take time out to pose for the photographer during a landing. An armored bulldozer is seen in the background, preparing the terrain. If it were not for some items of equipment such as swim fins, this could have been a scene from World War II.

While the UDTs conducted their operations without fatalities, they did not escape unscathed. One of them, Commander Robert J. Fay, was killed on April 28, 1965 when his jeep was hit by mortar fire. Fay, who had joined the navy during World War II, was serving as an advisor to MACV-SOG at the time of his death, rather than as part of a UDT.

SEALs Go to War

While the UDTs were conducting operations, the SEALs continued to instruct the South Vietnamese. For much of 1965 it appeared that the U.S. Navy was not convinced that using the SEALs in a combat role was a good idea. This was in spite of the fact that Captain Phil Bucklew, a veteran of navy special operations, had argued for their employment in a direct action role as early as January 1964. This changed in February 1966. Eighteen members of SEAL Team One deployed from their base in San Diego for direct action operations in South Vietnam. There was a problem in that the naval planners in the region were not altogether certain as to how they could best use the group and had not seen any immediately obvious tasks for them to perform. Consequently, the SEALs were sent on operations against Viet Cong units operating in the Rung Sat Special Zone in the Saigon region. The Rung Sat Special Zone (RSSZ) was an unfriendly operating environment. The

Below: A UDT member maps a beach in Vietnam. The lack of weapons and the fact that he is able to stand casually for a photograph suggests that enemy interference is clearly not expected.

zone was a muddy swamp spread over some 400 square miles (1036 sq km) and had a swift, deep running current. The Viet Cong had been using the area as a base, given the area's close proximity to the South Vietnamese capital. Shipping to and from the city ran through the area, giving the guerrillas ample opportunity to attack passing merchant vessels.

The SEALs were well suited to countering the threat posed by the Viet Cong and set about engaging the enemy. The SEALs made use of intelligence on enemy movement gathered by aircraft employing infrared sensors, and from this worked out which locations were the best sites for ambushes. The arrival of the SEALs meant that the Viet Cong could not operate at will in the area. Although they might be able to attack merchant shipping, there was a high risk that they would come under attack and would not be able to escape, which was, after all, an integral part of a successful operation for the guerrillas.

The SEALs enjoyed success in this role but were still without any formally defined operational tasks. This gave them considerable latitude in how they went about their business, since the instructions they received were rather vague. This led to rather simple operation orders—as T. L. Bosiljevac noted in his history of the SEALs in Vietnam, one such order was three sentences long and effectively boiled down to "Patrol, kill as many of the enemy as you can, then leave." This was admirably simple and effective, but did not

Above: UDT members and special forces hold a conference on a Vietnamese beach near Da Nang in 1965. The weapons carried are M16s, although their magazines are not fitted, suggesting that they do not currently feel under threat from Viet Cong attack.

Right: Part of the myriad
duties for the SEALs in
Vietnam included checking
out local craft for supplies
that might be heading for
the Viet Cong. The
SEALs were not averse to
using such local craft
themselves on occasion,
when it would help to
disguise their presence
from the enemy.

last. Navy planners began to come to terms with the SEALs' presence and worked out
how they could use them. This meant that riverine patrol vessels and helicopter gunships
could be made available to support the SEALs. Although these support assets were of
great use and added to the SEALs' flexibility, operations remained based around small unit
commando tactics. The complementary nature of these tactics and the fire support assets
was perhaps best exemplified when the SEALs ambushed and killed a high-ranking Viet
Cong member in a classic small-unit operation. They then discovered the exact time and
location for the dead man's funeral, and returned to the area with helicopter gunships.
The funeral party was attacked and several more senior Viet Cong officials were killed in
the process.

CAN GIO

On July 27, 1966 18 SEALs were inserted near to Can
Gio village. One six-man patrol discovered fresh
footprints, and as they tracked them, ran into three
guerrillas. Unfortunately for the VC concerned, the point
man was carrying an M79 grenade launcher and
immediately fired a round at the enemy, killing one of the
Viet Cong with the grenade. The SEALs then swept
through the area, and discovered an enemy encampment
clearly designed to house a considerable number of
people. A substantial haul of Viet Cong ammunition,
weapons, and equipment was seized, along with
documents, boats, and a stock of rice. The SEALs
destroyed everything except the documents, which were
sent on for analysis at headquarters.

Larger Scale Operations

The SEALs and UDTs did not always operate in small parties, though. Between March 26 and April 7, 1966, they combined with regular Marine forces in Operation Jackstay to interdict guerrilla forces at the mouth of the Saigon River. Among other actions, members of UDT 11 ambushed a Viet Cong junk, inflicting heavy casualties on the occupants, then demolished a guerrilla camp. The operation was judged to be a considerable success, since it had a major disruptive effect upon VC operations in the area. This was soon followed by several other missions for the navy men.

One operation on August 5, 1966, led to the capture of three sampans and over 6000 pounds (2700 kilograms) of rice. Two days later, a squad ambushed a junk and two sampans and killed seven Viet Cong. On August 18, a patrol discovered two silos containing huge amounts of rice, clearly designed to feed guerrillas in the area. The SEALs called in an air strike and naval gunfire and this destroyed over 300,000 tons of rice. While destroying rice silos does not on first examination appear to be particularly significant, it should be recalled that this represented a massive blow to the enemy's logistics and the sustainability of the VC in the region with a consequent disruption to their ability to operate effectively.

Below: SEALs make their way ashore from a landing craft during operations in 1966 in the Rung Sat Special Zone. The landing craft gave the SEALs mobility around the Delta, although they presented tempting targets. There were several instances where the landing craft were subjected to heavy attack, and only determined resistance by the SEALs and the craft's crewmen prevented a disaster.

The next day, August 19, 1966, was not such a good one. A small group of SEALs was conducting a reconnaissance mission along the Dinh Ba River when a report came in that a helicopter pilot had seen what appeared to be camouflaged sampans farther up river. The SEALs were moved to the area of the sighting and discovered fresh tracks. As they followed the tracks, the SEALs saw the sampans some 550 yards (500 meters) ahead of them and slowly moved toward them. When they reached a jungle clearing, the point man, Petty Officer Billy W. Machen, stopped the patrol and moved forward to investigate. As he scanned the jungle, he realized there were VC waiting in ambush positions. Rather than dive for cover, Machen immediately opened fire and forced the VC to initiate the ambush before the rest of the team had entered the killing zone. The SEALs were able to gain cover and then returned fire. A vicious combat then ensued, ending with the arrival of helicopter gunships to give the patrol covering fire. Sadly, Machen was killed in the initial contact. Determined not to leave him behind, another member of the patrol recovered Machen's body and carried him out of the area. Billy W. Machen was subsequently awarded a posthumous Silver Star for his gallantry. He was the first SEAL fatality in combat in Vietnam and his death demonstrated that the war was becoming ever more serious.

The SEALs and UDTs continued their operations in the RSSZ, killing enemy troops, and capturing weapons, sampans, and equipment. As Machen's death demonstrated, the Viet Cong were not passive participants in this process and responded vigorously. However, the superior training of the SEALs usually gave them the advantage even when confronted by a substantial enemy force. A prime example of this came on October 7, 1966, when a patrol from SEAL Team One ran into serious opposition. The patrol, made up of two seven-man squads, was moving along the Long Tau River in a Landing Craft,

Rather than dive for cover, Machen immediately opened fire and forced the VC to initiate the ambush before the rest of the team had entered the killing zone.

Left: SEALs aboard a patrol boat check a junk for any war material. Most of these routine searches produced nothing, but on occasion, they revealed substantial amounts of supplies heading for the VC hidden in the jungle of the Delta.

Mechanized (LCM), as it headed toward a dropping off point for the SEAL patrols. Unfortunately, the Viet Cong were lying in wait in battalion strength to ambush river traffic and the LCM was a tempting target. They initiated an ambush and the LCM immediately came under very heavy fire. One mortar round scored a direct hit on the LCM, causing casualties. The initial salvo from the VC wounded 16 of the 19 men aboard the LCM to varying degrees, some of them seriously. Although the VC had gained an advantage it did not last. The LCM had been provided with armor and a number of weapons, including a 20mm (0.78-inch) cannon, two .50-caliber (12.7mm) machine-guns, and a mortar of its own in addition to other .30-caliber (7.62mm) automatic weapons and the SEALs' personal small arms.

The Viet Cong mortar round wounded both of the .50-caliber gunners but they carried on firing regardless. In fact, the two SEAL gunners put down such a volume of fire that the machine-gun barrels were white hot and glowing at the end of the engagement. Despite his

Unfortunately, the Viet Cong were lying in wait in battalion strength to ambush river traffic and the LCM was a tempting target. They initiated an ambush and the LCM immediately came under very heavy fire.

wounds, one of the SEALs, Chief Petty Officer Churchill, noticed that a fragment from the enemy mortar hit was in danger of setting off the LCM's own mortar ammunition. Churchill managed to pick up the piece of hot shrapnel and heaved it overboard. As he did so he realized that one of the .50-caliber machine guns had stopped firing and saw that the wounded gunner had fallen unconscious. Churchill tried to take over the weapon. The patrol officer then moved over to the position and relieved his injured subordinate. Rather than do nothing, Churchill then began to give first aid to the wounded SEALs, which further exposed him to incoming fire. While the casualties were substantial, the sheer aggression of the SEALs proved to be the decisive factor. Later investigation revealed that the savage return fire from the LCM had killed more than 40 VC and wounded others. These losses caused the VC unit to break contact and retreat; for the next two weeks, the enemy battalion was noticeably quieter than it had been. On the American side, three of the SEALs were so badly hurt that they were discharged from the navy on medical grounds, while CPO Churchill was awarded a Silver Star for his actions.

A small number of men were having a considerable effect so the activities of the SEALs could not fail to go unnoticed. The U.S. Navy decided that it should increase the number of SEALs in theater, expanding the teams to a total of seven officers and thirty enlisted men, while SEAL Team Two was ordered to begin preparations to send five officers and

Below: A SEAL watches the shoreline through the sight on a recoilless rifle while on patrol in the Rung Sat Special Zone. The recoilless rifle had largely fallen from favor in its original anti-tank role by this time, but was still useful. The heavy firepower that it could deliver against an enemy target made it particularly useful for engaging VC hidden in bunkers.

Left: SEALs in a patrol boat in the Mekong Delta during 1967. This could be a routine patrol, or the patrol boat may be on its way to insert SEALs for a direct action mission.

Below: This plan of the Mekong Delta shows the extent of the area that the SEALs covered. The scale does not allow the countless small streams and tributaries that covered the Delta to be seen. Each waterway could have VC hiding somewhere along the banks, waiting in ambush.

twenty men to Vietnam to boost numbers still further. The pace and success of operations in the RSSZ gave clear justification for the decision to increase the number of special forces present. When Operation Charleston took place on December 3 and 4, 1966, the SEALs worked in support of the U.S. Army, exploiting intelligence information from sources that they had developed during the course of the year. A six-strong SEAL patrol discovered a weapons cache on December 3, which included a 57mm (2.24-inch) recoilless rifle, two German machine-guns dating from World War II, and 10,000 rounds of ammunition. (The recoilless rifle subsequently found its way to the U.S. Navy museum where it went on display.) The SEALs finished the year with raids on enemy facilities on December 13 and 21, destroying a particularly large (but unoccupied) VC camp on the latter date. They also captured a number of documents and several hundred thousand pounds of rice that would have been used to sustain the VC during some of 1967.

The small SEAL Team One detachment never had more than 40 men. Yet during 1966 it had conducted

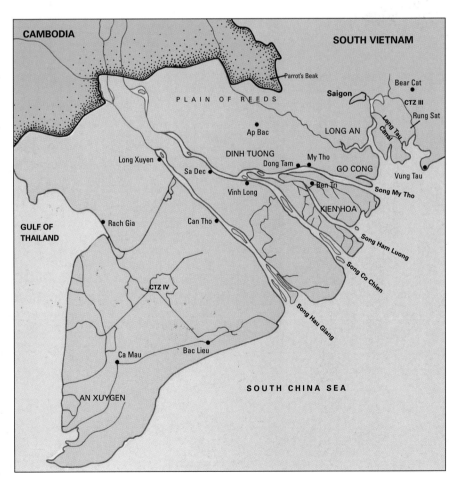

It is as well to note that for the VC, a wounded guerrilla was far more of a problem than a dead one— the dead body could be left where it fell but the wounded man, more often than not, had to be extricated from the scene and then treated.

Right: A SEAL stands waiting to assist in tying up a patrol craft as it returns to shore on the Bassac River. The patrol craft were not manned by SEALs alone, since a dedicated band of sailors operated the patrol boats and landing craft that took the SEALs on operations, facing the same risks as the Navy commandos.

153 combat operations, with impressive results. It was estimated that 101 Viet Cong guerrillas had been killed, while 21 sampans, 2 junks, and 33 assorted buildings had been destroyed. Furthermore, the SEALs had captured over 500,000 pounds (227,000 kilograms) of rice, a variety of weapons and many valuable enemy documents. These figures do not tell the whole story, however. It is as well to note that for the VC, a wounded guerrilla was far more of a problem than a dead one—the dead body could be left where it fell but the wounded man, more often than not, had to be extricated from the scene and then treated. The provision of treatment, or moving the wounded to a place where they could receive it, added to the logistical burdens of the guerrillas, who naturally enough did not have the sort of medical organization available to them that the U.S. forces did.

In addition to this, the very presence of the SEALs and their robust manner of engaging the enemy (as evidenced by their response to the attack on the LCM) had a number of unfavorable implications for the VC. They could no longer operate in the RSSZ at will, as they had done before, while the loss of personnel, supplies, and equipment must have had an adverse effect on morale, although this is almost impossible to quantify. Finally, the SEALs appear to have been quite successful in developing human intelligence sources in the area, thus creating another headache for the VC, who had previously not had to worry about their operational security to any great extent.

Above: The machine gunner on a patrol craft opens up with a 0.5-inch (12.7mm) machine gun against a target on the river bank on January 20, 1967, some 15 miles (24km) south east of Saigon. In the foreground, an M79 grenade launcher is brought forward. Four Viet Cong were killed during the operation, and significant amounts of rice destroyed by the SEALs.

NEW TECHNIQUES

The SEAL teams began to develop new operational techniques in Vietnam. It became clear that wearing combat boots was problematic. Their footprints immediately gave away the presence of U.S. forces to the VC, who did not wear such footgear (if they possessed any footwear at all). The SEALs responded by wearing tennis shoes, or even by emulating the Viet Cong. Conventional uniform began to be replaced by the use of jeans instead of issue trousers, since many SEALs felt that the material stood up better to the harsh conditions in the Delta.

As 1966 drew to a close, it was clear that the SEALs had been operationally successful. They had provided a valuable, if relatively small-scale, means of inflicting damage on the VC in a way that conventional forces could not. The results achieved by the SEALs and the UDTs meant that their skills soon came to be considered in a very different fashion to that at the start of the year. The planners moved from regarding the SEALs as an awkward presence for whom it was difficult to find a role to seeing them as an important weapon in the sort of unconventional warfare that the U.S. found itself fighting in Vietnam. It was, therefore, almost inevitable that the early efforts of 1966 would be followed by the commitment of more SEALs to Vietnam, in greater numbers than before.

1967

The growth in the number of SEALs assigned to Vietnam mirrored an increasing commitment by the U.S. government to the war. By the start of 1967, there were nearly 400,000 personnel involved in the conflict as efforts were made to coerce the North Vietnamese into withdrawing their support for the Viet Cong. Despite the massive efforts being made in the Rolling Thunder bombing campaign (which was notably hamstrung by

Right: SEALs in a typical Vietnamese village in an enemy-infested area along the Bassac River 67 miles (107km) south west of Saigon in September 1967 during Operation Crimson Tide. Villages could be hiding places for the VC, or they could contain villagers with little time for the communist/ nationalist cause. As the VC were effective guerrillas following Maoist principles of guerrilla warfare, it was extremely difficult to tell whether the village was used by the VC or not.

Left: A SEAL practices stalking an enemy sentry (played by another SEAL complete with stereotypical hat and Soviet submachine gun) during training in California in 1967. In most instances, SEALs would seek to neutralize sentries with a silenced weapon if one was available.

Below: SEALs fast rope from a Bell UH-1 Huey during operations in 1967. While the men were vulnerable hanging beneath the helicopter, they were able to get on the ground far more quickly than if the helicopter landed first.

political limitations over targeting), the enemy did not display any signs of giving in. Indeed, the Viet Cong increased their efforts against targets in the South. This was particularly true in the RSSZ and attacks on shipping increased. While the buildup in numbers was underway, operations continued. Information gathered from the documents seized in Operation Charleston enabled the SEALs to destroy wells used by the VC; two teams destroyed eight wells on January 12. Again, this apparently simple task had a considerable impact: it compelled the VC to carry water with them. Previously, they had been able to make for a reliable and constant source of water and had needed only enough to sustain them between visits to the wells. Now they had to carry all the water they required for the duration of their operations.

At the end of the month, the elements from SEAL Team Two arrived, and based themselves at Nha Bhe. Some operations with SEAL Team One were undertaken as the new SEALs acquainted themselves with their area of responsibility, before SEAL Team One moved to their operating areas in the Mekong Delta.

The SEALs also made changes to the way in which they entered their patrol areas. While they continued to use the standard PBR patrol boat as their preferred conveyance, some teams swam to shore rather than have the PBR pull alongside, giving away the patrol's location to any VC who happened to be in the area. In a further refinement of this approach, a SEAL Team One patrol

Right: Although not depicting SEALs, this photograph epitomises the routine work carried out on the Mekong Delta. The crew of a Patrol Air Cushion Vehicle (PACV) bring captured VC prisoners aboard. The hovercraft were a great success in operations in the Plain of Reeds.

Below: SEALs watch the detonation of explosive charges that they have planted in VC bunkers from the safety of a "Mike" boat. The SEALs often did not encounter the VC, but found their hiding places. In such instances, they would destroy them and any equipment.

jumped from the stern of the PBR as it was still moving. This method had the advantage that the engine note of the PBR did not change at all, giving any eavesdroppers the impression that the boat had not landed any personnel. The sound of the PBR's engine was loud enough* to mask the sound of the SEALs jumping into the water. Some other developments in technique saw the use of deception in an attempt to trap the opposition.

The deception methods included the use of "false insertions" and "false extractions." In the former, the SEALs would not actually land, but the PBR would make as if it was about to disembark patrols, stopping near to the shore. This had the benefit of making the VC uncertain as to the location of the SEALs, forcing them to move. If any movement was detected the SEALs would then insert for real to lay an ambush. False extractions were also an effective means of trying to lure the enemy into an ambush. Part of a patrol would extract from the area, leaving the remainder hidden in ambush positions. When the VC saw part of the patrol leave, they tended to assume that the whole unit had left. They would then move and blunder into an ambush. These techniques all depended, of course, on the elusive VC being in the patrol area in the first place. Although intelligence was good, it was not so good as to guarantee that every patrol would find numbers of Viet Cong to ambush every time they went out. Further trickery came with the so-called "double-back ambush," which was as simple in conception as the name suggests. The entire patrol would depart its area but instead of leaving would double back on its own path. Eventually, the whole patrol would be lying in wait to engage anyone who might have been tracking them.

Intelligence Gathering

These new techniques contributed to the increased use of the SEAL teams in intelligence-gathering operations. Patrols were sent out to set up observation posts concealed in the dense jungle and they would remain in place for days at a time. The demands of living in an observation post were—and still are—acute. SEALs engaged in such activity would usually be forced to remain in place, moving only rarely. Bodily functions had to be undertaken in the confined area of the observation post and cooking food could prove particularly difficult, since the aroma given off would be easily detected by a guerrilla unit. Although patrols were well armed, contact with the enemy would not be initiated, except in dire emergency: fighting would defeat the entire purpose of using a covert observation post. By April 1967, more SEALs were in Vietnam to undertake such tasks, since SEAL Team One's Kilo and Lima platoons arrived during the first week of the month. On April 7, however, Kilo platoon received a very unpleasant introduction to Vietnam—the LCM in

Left: William Langley applies camouflage before heading off on a SEAL mission along the Bassac River in November 1967. Although far from "high-tech," the simple camouflage stick remains an important military tool, particularly for those on ambushes. His facial hair, however, is not standard military issue.

which members of fire teams 3 and 4 were traveling was ambushed. Unlike the incident from 1966 recounted above, the Viet Cong were more vigorous in their efforts.

The trouble began with the use of the LCM for what was known as "recon by fire." The idea of behind this process was admirably simple—the LCM would cruise along the river, firing its weapons in an attempt to gain a response from the enemy. Once contact was initiated, the SEALs aboard the LCM would return fire and call in air support, which would be sufficient to inflict serious damage on the VC. The only problem was that this noisy activity revealed the location of the LCM and might permit a reasonably organized band of VC to lie in wait for the LCM farther along the river. Rather than have the element of surprise, which the SEALs sought to obtain in their direct-action operations, this advantage could easily be ceded to the enemy. This was to be the case on April 7. The ambush was initiated and the LCM returned fire; all appeared to be going as well as could be expected in a vicious firefight when there was a large explosion directly above the landing craft. The source of the explosion has been disputed but it was either a large caliber mortar round or perhaps one of several B-40 rockets that was fired by the VC. The blast and shrapnel from the explosion caused serious casualties. Two SEALs were killed instantly and another twelve were wounded, one of these men later dying from his wounds. The LCM was forced to limp away from the ambush site. Once it had

Below: SEALs watch another Viet Cong hideaway get blown sky high by the explosive charges they have placed. The men must be confident that the enemy are not nearby— "beaching" the boats on the bank left them vulnerable to attack.

successfully extricated itself, the dead and wounded were evacuated by helicopter.

The incident demonstrated another truism about special forces, which is that although they are trained to be highly aggressive, expecting them to act as such all the time can have serious disadvantages. In their after-action report, the SEALs pointed out that they had never been entirely in favor of the recon-by-fire technique, since it offered an invitation to the VC to engage them from a position of strength—just as they had on April 7. The SEALs made clear their view that the LCMs would be better employed assisting the SEALs in their infiltration of a patrol area. Once ashore, the SEALs would be in a much better position to initiate offensive action with the benefit of surprise. Risking casualties among the SEALs was hardly sensible, since they were not available in large numbers. If the SEALs in theater were reduced in number by death and wounds, it would not be a simple task to replace them with an equal number of men from the United States, since this sort of manpower did not exist. While training and selection classes were increased to meet the demand, there was no guarantee that the increased number of potential recruits would lead to an increased number of SEALs. Not all recruits would pass the rigorous selection process. In fact, it was far more likely that the majority of trainees would not end up as SEAL team members.

A more satisfactory use of the SEALs was in combining listening-post duties with ambush operations. This gave the team the opportunity to gather intelligence and if a suitable opportunity arose, engage small parties of the enemy. They could also avoid fighting vastly superior numbers, which could only end in serious difficulties.

Conversely, a similar operation on April 18 did not have such problems: a three-man listening post found itself confronted by three VC personnel, whom they promptly shot and killed. Of course, once contact with the enemy took place, the listening post was forced to withdraw, since its position was compromised.

Above: Two PBR patrol boats make their way along the Mekong River, their machine guns aimed at the enemy. Overhead in the background, a UH-1 Huey gunship provides fire support with the use of unguided rockets.

CLOSE ENCOUNTER

SEALs could get very close to the enemy. In one instance, a patrol led by Lieutenant Michael Troy (a gold medallist in the 200m butterfly event at the Rome Olympics of 1960) discovered that the ambush it planned to conduct would be a very bad idea, since the enemy force numbered around 60 personnel. Troy and his team took to the water and stayed there for around 12 hours with only their heads above the water. Because they were wearing camouflage face paint and were well hidden the VC did not spot them, although Troy later remarked that one member of the VC patrol came so close to him that he could have reached up and touched the man.

Right: A SEAL patrol in country near Vinh Binh in December 1967. The point man carefully moves forward while his colleagues wait after discovering a punji stake booby trap. Jungle patrolling was a slow business—rapid movement generates noise that gives patrols away to the enemy. Rather than crash through the foliage, patrols would move extremely slowly and methodically, remaining as quiet as possible. They would also normally avoid cooking food or smoking (despite the SEAL smoker shown here), since such smells were just as much a giveaway as noise.

Four VC were heading toward a well and the observation team signaled the patrol that the enemy was present.

Direct Action

Although there was an increased focus on covert observation tasks, the SEALs continued to undertake aggressive, direct-action operations. On July 2, 1967, SEALs from Team One's Juliet and Kilo platoons combined with elements of the 2/7 Air Cavalry, the U.S. Coast Guard cutter *Point White*, and the destroyer USS *Brush* for Operation Shallow Draft 11-A. Intelligence had revealed the location of a VC headquarters some 20 miles (32 kilometers) northeast of Phan Thiet. It was suspected that several senior VC officials would be in the stronghold. The SEALs were tasked with capturing as many of these officials as they could. They began the raid by launching in inflatable boats from the *Brush*. Once in range of the shore, a number of the SEALs left the boats and swam in to reconnoiter the beach. Once the beach was found to be clear, the scouts signaled to the boats, and the team came ashore. They concealed the boats and moved inland, stopping to establish radio contact with the *Brush*. Once this was done, the team climbed a hill and established an observation post. Then they settled down to try to get some rest. During the course of the following day, the team remained hidden in the observation post, carefully watching the surrounding area. As the light fell, six SEALs left the observation post and headed down to the target area. Shortly after they had arrived in their patrol zone, the men in the

Above: A SEAL instructor oversees training on a 40mm (1.57-inch) automatic grenade launcher in January 1968. This weapon is one of the early models of grenade launcher, since the rounds are being cranked in by the handle on the side of the weapon. Such weapons offer a means of delivering large amounts of firepower against point targets, and were an extremely useful weapon to have on patrol boats in Vietnam.

Left: A patrol boat crewman takes time to relax behind his 0.5-inch (12.7mm) machine gun. His flak jacket is notable, while his helmet can just be seen at the bottom right of the picture. The thick jungle in the background gives some idea of the difficulties of patrolling—staring into the trees for hours at a time, trying to spot any movement, was a fatiguing task.

The next day saw an operation disrupted by hostile action of an unusual sort—a wild boar charged a group of SEALs who were compelled to shoot the beast to protect themselves.

observation post spotted movement. Four VC were heading toward a well and the observation team signaled the patrol that the enemy was present. They also notified the *Brush*, which was to provide fire support if necessary. The team's interpreter hailed the VC as they approached the well. Rather than stand their ground, the four VC—two men and two women—turned and ran. The SEALs pursued them, and one of the women was killed by a gunshot. One of the male VC was slightly wounded, while the other two guerrillas were overpowered. As the SEALs moved to their exfiltration point, awaiting the arrival of helicopters, the *Brush* began firing to suppress any enemy efforts at interfering with the departure of the SEALs. Once the SEALs returned to base, they discovered that the two male prisoners were leaders of VC cells, while the dead woman was the head of one of the VC's women's organizations. The raid also netted a useful haul of documentation. The results of this spectacular raid were judged to be particularly worthwhile and prisoner abduction was to become an important part of the SEALs' operations for the remainder of the Vietnam War.

As well as the raid, the SEALs undertook a number of other operations. Over a period of two weeks in July, Kilo platoon managed to kill several VC in ambushes and recovered a number of documents that were well received by intelligence analysts. A Team Two platoon captured important documents relating to the VC's command structure in the

Below: A SEAL crouches at the front of a small patrol craft, his M16 rifle at the ready. The M16 made its name in Vietnam, albeit after initial difficulties, providing automatic firepower in a lightweight package.

Left: SEALs come ashore in the Rung Sat Special Zone in early 1968. The use of small boats to ferry SEALs to their operating areas provided the main means of infiltration where it was necessary to avoid alerting the enemy. The whalers also provided a rapid means of departure if required by the SEALs.

Binh Dai zone on July 9 and followed this up by killing four VC on the last day of their patrol, recovering yet more documents. The latter batch of documents included two maps and a list of Viet Cong personnel; information garnered from the maps led to an operation by the South Vietnamese army on July 17. An operation by two SEAL squads against a suspected command post on the 20th did not net the VC commander who was thought to be there but the SEAL teams engaged a number of sampans as Viet Cong attempted to leave the area; four VC were killed. The next day saw an operation disrupted by hostile action of an unusual sort—a wild boar charged a group of SEALs who were compelled to shoot the beast to protect themselves. The sound of the gunshot was enough to mark the end of the mission for the team—they could not be certain whether the noise had been heard by the VC. Rather than take the chance that they might have been compromised, the SEALs returned to base. On August 11, another team was forced to extract from an ambush position. One of the men sustained a bite from a

SAVING THE ENEMY

A series of operations in October 1967 led to the death of seven enemy troops and the capture of several others, one of whom was wanted for the murder of the South Vietnamese national police chief five years previously. Having expended considerable effort in attempting to kill this particular man, the SEALs then had to protect him from the South Vietnamese soldiers accompanying the patrol, who wanted to shoot the prisoner there and then. It appears that the SEALs made clear that the man was not going to be killed in their customary forthright and concise fashion, since the South Vietnamese troops lost interest in executing the captive.

Above: A bird's-eye view of patrol boats making their way along the Mekong Delta. While the SEALs carried considerable personal firepower on operations, the presence of air support was always a comfort, since it provided a fast-responding means of bringing fire to bear on the enemy when a situation became difficult.

venomous spider and he had to be evacuated to hospital. It was not just the Viet Cong who caused problems.

On August 16, twenty SEALs launched an offensive sweep on the island of Culaodung after intelligence from a VC defector suggested that there might be as many as 200 VC there. The SEALs landed at dawn and from 0900 hours were provided with air support from UH-1 "Huey" gunships. The SEALs exchanged fire with several VC (although the exchanges were brief, with the VC running after firing their first shots) and located a number of bunkers and barrack buildings. Fourteen bunkers and more than fifty buildings were destroyed. The SEALs also discovered a cache of some fourteen tons of rice and destroyed this as well. Finally, they added some half-dozen sampans to the list of items that would not be of any further use to the enemy. Although the VC had fired shots, it was hard to tell how accurate the defector's report of up to 200 men had been. The SEALs certainly killed three guerrillas, but of the others there appeared to be no trace. This operation demonstrated the value of establishing an effective intelligence network that could, on occasion, "turn" an enemy soldier, who would then provide valuable information. This point was reinforced just two days after the Culaodung island mission, when another former VC led a SEAL patrol to an enemy encampment. In the short and vicious firefight that followed, three Viet Cong members were killed, and the camp's armory was blown up.

New Techniques

Although there was little doubt that the SEALs were enjoying considerable success in their missions they did not rest on their laurels. Attempts were made to improve operational techniques at all levels. While not always obvious on an individual level, some of the changes were easy to spot. One of these came with the decision to put small, high-speed "Boston Whaler" boats to trial. SEALs had noticed that the relatively flimsy sampans used by the guerrillas tended to sink very quickly after an engagement, undoubtedly taking useful intelligence information with them. The whalers were deployed to allow the SEALs to make a rapid approach to any sampans that they had hit, so that they could secure the small craft and make certain that it did not find its way to the bottom of the river. The whalers fulfilled the expectations of the SEALs, leading to the recovery of a great deal of documentation and equipment. In fact, the boats were so successful that they remain in use.

As 1967 drew to a close, the SEALs began to place more emphasis on ambushes rather than just reconnaissance patrols. While the VC had shown some reluctance to engage the SEALs on occasion, they did not on October 13, when a sizeable group of VC reacted to

Below: A SEAL boat crewman keeps a careful lookout along the river bank over the barrels of his twin 'fifty-cal' Browning M2 machine guns. Although old, the 0.5-inch (12.7mm) machine gun delivered a formidable amount of firepower, and nothing better has been found to replace it in service, even today.

Above: A Huey gunship fires a 2.75-inch (70mm) rocket from one of the seven-round pods mounted along its sides. Outboard of the rocket pods are two M60 machine guns. Some Huey gunships replaced the M60s with XM134 Miniguns, formidable Gatling-type weapons that can fire at the rate of 100 rounds *a second*. The Hueys also carried two M60s for use by the door gunners, making for a formidable amount of firepower.

the SEALs' initiation of an ambush by attempting to overrun the Americans. Unfortunately for the VC, one of the SEALs was equipped with a 40mm (1.57-inch) grenade launcher and put a barrage of grenades on them. Seven VC were killed as a result of the grenades, and the rest—perhaps wisely—decided that they would rather disengage than continue their attack.

At the end of October, another patrol encountered aggressive VC resistance when they ambushed a group of enemy soldiers and killed two of them. As was normal procedure, the SEALs then followed up the ambush with a sweep of the area only to come under heavy fire from more VC who were in a bunker complex. The SEALs took the enemy under fire and killed two more VC, before moving forward again and securing the complex. On investigation, they discovered 14 well-concealed bunkers and a large quantity of ammunition. The bunkers were blown up, while the ammunition was removed, possibly to allow the SEALs and other special forces to make use of AK-47 Kalashnikov assault rifles (and their derivatives). The AK-47 was (and still is) famed for its ability to operate in the harshest conditions and, despite its faults, special operations units prized its reliability. At this time, the M16—a relatively new design which was in the process of becoming the standard assault rifle for the U.S. armed forces—suffered a reputation for not functioning at the critical moment and there were a number of instances where troops made use of captured rifles instead.

Left: This photograph of a clean-cut commando (actually seen during training in the United States) has obviously not been taken in Vietnam on operations, since he is far too smartly dressed. His face is not camouflaged, and the same is true of the shiny black forestock of his M16. In the Mekong Delta, it was often difficult to find time to shave. SEALs pictured in the Delta were often seen with long hair and bushy beards which made their appearance even more frightening to the VC.

Unfortunately for the VC, one of the SEALs was equipped with a 40mm (1.57-inch) grenade launcher and put a barrage of grenades on them. Seven VC were killed as a result of the grenades, and the rest—perhaps wisely—decided that they would rather disengage than continue their attack.

November and December 1967 saw similar ambushes and captures. Between November 15 and 25, elements from SEAL Team Two were particularly busy. On the 15th a patrol killed a VC district security officer who had been hunted for a considerable length of time. Over the next nine days, during the course of Operation Cuu Long, 7th Platoon killed 15 guerrillas and captured 11. They also seized an AK-47, a rocket launcher, and 16 Chinese-made versions of the SKS carbine. This was not all that 7th platoon achieved, since they also destroyed 80 enemy bunker positions and half a dozen sampans. Having completed a particularly successful operation, the platoon then went on to kill three more VC and capture another in a sweep operation near to My Tho.

The rest of SEAL Two was not inactive either.On November 25, a patrol discovered a number of "hooches" (the term used to describe any VC dwelling, from a reed-roofed shack to a Quonsett hut). They observed the area for movement and were rewarded just after nightfall when two VC attempted to leave the area. The SEALs fired on both, but as they did so, it became clear that the hooches were occupied by over a dozen more VC, and possibly as many as 20. The SEALs swiftly began to exfiltrate from the area, calling

Below: This almost timeless picture shows a UDT member in the Vietnam War, but could just as well be from 1944—apart from the sunblock on his nose. He is stripped to the waist and wears a helmet that had not changed in design since World War II.

for a riverine craft to come and retrieve them. As they made their way to the rendezvous, they ran straight into a bunker occupied by Viet Cong. While the SEALs were surprised, the Viet Cong were more so. They were also slower to the trigger and the SEALs killed them all. The patrol was recovered safely and it soon emerged that the operation had resulted in the deaths of six Viet Cong.

The year did not end altogether successfully, however, for the SEALs. On December 23, SEAL One's Bravo platoon began a reconnaissance/ambush patrol but after moving only a short distance came under heavy fire. It later transpired that the patrol had penetrated the outer perimeter of a Viet Cong camp. The point man of the patrol, Seaman Frank G. Antone was hit by the initial burst of fire and was killed, as was a South Vietnamese commando. The platoon returned fire and immediately began to exfiltrate toward their extraction point. Three more SEALs were wounded before helicopters recovered all of them.

By the end of 1967, any doubts that the SEALs represented an extremely effective means of carrying the fight to the enemy had gone. The ambushes launched by the SEAL patrols during 1966 and 1967 had changed the nature of the war for the Viet Cong, who knew that they could no longer operate at will. The arrival of the SEALs meant that the VC could never be certain whether or not they would be ambushed when moving. Nor could they be sure that their strongholds were safe from attack. As well as

spreading doubt and imposing psychological pressure on the enemy, the SEALs had achieved results that were easier to define in terms of enemy personnel killed and captured, in weapons, equipment, and documents seized, and in material destroyed. While the SEAL teams represented a very small proportion of the personnel deployed to Vietnam (by the end of 1967, there were almost 500,000 Americans serving in the country) their results were out of all proportion to their numbers and were of clear significance. Despite the high level of achievements during the first two years of operations, the SEALs would reach new peaks of performance as the war went on. This was as well: despite the setbacks caused by the SEAL teams, the Viet Cong were most emphatically not finished and their defeat, if it was to be achieved, was seen to be a long way off. The events of 1968 would display this fact all too clearly.

1968

The SEALs did not have to wait long before they commenced operations in 1968. On January 2, a patrol was led to a VC camp hidden on May Island (in the middle of the Bassac River) by a defector. The occupants were engaged in swift and decisive combat. Six enemy soldiers were killed and two buildings and a quantity of rice were destroyed. The patrol had not yet finished its work for the day, since they later captured an enemy courier. The

Above: SEALs clean their weapons in preparation for their next operation. Although the M16 was—remarkably—touted as a "self-cleaning rifle" when it first entered service, the SEALs did not believe this and took scrupulous care to maintain their weapons. In common with other special forces troops, they had far fewer problems with the gun as a result.

Right: An image from a SEAL recruiting poster from 1967 tries to demonstrate some of the aspects of the SEALs' work—arguably not particularly well! The camouflage jacket/beach shorts combination appears a little unlikely, but given the SEALs' penchant for unsual clothing is not impossible. The diver, meanwhile demonstrates the latest in scuba gear, looking rather poorly equipped to the modern eye.

Unknown to anyone on the American side the bunker was occupied by five VC guerrillas who were preparing to conduct attacks with a rocket launcher.

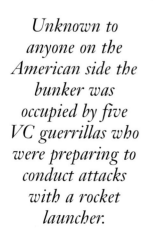

courier was a potentially valuable source of information and he knew it. As the SEALs moved toward their exfiltration point the prisoner attempted to escape and was shot. His wound proved fatal and the SEALs went home empty-handed. Before the first week of the year was over, 7th Platoon, accompanied by two members of the South Vietnamese equivalent of the SEALs, the Lien Doc Nguoi Niha (LDNN), ambushed a convoy of three sampans traveling down a small river, killing all four occupants of the small craft. Thus, the events of the first seven days of 1968 seemed to suggest that the war would continue in much the same vein for the SEALs. There was a worrying omen just four days later, however. On January 11, a squad from Bravo platoon was sent to deal with a VC bunker in the Ba Xuyen province. Unknown to anyone on the American side the bunker was occupied by five VC guerrillas who were preparing to conduct attacks with a rocket launcher. One of the VC ran from the bunker, firing his AK-47 as he charged toward the approaching SEALs. The burst of fire hit Seaman Roy B. Keith, mortally wounding him. Keith's colleagues reacted instantly and the VC with the AK-47 was killed. The patrol then moved in on the remaining VC, killing three of them. One VC managed to escape, but it was believed that he had been wounded, possibly quite badly. The Viet Cong rocket launcher was captured, along with three assault rifles. Seaman Keith was the first of 16

MISTAKEN IDENTITY

On January 22, 1967 two SEAL squads were operating along the banks of a canal on the Tien Giang River. While patrolling on one side of the waterway the SEALs in the first team spotted an unlighted sampan and fired on it, killing the four VC aboard. The squad moved away from the area, and came across another unlighted sampan, this time with two men on board. Again, they opened fire and riddled the small craft with bullets. Again, the crew was killed. The second outbreak of firing did not go unnoticed, and a small force of VC on the other bank reacted. Their reaction was misjudged, however, since they were not exactly certain of where the American fire had come from. Their misjudgment meant that rather than firing at the SEALs, they were firing at another

group of VC, who promptly returned fire. The SEALs were treated to a grandstand view as the two groups of VC shot at each other with increasing ferocity. The second SEAL squad, which was beginning to feel a little left out of matters, discovered that it had chosen an ambush position that was perfect for engaging both sets of VC, which it promptly did. As if this was not enough, a lone sampan blundered into the middle of the firefight and the SEALs set about it and the unfortunate VC crewman with gusto. The SEALs decided that it was probably a good time to leave and moved toward their extraction point, killing yet another Viet Cong soldier as they left. The two SEAL squads then linked up and made their way out of the area.

SEALs to die in 1968—this was more than twice the number of men killed in 1966 and 1967 and was to demonstrate the intensity of the year's fighting. A week later, Gunner's Mate First Class Arthur Williams was killed as his team was being extracted while under fire from the enemy.

This did not mean that the SEALs had suddenly begun to suffer reverses at the hands of the Viet Cong, though. In the late evening of January 22 and the early hours of the following morning, there were two notable actions involving SEAL teams. In one of them, a squad from Alfa platoon joined five members of the Australian Special Air Service (SAS) to conduct an ambush operation in the RSSZ. The party was inserted by helicopter into a mangrove swamp at 1830 hours and dug in to their ambush positions. The ambush team had to wait for something to materialize. At 0530 hours the next morning, the team heard the sound of several boats approaching. The SEALs and SAS became more alert, waiting to see what came into view. They did not have to wait long, since three sampans containing somewhere between eight and twelve VC (the poor light made it difficult to tell exactly how many guerrillas were on board the boats) were quickly sighted. This was a tempting target but it soon became obvious that the sampans were moving away from the ambush site into another part of the swamp. It was obvious that the ambushers would have to act quickly, so they called for the LCM that would recover them at the end of the mission to fire illumination rounds from its 81mm (3.1-inch) mortar. Incredibly, every single round failed to detonate. The situation was saved by the fact that the SEALs were equipped with hand-held parachute flares, which they fired to illuminate the ambush

Below: A map of the Tet Offensive, which caught the U.S. forces in Vietnam by surprise.

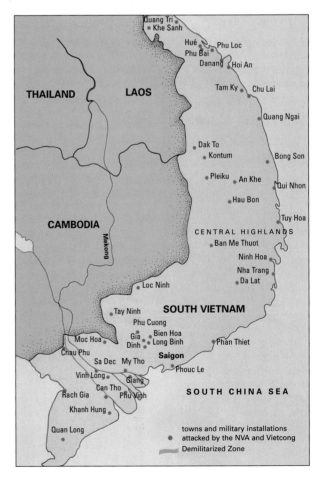

towns and military installations
● attacked by the NVA and Vietcong
▬ Demilitarized Zone

Above: Caked with mud, this SEAL endures the rigors of training during 1967/68. Mud has been an integral part of SEAL training, and many recruits will encounter more of it in a few months than most human beings will in a lifetime.

Right: Wearing a flak jacket, a SEAL practices his explosives technique. SEALs must be adept with demolitions work, since it forms an important part of their work. In Vietnam, most explosives work was used to destroy VC bunkers and storage areas. The UDTs also made great use of explosives.

site. Once the area had been lit up, the ambush team laid down heavy fire against the sampans. Two VC were killed and one of the sampans was captured along with several grenades and the personal kit of the dead men. Interestingly, the two dead enemy soldiers were wearing the uniform of the North Vietnamese army. Although North Vietnamese regulars had been killed elsewhere in South Vietnam, the appearance of regular troops was a useful indicator to the intelligence services that there was something unusual taking place: the problem was that they were not able to be sure exactly what that something was.

All of this success was quickly forgotten, however. On January 31, to coincide with the Vietnamese New Year, the North Vietnamese and the Viet Cong launched a massive offensive in the South in the hope of sparking a nationwide uprising.

Tet

The Tet offensive began with a series of attacks against key targets in certain South Vietnamese cities and the communists enjoyed some early successes thanks to the element of surprise. But the fierce fighting rapidly turned away from the sort of guerrilla warfare at which both the Viet Cong and North Vietnamese army excelled into a more conventional, urban-based conflict —in which the United States Army excelled. This was not least due to the fact that this was the very sort of combat that American soldiers had been preparing for—it was anticipated that urban warfare would be an integral part of a possible World War III. Despite the more

conventional manner of the fighting, this did not mean that the SEALs were without work. SEAL detachments went to work to ensure that the towns that they used as bases and staging posts did not suffer too heavily from the enemy attack. In My Tho, three VC battalions attempted to seize all the bridges into and out of the city, supported by an armored sampan. Two SEALs set about the sampan with 66mm (2.6-inch) anti-tank rockets and disabled it, while others joined army units in the defense of the city.

For the men of SEAL Team Two's 8th Platoon, the situation was even more dramatic. The platoon, operating from Chau Doc, had been inserted by a PBR (Patrol Boat, River) on a reconnaissance mission just after midnight on January 31. The platoon became uncomfortably aware of the fact that enemy forces were massing near the city in large numbers. The SEALs were well aware that they were unable to do anything to stop this and withdrew from the area as quickly as they could to report their discovery. The enemy attack commenced just after 0300 hours and it soon became obvious that the communist forces intended to cut the town off and to capture it. The SEALs were not alone. As well as local forces, a team of U.S. Army advisors was in the city. Even with these men, though, the American strength in the town was insufficient to hope to stop the advance, not least since the patrol and the Army team had only their personal weapons. The officer commanding the SEAL team learned that there was a training camp from the American CORDS (Civil Operations and Revolutionary Development) aid organization about a mile down the river and the camp possessed some weaponry. He promptly sent half of the

Above: SEALs prepare to come ashore from a patrol boat. The two M60 machine guns (one jutting out from each side) are a notable part of the patrol's weapons. Note the large dome containing a radar.

Left: Crew on a large patrol craft exchange pleasantries with locals passing by in a sampan. The man nearest the camera has an M79 grenade launcher slung over his shoulder. The formidable looking mounting in the center of the deck is a dual machine gun and mortar. The 81mm (3.1in) mortar was not designed to fire horizontally from a deck mounting, but there was nothing to stop it from being so operated either. The mortar offered the boat a means of delivering heavy and accurate fire on to enemy positions.

The enemy attack commenced just after 0300 hours and it soon became obvious that the communist forces intended to cut the town off and to capture it.

Right: A bandanna-toting SEAL briefs a helicopter pilot before they head off on another mission. The helicopter is operating from the back of a transport ship. The pilot's knife is prominent, and he carries a handgun in a shoulder holster beneath his left arm. The string of bullets across his chest suggests that he intends to be well-prepared if he has cause to use his gun.

The VC scurried out of the line of fire while Dix and the two SEALs grabbed the nurse. Scrambling onto their jeep, the Americans sped away as the VC reached the front of the house, firing at the retreating rescue party.

platoon and a PBR to the camp where two jeeps and a .5-inch (12.7mm) machine-gun were discovered. The SEALs mounted the gun on one of the jeeps and drove them both to Chau Doc as quickly as they could.

On their arrival, the SEALs reported that ten U.S. civilians were missing from the CORDS camp. One of the Army Advisors, Drew Dix, took a break from leading the defense of the city to suggest that he lead a team to locations where the missing personnel might be hiding. The SEAL officer approved and Dix and half a dozen men went out, trading shots with the attacking forces as they went. The first house they went to was the home of a civilian nurse. The VC had already broken into it and the nurse, understandably terrified, had hidden in a cupboard in a downstairs room. As she heard the footfalls of the VC on the stairs, she panicked, and rushed toward the back door. She threw it open, only to run into more guerrillas. At this point, two of the SEALs kicked down the front door. This left the nurse in the unfortunate position of standing in between two groups of armed men. Recognizing the men at the front door as Americans, she made toward them but fell in her haste to get to them. This simplified matters for the SEALs, who promptly opened fire on the VC. The VC scurried out of the line of fire while Dix and the two SEALs grabbed the nurse. Scrambling onto their jeep, the Americans sped away as the VC reached the front of the house, firing at the retreating rescue party. The first recovery was by far the most dramatic and the other nine Americans were safely retrieved. For this and for his actions during the rest of the fighting, Dix was later awarded the Medal of Honor.

After the successful conclusion of the rescue the SEALs continued to assist in the battle against the enemy for the next two days as South Vietnamese forces arrived. As the friendly troops made their way to the center of the town they encountered fierce resistance around the marketplace. To help matters along, the SEALs put in an attack against the Viet Cong's rear, fighting their way in toward the market. As the SEALs took up position in a three-story building to obtain a better vantage point, Petty Officer Third Class Ted Risher was hit by a single round fired from retreating VC. His colleagues commandeered a station wagon and rushed him back to the PBR where Risher received treatment. Despite the efforts of the SEALs and the nurse who had been rescued earlier, Risher succumbed to his wounds.

The events at Chau Doc were representative of a whole array of fighting during Tet. The VC and the North Vietnamese would enjoy some temporary—but often spectacular—success before being driven back, usually at heavy cost. Unfortunately for U.S. forces, the fact that the Tet offensive was a military disaster for the Viet Cong was not appreciated at home. Television coverage of events appeared to suggest that the Viet Cong had enjoyed great success. In a way this impression was correct since the communists gained massively from the interpretation placed on the offensive by the American public. Pressure for an American withdrawal from Vietnam intensified leading to President Johnson's decision not to run for reelection and to the beginning of the de-escalation process that would see America's final departure from the country. Before this happened, though, there was a great deal more fighting to be done and the SEALs would play a full part.

Below: "The forgotten SEALs." The SEALs worked closely alongside their Vietnamese counterparts, the LDNN, seen here on a patrol boat. The LDNN were tough individuals, and played a full part in the whole range of SEAL missions during the Vietnam War.

Chapter Three

From Tet to Final Withdrawal

By 1968, the SEALs had established themselves as a force to be feared by the Viet Cong in the Mekong Delta. However events elsewhere were to lead to their withdrawal within a few years.

Left: A U.S. Navy SEAL partially submerged in a waterway in the Mekong Delta, searching for traces of the Viet Cong's presence.

Below: One of the "classic" SEAL photographs from the Vietnam War. The SEAL wears decidedly non-standard headgear along with the famous "Tiger-Stripe" fatigues that became so associated with the SEALs during the war. He carries a favorite SEAL weapon, the Stoner 63 light machine gun.

Once the Tet offensive had died away, U.S. forces resumed their normal activities. In the case of the SEALs, this meant returning to their aggressive patrolling and reconnaissance activities. On February 17, a SEAL officer led a force of 60 local fighters (known as PRUs from "Provincial Reconnaissance Unit") on a mission against the VC in Ba Xuyen province. The operation netted 23 VC prisoners and it was estimated that another 20 or so Viet Cong were killed. Such operations, with the SEALs working alongside friendly irregular forces, increased in their intensity. On March 6, 7th Platoon joined forces with a PRU and attacked an enemy company in an engagement that lasted for nearly eight hours: six VC were killed. Three days later, another squad from Team Two went into action with a large PRU group and were responsible for killing at least six enemy guerrillas. However, while the actions with the PRUs had been successful, the SEALs made it clear that they were not happy working with such large groups; the essence of SEAL operations was the small-team operation. The SEALs had a point. There has always been a danger of viewing elite forces like the SEALs as being able to achieve any task allotted to them and when a

Left: A SEAL and his canine friend Silver, somewhere in the Mekong Delta in July 1968. Silver was employed on operations to sniff the enemy out, or detect his booby traps. Here he is being exercised by his handler in river water.

task seems to demand the use of relatively large numbers of men, simply trying to use the special forces as conventional infantrymen. The best units to employ in the manner of conventional infantry are, unsurprisingly, infantry. The SEALs—and their counterparts in the U.S. and British armed forces—have always made strenuous efforts to ensure that their successes in small group operations does not seduce planning staff into thinking that combining them in large numbers and changing their *modus operandi* will bring similar levels of success. The small team operations in Vietnam were dangerous enough without trying to employ the SEALs in roles for which other forces were better suited.

Patrols and Raids

This level of danger was demonstrated on March 13, 1968, when 7th Platoon was inserted east of My Tho, deep inside VC-held territory. The platoon moved forward for about a mile, then split into two groups. The first squad ran into two Viet Cong, and engaged them. The firefight was short and effective, both VC being killed. As the SEAL squad regained its hearing after the gunfire had died away, they could detect the sounds of what appeared to be a large force of Viet Cong to the east. The team evaded to the north, calling in fire support from helicopters and fighting off some 20 guerrillas as they left the area.

The first squad ran into two Viet Cong, and engaged them. The firefight was short and effective, both VC being killed. As the SEAL squad regained its hearing after the gunfire had died away, they could detect the sounds of what appeared to be a large force of Viet Cong to the east.

Right: Not a still from an early exercise video, but SEALs warming up on the helicopter deck of an assault ship moored off Vietnam. If aboard ship, SEALs will do their best to exercise as often as possible to maintain the formidably high fitness levels that they require for their job. It is more difficult to find the room to exercise aboard a submarine, but even this has been known not stop the SEALs from finding some way of carrying out physical conditioning.

They discovered 30 or so VC asleep in the building but were then spotted by an enemy sentry who opened fire. A vicious close-quarter battle broke out and the SEALs suffered five casualties,

The second squad had an even more torrid time. It discovered an enemy base camp and cautiously moved forward. They halted outside what appeared to be a barracks building and a three-man party led by Interior Communications Electrician Senior Chief Bob Gallagher moved ahead of their colleagues to investigate. They discovered 30 or so VC asleep in the building but were then spotted by an enemy sentry who opened fire. A vicious close-quarter battle broke out and the SEALs suffered five casualties, including Gallagher, who was hit in both legs. This did not prevent him from killing five of the enemy, while the rest of the SEAL squad accounted for approximately half of the VC who had been in the barracks. It was clear that the SEALs needed to leave the area quickly and Gallagher, helped by his colleagues, led the party away from the area, pursued by the VC. The SEAL team concealed itself and called for air support. The U.S. helicopters were on the scene quickly and the SEALs revealed their location by firing tracer into the air. Although this gave away their location to the helicopters, the VC were also firing large amounts of tracer and could not tell which was theirs and which was originating from the SEALs. The helicopters came in to recover the SEALs under fire. As the helicopters were loaded, Gallagher allowed others to be taken onboard first and continued to fight off the approaching VC, even though he was hit again. Once loaded, the helicopters lifted off, taking with it a SEAL team that was battered but alive. Gallagher was carefully removed from the helicopter and the doctors told him that his leg wounds were so serious that he would almost certainly never walk again. Gallagher demurred. By the end of the Vietnam War he had not only walked again but had completed his fourth tour of duty against the VC. Gallagher was awarded the Navy Cross for his gallantry. Gallagher had severely damaged the VC camp. Artillery fire and an air strike later destroyed what was left.

AMBUSH

March 14, 1968 saw 8th Platoon establish an ambush along the bank of a river. After an hour of waiting, a lone VC in a sampan appeared. Rather than kill the man, two SEALs jumped from the bank into the boat and overpowered him after a brief and very one-sided struggle. The SEALs then settled into their positions again. After waiting for another 30 minutes they were rewarded by the appearance of a sampan carrying a six-strong group of VC. The SEALs already had their prisoner for the evening and engaged the VC craft with heavy fire, killing all of them. They then retrieved the captured sampan from its hiding place and recovered the second boat. After the SEALs had extracted their haul to a nearby South Vietnamese outpost it was discovered that the dead men included the deputy commander of the local VC battalion, a VC company commander, and a reporter from Hanoi. The loss of the two commanders and the communications equipment that had been recovered from the second sampan put the local VC battalion out of action for a short period and prevented it from launching a planned attack on an airfield. It was a classic example of a efficient patrol action typical of many carried out by the SEALs.

March ended with two more hugely effective missions on the 29th—7th Platoon combined with a squad drawn from Team One's Delta Platoon for a raid on a reported arms factory in the upper Mekong Delta near Ben Tre. Guided by a Viet Cong defector, the SEALs, inserted by a PBR, traveled inland toward the target. The patrol stopped outside a small village, with four huts being pointed out by the defector as being of particular interest. Before the SEALs could begin their search, two armed men walked right into the security element that had set up position on the perimeter of the village. Since it was imperative that surprise be maintained, the security element jumped the VC and killed

Left: A gunner gets a soaking as his patrol boat proceeds at high speed down a river during the SEA LORDS operation. The large size of the man's helmet stems from the need to accommodate radio headphones beneath it so that he can communicate with the bridge or other members of the crew.

them in hand-to-hand combat. Demonstrating that close-in fighting using knives is an unpredictable and dangerous business even for the highly trained, the SEALs suffered one casualty with a knife wound to the leg. The rest of the SEAL team then attacked the huts, killing two more VC in the process. The defector located a well-camouflaged arms cache but was convinced that there was more than one to be found in the village. The villagers were questioned and one of them revealed that there was a second cache in a nearby underground bunker. He led the SEALs to the site and they discovered a treasure trove of weapons and equipment. The SEALs called in the PBRs but the extent of the cache was such that all of it could not be removed and some of it had to be destroyed at the scene. The cache was the largest discovered in the Mekong Delta up to that time. It included more than 50 different mines, two German MP 40 submachine guns, and two American M1 Carbines, all of World War II vintage, an array of hand grenades, numerous fuzes, blasting caps and gunsmith's tools, and stacks of documentation amounting to 20 pounds (9 kilograms) in weight.

While the first squad from Delta Platoon was busy assisting 7th Platoon, the second squad was dispatched by PBR to investigate reported sightings of a group of armed men. While looking for the men, the squad came across five VC in a small hut and opened fire on them. The gunfight was brief and all five VC were killed. As the SEALs examined the site, they discovered the remains of an old VC base camp. While they were in the process of doing this, the squad came under fire from automatic weapons and two of the party moved toward the location of the gunfire. As they did so, they heard whistles being blown, which was clearly a rallying sign for a large force of VC. It was obvious that the VC had been attempting to conduct a reconnaissance by fire, drawing the SEALs into an ambush. The SEAL team immediately radioed for assistance and their PBR arrived to pick them up without incident. As the PBR left the scene, the SEALs called in helicopter gunships, which attacked the area using rockets and machine-guns. Later investigation suggested that 27 Viet Cong had been killed as a result of the SEALs' gunfire and the intervention by the helicopters.

Joint Operations

Although the SEALs continued to enjoy success through April and May, the price they paid increased. Boatswain's Mate 1st Class Walter Pope; Petty Officer 2nd Class David Devine; Storekeeper 2nd Class Donald Zillgitt; and Chief Electrician's Master Gordon Brown were all killed as activity intensified. By now the SEALs were operating almost every day, deep inside enemy-controlled territory. In addition, the enemy were behaving more aggressively, operating in large numbers and attempting to conduct ambushes against the SEALs.

Five days later, SEALs working with a PRU attempted to locate a VC team that had mortared Chau Doc, only to come under heavy fire themselves. A massive gun battle broke out near a small pagoda, with the SEALs calling in helicopters for additional fire support.

Above: An 81mm (3.2-inch) mortar aboard a landing craft about to be fired. The awkward nature of loading this weapon when mounted horizontally is clear from this picture, but the benefits provided by the mortar's firepower offset this problem in the minds of the boat crews. The mortars were instrumental in beating off VC attacks on SEAL landing craft on more than one occasion.

DECEPTION ATTEMPTS

The VC had often attempted to draw SEALs toward ambush zones, either by radio calls or the use of signal lights. The SEALs had always managed to prevent this, in one instance by locating the position from which the enemy was using the signal light and blasting it with heavy automatic gunfire. It was not just deception attempts that were problematic. On May 11, 3rd Platoon ambushed a large guerrilla force but the VC responded robustly, pinning the SEALs down. Air support was requested and in conjunction with a counter-attack by the SEALs the platoon was extracted safely. Three days later, 8th Platoon found itself in a firefight with more than 80 VC near the Cambodian border. The enemy fire kept the SEALs pinned down for four hours. The SEALs were trapped in a cemetery, using tombstones as cover. On more than one occasion it appeared that the SEALs were finished but they always managed to beat the VC off. Again, air support arrived in the nick of time, along with suppressive fire from friendly artillery. Despite the intense enemy fire, the SEALs' commander was able to lead his team back without a scratch. It later emerged that the enemy had 24 fatalities and 40 men wounded.

As the light fell, the SEALs and PRUs moved to a clearing and were safely extracted. A sweep by South Vietnamese army patrols the next day discovered the remains of 36 VC who had been killed in the fight.

In all of these cases, air support and the aggressive manner in which the SEALs operated made the difference between being overwhelmed and achieving good results. It is not unfair to suggest that the provision of air support enabled the SEALs to operate with great confidence. In one instance, this confidence led to an incredible moment when a SEAL team attacked a group of VC who turned out to be part of the security element for two VC battalions. The SEAL team took the rest of the enemy troops under fire and then landed

Right: A landing craft makes its way down the Mekong Delta, carrying SEALs on another mission. The landing craft was an extremely useful means of transport for the SEALs as they made their way about the river network. Early efforts to use the craft to carry out "reconnaissance by fire" missions were abandoned after incidents where the VC caused serious damage to the landing craft, which were not able to manoeuvre away from the threat at the sort of speed that a patrol boat could.

to continue the fight. After a quarter of an hour the Viet Cong forces retreated. They were convinced that they were under attack by a far larger force than they actually were. On another operation, a SEAL team located three huts. A reconnaissance by a single man revealed that there were eight weapons and a number of sleeping men inside. Although a quick calculation suggested that there might 18 to 24 guerrillas in the three huts (which meant that the SEALs might be outnumbered four-to-one), the SEALs did not take what might have been considered to be the sensible option of quietly leaving the scene. Using some degree of cunning, the SEAL team officer split his six-man patrol into three and each element planted Claymore mines around each of the three huts. After making sure that the mines were correctly set, they withdrew and detonated the mines. Nineteen guerrillas in the three huts were killed in the blast and the SEAL team extracted without having fired a single round of ammunition from their personal weapons.

Dominating the Enemy

The SEALs spent the remainder of 1968 conducting similar operations, becoming more practiced as they did so. Whereas in 1967, many of the SEALs were entering combat for the first time, by the fall of 1968, every SEAL squad contained extensive operational experience, which had been gained in a variety of places in South Vietnam. The constant pressure applied to the VC through the SEALs' operations meant that the guerrillas' activities were seriously hampered. This in turn imposed psychological burdens on the VC,

Above: One SEAL keeps watch while the other prepares to demolish a VC bunker in February 1969. The photograph illustrates the contrasting terrain of the Mekong Delta: thick jungle in some places gave way to swamp conditions elsewhere. The jungle itself presented almost as many challenges as the VC to the SEALs, although careful training ensured that these difficulties could be overcome by those determined enough to deal with them.

Above: A SEAL prepares explosives to destroy a VC bunker located on a search mission in the Delta. The VC constructed a huge number of positions in the Mekong Delta and South Vietnam, using them to store food and munitions, and as staging posts to and from operations. The SEALs played a major part in dealing with the bunkers, destroying all the supplies that they found.

many of whom began to believe that SEALs would be waiting for them behind almost every tree or turn in the river. This belief was not altogether without foundation, given the style in which the SEALs operated.

An operation on September 14, 1968 added to the psychological burdens endured by the VC, albeit not through the initial action itself. A SEAL squad set out on an ambush mission in a fast patrol craft (PCF), transferring to Boston Whalers for the insertion. Their patrol was uneventful and the SEAL team then established an ambush position on the riverbank. Here they would lie until they made a contact or until the time for extraction came. A South Vietnamese LDNN member accompanied the team to provide translation services and it was not long before he was required. The team heard voices coming from the nearby tree line and put the LDNN man to work. After listening carefully to the conversations for a few minutes, the Vietnamese sailor concluded that the voices were coming from a party of VC rather than from locals going about their business. This increased the possibilities of a contact and the SEALs were not disappointed. A short while later, a sampan appeared, carrying three men. Since one of the men was armed, it seemed reasonable to assume that the boat was carrying VC and the SEALs opened fire. As was customary, the SEALs employed overwhelming firepower to ensure that the ambush was short. They fired more than 250 rounds of 5.56mm (0.22-inch) ammunition, eight grenades from a grenade launcher, three hand grenades, and two dozen rounds from a submachine gun. The SEALs then searched the sampan and the bodies, recovering a pile of documents. This was an interesting aspect to the Viet Cong's campaign, since the SEALs managed to recover an enormous amount of documentation during the course of the Vietnam War, much of it being of considerable intelligence value. Being mobile, the VC were faced with the problem that much of this documentation had to travel with them, risking compromise should the men carrying the paperwork be killed or captured or the documentation lost. Given this, it seems odd that the VC appeared to make little effort to ensure that the information in documents was not quite so easy to interpret. Had they done so, the information obtained from ambushes like that on September 14 might have been less damaging in its nature.

The documents retrieved from the sampan revealed that one of the dead men was the Viet Cong district chief, a company commander, and a courier. The papers also gave away a plan for an attack on Qui Nhon, the operational reports of the local battalion, a complete

Left: Patrol craft head upriver during Operation Slingshot in February 1969. Such fast-moving craft presented harder targets for any potential VC ambusher to hit.

list of the weapons available to the Viet Cong, and most damagingly, a personnel roster for the battalion. This sort of haul was not common, but it was not exactly rare, either. Information of this kind certainly eased the task of the SEALs in one of their other missions, that of the abduction of members of the VC. Using intelligence garnered from recovered documents, defectors, and informers, the SEALs were able to build up a picture of where VC operatives were living and hiding and then went and captured them. The SEALs made a specialty of approaching isolated villages and hamlets in the middle of the night in almost complete silence, creeping up on the house of the wanted man, and then forcing an entry. They would wake the suspect and subdue him (although the presence of heavily armed men was normally enough to make the target quiescent), before spiriting him away from the village. This added to the reputation of the SEALs among many of the VC, who began to believe that they were not guaranteed safety from the attention of the

LOCAL HELP

As well as the negative impact on the VC of SEAL operations, the frogmen's successes instilled confidence in the local population. While the VC enjoyed support from villages and hamlets, this was often given reluctantly and only because of the brutality exacted on the inhabitants by the VC if they did not cooperate. As the British had discovered in Malaya a decade before, if the local villagers could be persuaded that they would receive some degree of assistance and that the guerrillas were not invincible, they could be relied upon to provide useful intelligence.

The SEALs made a specialty of approaching isolated villages and hamlets in the middle of the night in almost complete silence, creeping up on the house of the wanted man, and then forcing an entry.

Right: When not on operations, the SEALs and the men who operated the riverine patrol boats made use of barracks ships for accommodation purposes (also planning their missions aboard these vessels). A pontoon was moored alongside the ship, and the patrol craft were tied up alongside. Here, Vietnamese troops clamber down to the ships before setting off on another patrol.during Operation Sivler Mace II.

"Men with Green Faces" anywhere. Although it would be easy to overstate the psychological effect of this reputation, it should not be ignored, since it was significant. It made the VC very careful in what they did and was enough to encourage more than a few communist guerrillas to change sides, as the defectors admitted.

One such instance came in October 1968, when a Vietnamese woman gave the SEALs information about a VC prison camp. Her motives were clear—her husband was being held at the camp and she hoped that the SEALs might rescue him. A combined force of SEALs and a PRU went to the reported location on Con Coc Island (some 80 miles/129 kilometers from Saigon), inserting from six PBRs. They overran the camp, capturing two guards and large amounts of documentation. Twenty-four prisoners were recovered. The SEALs moved the captives to the PBRs, destroyed the camp with explosives, and then returned to base.

On the same day, another SEAL/PRU force attacked a further prison camp, once again being helped by inmates' wives. This time, the women led the SEALs to the area. The SEAL/PRU force assaulted the camp with the SEALs aiming to cut off the prisoner holding area from that occupied by the guards. This was done with the intention of ensuring that the VC did not have the opportunity to fire into the prisoner cages. The SEALs killed seven guards and captured two more. Twenty-six prisoners were freed. As before, the prisoners were helped back to the PBRs that would extract the raiding force while the SEALs finished their day's work by demolishing the camp.

SEA LORDS

In September 1968, Admiral Elmo R. Zumwalt Jr. took over as commander of naval forces in Vietnam. Zumwalt had a particularly high level of admiration for the SEALs and his

Above: A patrol made up of several boats makes its way carefully down the river, watching out for any VC who may be hiding on the bank. As well as the 0.5-inch (12.7mm) machine gun, at least two M60s are available to provide fire on any targets that present themselves as the boats pass.

Right: Admiral Elmo R Zumwalt, (left, with back to camera) the commander of naval forces in Vietnam, chats to a group of SEALs. Zumwalt held the SEALs in high regard, and based his SEA LORDS strategy around their activities, with the intention of interdicting supplies carried to the VC by boats. The SEALs carried out intelligence gathering and ambush missions under the program.

SEA LORDS demanded that U.S. forces intercept the supplies using a variety of approaches based on direct action and patrolling. To Zumwalt's eyes, the task of enacting SEA LORDS was perfectly suited to the SEALs.

tenure was punctuated by several signals to the United States expressing the view that he required more of the frogmen to fight the war. Zumwalt was particularly aware of the fact that a great deal of the Viet Cong's supplies were being brought into South Vietnam down the so-called Ho Chi Minh Trail that ran from North Vietnam via Laos and Cambodia. However, a large amount of equipment was also reaching the guerrillas through the Cambodian ports on the Gulf of Thailand. Zumwalt was determined to try to interdict this route and came up with a new plan—the South East Asia Lake, Ocean, River, and Delta Strategy (SEA LORDS). While the name of the plan was long-winded (no doubt to produce the catchy acronym), the wisdom behind it was clear. For the Viet Cong, moving supplies at sea and then through the river network meant that the supply trail was much shorter than the Ho Chi Minh Trail. It was also the case that while the Trail had received an enormous amount of attention from U.S. air power the sea and river routes had been left largely alone. A further advantage was that the river network contained hundreds of waterways from large rivers to small tributaries that were just about navigable by boats. SEA LORDS demanded that U.S. forces intercept the supplies using a variety of approaches based on direct action and patrolling. To Zumwalt's eyes, the task of enacting SEA LORDS was perfectly suited to the SEALs.

This supposition was correct but there was a difficulty. For the SEALs to be able to interdict the supply routes effectively they needed to know when and where the cargoes were. While intelligence information provided by headquarters was often accurate, it was

SEAL DISGUISES

In areas where the locals were known to be sympathetic to the VC, SEALs would dress in the fashion of the Viet Cong, or in nonstandard or civilian clothes. Carrying Soviet- and Chinese-made weapons, they would patrol in the company of local forces, who were also attired in the black pajamas associated with the VC. The SEALs found that the locals in the hostile areas always assumed that the indigenous forces were VC and that the men of European appearance accompanying them were Russian advisors. In fact, a number of intelligence reports from agents suggesting that Russian advisors were operating in certain parts of the South were found to be describing SEAL patrols. The information obtained by these operations was usually of high quality and extremely useful in the prosecution of the campaign against enemy supply lines.

also often outdated by the time it reached the SEAL teams and therefore useless. The SEALs set about the problem in a no-nonsense fashion. Having already developed an intelligence network of their own for the patrol and ambush operations, the SEALs simply expanded this. SEAL team officers were called to a meeting in Saigon and handed large bundles of cash with which to pay informants. This meant that the SEALs could obtain timely information and then act on it almost instantly, rather than have to wait for analysts to process it at headquarters before communicating it.

The year drew to a close with a notable operation against a VC camp on the Cambodian border. On November 26, Alfa squad from 4th Platoon was inserted on an intelligence-gathering operation and while patrolling, they encountered a lone Viet Cong soldier. Two SEALs were detailed to capture the man but as they approached he saw them and opened fire. The SEALs instantly returned fire and killed the man but the noise had alerted the base camp. The capture team was visible from the perimeter of the camp and the fire was directed against them, including mortars and heavy machine-gun fire. The rest of the SEAL squad laid down covering fire while the two SEALs ran for cover. As the SEAL patrol was forced back, a patrol of VC was seen to leave the camp with the clear intention of locating the capture team. The patrol leader called in a helicopter gunship to secure the area and then went out to locate the missing pair. They were soon found and the team extracted from the area in helicopters. This was not the end of the matter.

On December 7, the whole of 4th Platoon was deployed to the area and set up an observation post overlooking the enemy camp. Rather than attempt an assault on the camp, the Platoon called in helicopter gunships, which began a heavy attack on the VC positions. The SEAL team then added its own fire to the proceedings, although this provoked the VC into responding with mortars and the dispatch of troops in an effort to encircle the SEALs. Despite this threat, the SEALs were able to extract safely by

Below: The VC had established an effective river supply network which the SEALs sought to counter under the SEA LORDS program.

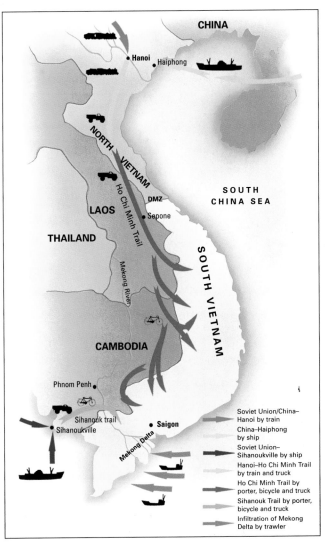

Soviet Union/China–
Hanoi by train
China–Haiphong
by ship
Soviet Union–
Sihanoukville by ship
Hanoi–Ho Chi Minh Trail
by train and truck
Ho Chi Minh Trail by
porter, bicycle and truck
Sihanouk Trail by porter,
bicycle and truck
Infiltration of Mekong
Delta by trawler

Right: A SEAL and a group of LDNNs pose for the camera after a mission. The LDNNs provided vital local knowledge and translation services to the SEALs, as well as being extremely useful men to have along when the enemy was encountered. While some South Vietnamese units had a poor reputation, this was not the case with the effective LDNNs.

helicopter, leaving behind a total of 15 dead Viet Cong, 29 wounded, and a distinctly battered enemy encampment.

1969

The new year began with the inauguration of President Richard Nixon, which meant that there would be a change of political direction of the war. Antiwar feeling in the United States had increased dramatically but the conflict was far from at an end. Although there was a clear sense that the United States would attempt to extricate itself from Vietnam, the way in which this was to be done was far from clear. The SEALs would have to undertake a great deal of hard fighting before there was any sign of a resolution to the conflict.

On January 10, seven men from 6th Platoon inserted along the Vam Co River and began to patrol inland. After traveling less than a mile they discovered signs of an arms cache. Further investigation revealed a massive stockpile of Viet Cong ammunition, which took more than three hours to clear. Over 300 mortar, rocket, and recoilless rifle rounds were discovered, along with 27,000 rounds of ammunition. On 14th, Signalman 1st Class David Wilson was killed by a VC booby trap, while in a separate operation a combined SEAL and South Vietnamese team attacked a North Vietnamese unit in a hamlet held by the Viet Cong. The leader of the NVA unit was killed along with two of his men and the VC's hamlet security chief—who had not done as good a job as he thought he had—was also killed. Two days later, another SEAL, Gunner's Mate First Class Harry Mattingly was killed. As T. J. Bosiljevac has observed in his history of the SEALs in Vietnam, 1969 "began with success, recognition, and fatalities. The only clear difference from the previous year's end was a mark on the calendar."

As T. J. Bosiljevac has observed in his history of the SEALs in Vietnam, 1969 "began with success, recognition, and fatalities. The only clear difference from the previous year's end was a mark on the calendar."

Although peace talks opened in Paris at the end of January, there was no let up in the SEAL's operations. On February 5, seven men from Team Two reacted to intelligence information by attacking a small hut where Viet Cong members had been reported. The five occupants were killed and it later transpired that they were operating a VC post office from the hut. The raid retrieved yet more valuable documents for intelligence analysts to sift through. Ten days later, another Team Two squad ambushed a VC group along the My Tho River, killing five high-ranking VC officers and wounding two others. The My Tho River was to prove a profitable hunting ground for Team Two at the start of the year, as a squad from 5th Platoon killed ten VC in two huts they located while on patrol in the area. The action was notable for the fact that the SEALs sent their translator into the two huts to mingle with the occupants, confident that he would be mistaken for a member of the VC. At a suitable moment, the interpreter returned to the patrol, revealed what he had seen, and the SEALs moved in. Although the VC sentry spotted them approaching and opened fire, he could do nothing to stop the SEALs from inflicting fatalities on his comrades.

Ham Tan Island

Also at the beginning of March, two VC defectors revealed that there was an important guerrilla intelligence unit and a team of engineers operating from Ham Tam Island in Nha Trang Bay. The island base was used as a relay station, since the VC intelligence team there consolidated the information brought back to them by their network of informers in Nha Trang itself. It was clear that the unit had to be stopped, but it was hoped that the agents could be taken alive, since they could be questioned to enable the whole ring of agents to be destroyed. This meant that a large conventional attack on the island would be of little utility and the task was handed to a seven-man SEAL squad headed by Lieutenant (Junior Grade) Joseph Kerrey. On March 14, Kerrey's team landed on the island accompanied by a Vietnamese commando and the two defectors who had given the information. The defectors had made it clear that their former colleagues would have noticed their absence. This would undoubtedly lead to suspicion that they had defected to the Americans and with it the departure of the VC agents from the island.

Kerrey's team faced their first obstacle in the form of a cliff some 350 feet (107 meters) high. The SEALs scaled this without ropes, putting the team in a position behind the

Above: Despite the almost comically short barrel, the grenade launcher being loaded by this SEAL could lay down a heavy barrage of explosives against an enemy position. The barrel length was an issue, though, since it meant that the launcher's accuracy declined as range increased. Later launchers had longer barrels to deal with this problem.

Above: Two SEALs crouch down in the jungle while on a mission: something appears to have gained their attention, although their relatively relaxed demeanor suggests that whatever it is does not pose a threat. The man with the M16 has taped two magazines together to facilitate rapid reloading, although this carries the risk of exposing the open magazine to dirt.

enemy encampment. This would enable them to launch their attack from a direction that would appear to be highly unlikely to the residents of the camp. As the team worked its way down toward the camp, they sighted a small group of enemy soldiers. Kerrey instructed three of his men to observe this group and moved on with the rest of the team to locate the rest of the VC. As they began their approach, Kerrey's team was spotted and the VC opened fire. It became clear that the information about the armament available to the VC had been less than reliable and the team came under heavy fire. Almost instantly, a grenade went off at Kerrey's feet, inflicting severe wounds to his lower legs. Undeterred, Kerrey began directing his team's response to the VC. The second part of the squad was directed to turn its attention to the VC force, catching them in a vicious crossfire. Four VC attempted to flee from the scene but were killed; three more tried to stand and fight, but were also cut down by the barrage of fire being laid in their direction by the squad. The SEALs then moved forward and captured several more VC, along with several large bags stuffed with documentation. Helicopters were called in to remove the SEAL team and Kerrey was flown to a hospital for urgent treatment. One other SEAL, the team's medic, lost an eye in the crossfire.

JOSEPH KERREY

Surgeons were able to save Kerrey's left leg but his right leg was so badly damaged that they were forced to amputate it. For his heroism, Kerrey became the first SEAL to win the Medal of Honor, awarded to him in May 1970. But Kerrey did not allow the loss of his leg to hold him back. He was forced to give up some sporting activities but on the basis that skydiving was more than possible with one real and one artificial leg, he invested in a parachute. Clearly an individual who enjoys a challenge, Kerrey later ran for gubernatorial office, winning in Nebraska, before representing the state in Congress. He would also run for the Democratic nomination for President in 1992. Now no longer a Senator, he is the president of New School University in Manhattan.

Other Operations

On March 23, elements of 7th Platoon were aboard two Navy helicopter gunships on a reconnaissance and strike mission near Da Dung Mountain, close to the Cambodian border. The helicopters were met by ground fire and began strafing the enemy positions but one of the helicopters was hit and forced down in a paddy field. One of the SEALs, Radioman 2nd Class Robert "R. J." Thomas, was thrown from the helicopter as it crashed, suffering some injuries. As he struggled to his feet, he realized that the helicopter had burst into flames and rushed to help the crewmen still trapped inside. As he did so the enemy began to fire on the crash site. The accompanying helicopter dropped a man to assist Thomas but he was wounded as the two men managed to pull the pilot out of the wreckage. Thomas then made several attempts to pull the remaining two crewmen who were trapped underneath the helicopter but he was driven back by the flames and explosions as the helicopter's ordnance began to "cook off"—in other words the helicopter's ammunition was detonated by the heat generated by the fire. Thomas and the man dropped by the second helicopter then moved the two crewmen that they had already rescued to a safer position. There was a further problem in that the VC had sent out a patrol to capture the four Americans. The situation was apparently desperate. Two of the men were in no fit state to fight, while Thomas had lost both his rifle and his pistol in the crash.

Below: Two patrol boats sit waiting for a SEAL patrol to return. The SEALs will be searching for any VC in the area, certain that they have a ready means of escape if they run into a much larger force.

Right: A SEAL take the opportunity to shave and freshen up. Patrols in the jungle could last for several days, without the chance to wash or to shave. At the end of their excursions, the SEALs would not only clean themselves up, but would make sure that ticks and leeches had not attached themselves to their bodies and dress any minor cuts or abrasions that they had picked up to ensure that they did not fall victim to infection or tropical diseases from the jungle.

In most cases, a man firing over any distance above about 20 yards (18 meters) with a pistol is hard-pressed to hit his target. Thomas, however, was known to be a remarkably good shot.

It seems that Thomas did not regard the situation as being particularly unfavorable: he borrowed a pistol from one of the helicopter crewmen and began to fire on the approaching VC. In most cases, a man firing over any distance above about 20 yards (18 meters) with a pistol is hard-pressed to hit his target. Thomas, however, was known to be a remarkably good shot. Lying on top of one of the injured men to shield him, Thomas used the man's back as a rest for his shooting arm and shot one of the approaching VC. He then switched fire to another and shot him as well. As the next VC fell to his well-aimed pistol shots the approaching group began to take a little more care and slowed down. At this point, an Army helicopter arrived and recovered the four men. The fighting continued and as the VC were driven back, two SEALs rappelled into the crash site from another helicopter and recovered the bodies of the two crewmen. Thomas was later awarded the Navy Cross for his outstanding action.

While the antiwar protests and the diplomatic efforts to secure a settlement went on, the war continued in much the same vein for the SEALs. On April 7, a combined SEAL and South Vietnamese team was sent on a rescue mission against a force of VC twice their size. The mission was generated when the VC took prisoner the family of a recent defector. The raid was provided with a considerable amount of air cover and artillery support and proved to be a stunning success. The defector's family was recovered, while 40 VC were killed. Such operations relied heavily on intelligence information and the quality of this was improving. Even though they had been successful before, the SEALs became increasingly confident of their ability to abduct or to kill senior Viet Cong officials.

Vietnamization

On June 8, President Nixon met President Thieu of South Vietnam, where Nixon announced that 25,000 U.S. troops would be withdrawn, the first notable attempt by the United States to disengage from the conflict. Although Nixon had spoken a great deal about ending the war—as public opinion in the United States demanded—he had not yet committed himself to a total withdrawal. The threat posed to the continuing existence of South Vietnam remained and it was obvious that the South Vietnamese were not yet in a position to put up an effective self-defense without American assistance, although aid to the country to enable this to happen would be increased. The announcement that the U.S. would remove its troops from Vietnam had an unintended consequence when morale in the armed forces in the country began to decline. The first incidents of racial tension, drug use, and the "fragging" (the term being derived from fragmentation grenade) or killing of officers and NCOs by their men began to be reported. The difficulty was that many of the troops in Vietnam were draftees, of whom a good proportion did not want to be there at all. Talk of withdrawal suggested that they were there for no good reason and their morale sank. Morale was not helped by the fact that it became clear that although the U.S. was going to withdraw at some point, this would not be in the foreseeable future. This left a problem where the U.S. Army in particular had a sizeable number of men who did not want to be in the army in the first place becoming more disillusioned by the notion that they were now fighting for no good reason. (If there was a good reason to be in Vietnam, they argued, why was the U.S. pulling out? And when would they be going home?) For the SEALs, the notion of withdrawal was not one with which they could readily identify. Morale remained strong and the SEALs were kept busy with their usual program of raids and ambushes.

On July 1, 5th Platoon attacked a VC base camp in Cai Lai District, killing four VC, while 8th Platoon found themselves involved in a slightly peculiar incident. While on patrol, they heard shots from the north of their position but it did not appear that the gunfire was directed at them. They moved toward the

Below: An ARVN trooper wearing "Tiger Stripe" fatigues atop a pair of jungle boots. He carries an M16 and a sidearm. Unlike the LDNNs, ARVN troops were of mixed quality: some good, some atrocious.

Above: A crewman aboard a UH-1 Huey looks down on two patrol boats speeding along the Delta. As well as providing fire support, the ubiquitous Huey was employed for the infiltration and extraction of SEAL patrols. The noise generated by a helicopter meant that infiltration had to be carried out some distance away from the objective to avoid alerting the enemy.

area where the fire had appeared to originate from and encountered an old man who helpfully told the team where they could find the enemy. The SEALs followed his directions and encountered a small VC unit. One of the VC was killed, while the others fled. To give further examples of the SEAL's proficiency in operations, Golf Platoon was responsible for killing 28 VC in four separate actions between July 3 and August 6, while 8th Platoon was busy investigating reports of VC prison camps during July. On July 10, the platoon conducted a heliborne raid on a camp reported to be holding prisoners of war (POWs) but none were found. They discovered a number of Viet Cong, however, and three of them were killed in a brief exchange of fire. Thirteen more were captured and another picked up when he was spotted trying to escape by swimming underwater. Two days later, 8th Platoon conducted an identical raid on a camp in Kien Hoa Province. This time, five POWs were found and liberated, while 14 VC were captured along with weapons and documents.

Although there was little doubt that the SEALs were continuing to conduct operations in a professional manner, this made little impact on the antiwar sentiment growing in the United States as 1969 progressed. There was little doubt that the SEALs were a highly successful element in the conflict. Their successes were not widely known, however, and other aspects of the conflict began to dominate coverage. Not least of which was the announcement in November that the U.S. Army was investigating reports that a platoon of soldiers led by Lieutenant William Calley had carried out a massacre of Vietnamese civilians in the hamlet of My Lai. Pressure for the war's end increased, yet the end of the conflict appeared to be no closer as the peace talks dragged on without result. Nixon's avowed intention of "Vietnamization" of the war—leaving the business of fighting to the Army of the Republic of Vietnam (ARVN) was beginning to have some effect in terms of the number of American personnel in the country but this was hardly noticed by the SEALs. Once again, as 1969 ended and 1970 began, the only difference that would have been noticed by the SEAL teams was that the calendar had changed and little else.

UDTs

Despite the fact that the SEAL teams were conducting the direct-action operations earned them most of the publicity for the use of U.S. Navy special forces in Vietnam, the UDTs were hardly inactive. Their work on beach reconnaissance and supporting raids by South Vietnamese commandos against the North should not be underestimated. The UDTs were responsible for the destruction of countless enemy bunkers in the aftermath of operations by the U.S. Marines and had begun the development of swimmer delivery vehicles, which became of considerable importance to the SEALs as well as time went on. Two incidents in January 1970 should serve as an illustration of the fact that the UDTs were operating just

Below: A fast patrol craft ploughs up the river, manned by a SEAL team. The SEALs made use of a wide number of boats, ranging from the speedboat-like Boston Whaler, to larger riverine monitors and even enemy sampans during the course of the war.

Left: A member of UDT 12 and Seafloat personnel carefully make their way through the dense jungle in a rigid patrol craft on a mission to plant sensing devices in the Delta to pick up VC movements. The UDT man in the front of the boat carries an M16 with a 30-round magazine. These were introduced when experience showed that the 20-round magazines, so familiar in pictures of the M16 in Vietnam, did not contain enough rounds when the weapon was being used on full automatic fire.

Despite the fact that the SEAL teams were conducting the direct-action operations earned them most of the publicity for the use of U.S. Navy special forces in Vietnam, the UDTs were hardly inactive.

Right: A boat crewman looks out at the bank while sitting behind an M60 machine gun. The belt of ammunition behind him is hanging from a similar weapon pointing in the opposite direction. While the M60 was far from perfect, it was a useful weapon to have, particularly when mounted aboard a vehicle or boat, where its weight was less of an issue for its operator.

as intensively as the SEALs and facing considerable danger. On January 21, UDT 12's Detachment Golf was supporting the 2nd Battalion, Fifth Mobile Forces Command in a sweep-and-clear operation in the Mekong Delta. Chief Hospital Corpsman Donnel C. Kinnard was serving as part of Detachment Golf and his exploits earned him a well-deserved Navy Cross. Kinnard recovered an enemy sampan that had been damaged by the 2nd Battalion, but as he did so, he came under fire from elements of the enemy who were still in the area. Managing to evade the gunfire, Kinnard captured the craft and the small arms in it. Later, Kinnard's team came under heavy fire by small arms and rockets and he was injured by shrapnel. This did not deter him and he replied to the enemy by hurling a number of grenades at their position. As the battle went on, a North Vietnamese officer felt that he had the chance to capture Kinnard and crept up on him from behind. He attacked

GUY E. STONE

Chief Shipfitter Guy E. Stone was accompanying a UDT team on a bunker destruction mission on January 27 when he encountered eight VC lying in wait for any Americans they might find. Stone yelled a warning to his teammates and dived for cover as the enemy opened fire. Stone directed the fire of his colleagues before charging the VC position. When he was within 15 feet (4.5 meters), he hurled three grenades which broke the VC's resistance. The UDT team moved in to secure the area. Stone then saw two more VC trying to escape and shot them with a weapon he grabbed from one of the other UDT men. Of the eight VC lying in ambush, six were killed and the other two captured. As was the case with Kinnard, Stone's bravery earned him a Navy Cross.

the wounded Kinnard but soon came to regret this. After several minutes of hard fighting, the North Vietnamese officer was lying on the ground, a captive of the man he had intended to take prisoner.

Disengagement

In spite of the fact that the SEALs were fighting just as hard as they had before, by Easter 1970 there was no disguising the fact that the Americans were determined to disengage from Vietnam. Even the SEALs began to notice as moves were put in place to cut back on their numbers. However, the way in which President Nixon sought to achieve this withdrawal was rather unconventional. Rather than meekly remove U.S. forces, Nixon attempted to inflict serious difficulties upon the North Vietnamese and the VC by authorizing operations in Cambodia. The operation had a dramatic effect on the VC as they discovered that their sanctuaries were no longer safe. While this meant that the communists were unable to conduct major offensive operations, the revelation of U.S. involvement in Cambodia sparked a new round of antiwar protests. In one of these, at

Below: A "Swift" class (or Patrol Class, Fast/PCF) patrol craft returns to base with elements of a UDT aboard. These boats were adapted from a civilian design used to support oil rig operations in the Gulf of Mexico, and were built in 1965–66. Around 200 were made, of which over half were transferred to South Vietnam between 1968 and 1970.

In spite of the fact that the SEALs were fighting just as hard as they had before, by Easter 1970 there was no disguising the fact that the Americans were determined to disengage from Vietnam.

Right: A UDT 12 lieutenant deals with a barricade placed across a waterway in the Mekong Delta. He is attaching explosives to blast it out of the way, but this does not tell the entire story. Before he has begun to place the charges, he will have made a careful examination of the barricade to ensure that the VC have not booby-trapped it. The VC were very adept at booby-trapping even the most innocuous items, and care had to be taken with almost every item to ensure that a nasty surprise had not been left.

Kent State University, National Guardsmen opened fire on protesting students, killing four of them. This did nothing to still the demands for an end to the war: if anything, it increased them.

The SEALS continued to operate, although the spring of 1970 saw relatively few contacts with the enemy. The SEALs became increasingly focused on the possibility of conducting raids on enemy POW camps, particularly since the issue of the maltreatment of American POWs had come to the attention of the American public. In response to intelligence reports, the SEALs were often tasked on short-notice raids against possible targets. The problem came in the lack of accurate intelligence, which meant that many of the camps turned out not to have prisoners. This did not prevent the SEALs from engaging the enemy and inflicting serious damage but it was not the intended use of the raids. There was some success on August 22, 1970 when elements of SEAL Team Two and a regional Vietnamese company were sent against a camp reported by an escaped POW. The team was inserted by helicopter, while the Royal Australian Air Force used Canberra bombers (the British-designed aircraft from which the USAF's Martin B-57 was derived) to cut off enemy forces on the other side of a canal adjacent to the camp. The SEALs spotted one VC and shot him as he entered a bunker and then entered the camp. It was clear that the VC had moved out with their prisoners and the SEALs immediately pursued them. The SEALs sought to hinder the VC's progress with the use of close air support and naval gunfire and remained on the trail of the VC for the next two hours. The VC had clearly begun to panic, since the SEALs found an array of

Above: A signalman from UDT 12 prepares to destroy a VC bunker in the Delta in October 1969. VC bunkers were usually well-hidden and could also be booby-trapped, so the demolitions men had to take particular care in their work.

Right: A SEAL with an adopted pet monkey. Local wildlife was easily tamed by bored U.S. personnel with the offer of food, and could make effective sentries—this monkey, for example, could make ear-splitting noise if it felt threatened by the presence of strangers.

The direct action patrols of the previous years would decline in number—but the last two years of the war would still see some remarkable achievements by the SEALs.

abandoned equipment and clothing as they closed in on the fleeing enemy. The VC decided that their safety was more important than retaining their POWs and fled. The SEALs were then able to locate 28 South Vietnamese POWs and evacuated them with the aid of Army helicopters.

The raids against POW camps were not the only activity for the SEALs, though, since they continued with their usual patrols and reconnaissance missions. On November 12, a combined force of SEALs and South Vietnamese troops discovered two large arms dumps. A week later, a similarly constituted force engaged three Viet Cong who fled to what appeared to be the safety of a bunker complex. The SEALs engaged the enemy bunkers as well and a total of seven guerrillas were killed. As the SEALs extracted, they called in air support, provided by jets rather than helicopters, and the bunker complex was flattened. Other similar operations punctuated the remaining days of 1970 and marked a turning point. Although the SEALs remained in Vietnam, the Vietnamization process began to reduce their numbers and many of those SEALS who remained were assigned to advise local forces. The direct action patrols of the previous years would decline in number—but the last two years of the war would still see some remarkable achievements by the SEALs.

The Final Months

The Vietnamization process was perhaps typified in 1971 by the beginning of Operation Lam Son 719 in the panhandle of Laos. While U.S. air assets were heavily committed in support of the operation, U.S. ground forces were conspicuous by their absence. Lam Son 719 was a success in its early days, but the North Vietnamese recovered their footing and threw the South Vietnamese back to their original positions. This demonstrated that although the South Vietnamese were clearly improving as a fighting force, they were not entirely ready to assume the full defense of their homeland just yet. Most notably, the South Vietnamese did not have anything like the air assets available to the United States and it was questionable as to whether they would be able to achieve any great success, even on the defensive, without such equipment and the personnel to fly it.

SEAL operations continued at a reduced rate and enjoyed similar levels of success as before. On February 24, elements of Team Two were landed by helicopter to investigate a complex of small huts in an enemy-held area. The platoon came under fire as soon as it had landed, but this did not prevent the SEALs from pressing home their attack. Eight Viet Cong were killed and a large arms cache was captured. Three VC prisoners were also taken and they revealed that one of the dead men was the communist hamlet chief. This was a swansong for 10th Platoon, since members of the platoon began to pull out of Vietnam shortly afterward; the same was true for personnel of the 8th and 9th Platoons. On March

Below: A combined SEAL and LDNN team on patrol. The SEAL wears two bandoliers of ammunition for a machine gun around his shoulders. The SEALs placed great reliance upon M60 and Stoner machine guns, since they provided a large volume of rapid fire that was of great utility in an ambush situation.

On March 7, 9th Platoon killed five VC and captured another five and then went on to kill two and capture three more when they made a heliborne raid on a VC wedding party.

Right: A SEAL seen through the foliage. The photograph is a useful demonstration of the value of camouflage. Even though the picture is taken at close range, if the SEAL was on patrol and wearing facial camouflage and some form of head covering (such as scrim netting), he would be almost invisible to anyone unaware that he was there. Attention to such detail provided the SEALs with a great advantage over the enemy on operations.

4, X-Ray Platoon ended its operational tour and was not replaced on its return to the United States. Although 8th, 9th, and 10th Platoons began to decrease in size, they were still active—on March 7, 9th Platoon killed five VC and captured another five and then went on to kill two and capture three more when they made a heliborne raid on a VC wedding party. 10th Platoon killed four VC on March 30 and it was clear that the SEALs intended to keep on fighting until the last of their number was withdrawn from the country. The drawdown continued and in November, President Nixon announced that the U.S. forces in Vietnam would only be used for defensive purposes. By this time, although U.S. special forces remained, the majority of special operations were conducted by South Vietnamese units. Although some SEALs were still in-country, they were there in case there was a need to conduct POW rescues. Combat operations were all but over by October, not least because the new Rules of Engagement meant that units had to announce that they were entering an operational area and then could fire only when they had been fired upon. Such conditions were not conducive to the type of operations that the SEALs had carried out before. Yet despite the fact that the war was virtually at an end, there was

Above: A member of UDT 13 aims his M16 down range. He may be practicing, but he may also be 'zeroing' his weapon sights to ensure accuracy the next time he comes to use the gun. The 'in-line' design of the M16 can be seen to advantage here; this helps contribute to accurate shooting, as do the M16 rifle's low recoil forces.

still time for the SEALs to carry out not one but two outstanding acts before they were finally gone from the scene.

"Bat 21"

Below: Off-duty, a SEAL and an LDNN converse. The close relationship between the SEALs and the LDNNs was vital to their effectiveness on operations; in the mission to resuce Colonel Iceal Hambleton, the role played by one LDNN was essential to the success of the operation.

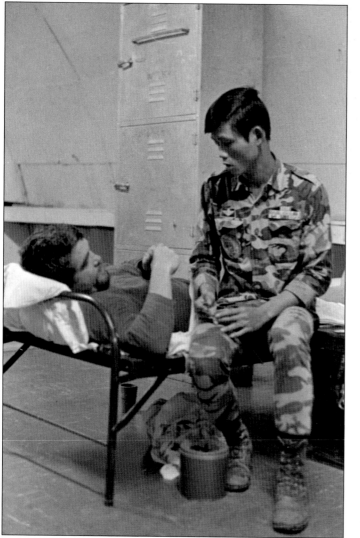

The opening months of 1972 were marked by the continuing withdrawal of American troops and a major miscalculation by the North Vietnamese. As U.S. force levels in Vietnam reached a new low, the leadership in Hanoi planned another major offensive. Their rationale for this was that the Americans would not be able to participate and that with a presidential election later in the year, Nixon would not be able to do anything to respond in fear of losing the election.

Unfortunately for Hanoi, they had forgotten some of the basic tenets of air power, one of which is that although aircraft may not be in a combat theater at the start of a battle, they are able to deploy rapidly if the need arises. Although there were only 76 American aircraft in Vietnam when the offensive was launched, Nixon ordered the dispatch of many more. Nixon was outraged by the North Vietnamese action and gave the air forces greater freedom of action than before. North Vietnam found itself on the receiving end of Operation Linebacker, in which air power was brought to bear against targets that had previously been off limits.

However, before the U.S. Air Force had begun its reinforcement of the theater, one of the most dramatic operations of the war had begun. On April 2, three B-52 bombers were conducting a raid on North Vietnamese forces near the Demilitarized Zone. The B-52s were supported by two EB-66 electronic warfare aircraft, which were pumping out signals to jam the fire control radars of North Vietnamese surface-to-air missiles (SAMs). While the EB-66s protected the bombers, one of them, call sign "Bat 21", was hit by a SAM and only one man was able to escape. He was Lieutenant Colonel Iceal Hambleton, one of the aircraft's electronic warfare officers. Hambleton was able to contact an OV-10 Bronco spotter plane, used for forward air control duties. The crew of the Bronco were able to pinpoint the spot where Hambleton landed, but the air force officer was in trouble: he had landed deep inside enemy territory and the North Vietnamese Army (NVA) were intent on capturing him. Thus began an odyssey that would culminate in a not entirely accurate motion picture and a less-well known act of heroism by a SEAL.

The NVA troops approaching Hambleton's position were engaged by a flight of Air Force A-1 Skyraiders leading a rescue force. The ancient

Left: Lieutenant Mike Slattery of UDT 13 gives his men a briefing before they depart on a demolition mission in Vietnam in early 1971. Like many SEALs and UDT men in the Delta, he is unshaven.

propeller-driven Skyraiders were hugely effective and carried a considerable amount of ordnance. While they kept the NVA under fire, a group of four Army helicopters attempted to recover Hambleton, but ran into heavy fire. One of the helicopters crashed, killing all the crew, while another made an emergency landing as the result of the damage. As they were unable to recover Hambleton with their first attempt, the Skyraiders were used to sow a minefield around the downed aviator, preventing the NVA from making a simple approach to their quarry. Efforts to recover Hambleton continued, with two OV-10s and an HH-53 rescue helicopter being shot down as each successive recovery attempt ran into difficulties. Although the losses of equipment and personnel sustained in the attempt to recover one downed airman seemed disproportionate, the U.S. Air Force maintained its steadfast determination not to leave any of its men to the mercies of the North Vietnamese if at all possible. It then emerged that Hambleton had spent part of his career working with ballistic missiles in Strategic Air Command, making him an even bigger prize for the enemy. While the NVA did not know this, the Americans could not risk allowing Hambleton's capture—

Efforts to recover Hambleton continued, with two OV-10s and an HH-53 rescue helicopter being shot down as each successive recovery attempt ran into difficulties.

Left: A UDT team aboard a patrol boat towards the end of American direct participation in the Vietnam War. The M60 and M16 are both prominent in the foreground, as is the rather scruffy nature of the men's uniform. While there is some truth in the adage that smart soldiers are better soldiers than scruffy ones, this was most definitely not the case with the men of the UDTs and SEALs. No matter how crumpled or non-regulation their uniform appeared, their professionalism and dedication to their task was unquestioned.

Although the losses of equipment and personnel sustained in the attempt to recover one downed airman seemed disproportionate, the U.S. Air Force maintained its steadfast determination not to leave any of its men to the mercies of the North Vietnamese if at all possible.

Right: A SEAL armed with an M79 waits to go on patrol in 1971. The M79 was a good weapon, but it did not allow the operator to change quickly between his rifle and the grenade launcher (in many instances, the M79 gunner did not carry a rifle). This led to the development of grenade launchers that could be mounted beneath an M16.

All rescue attempts had failed and there were concerns that the 53-year-old Hambleton might not be able to survive for much longer.

the brutal interrogation methods employed by the North Vietnamese meant that there was a risk that Hambleton might reveal his background if captured. The North Vietnamese would almost certainly have handed Hambleton over to the Soviets, and this, in turn, risked compromising the U.S. nuclear deterrent. While this represented by far the worst-case scenario, U.S. commanders became even more determined to rescue Hambleton.

A week after he had been shot down, the authorities began to become very concerned. All rescue attempts had failed and there were concerns that the 53-year-old Hambleton might not be able to survive for much longer. He was short of water, his survival radio batteries would not last for a great deal of time, and the lack of food meant that Hambleton was likely to be in a deteriorating physical condition. Since it seemed apparent that extraction by helicopter was not likely to succeed, rescue coordinators turned to a SEAL officer, Lieutenant Thomas Norris.

Norris was part of Strategic Technical Directorate Assistance Team 158, which was intended to give advice to the South Vietnamese. His special-forces background meant that he was ideally suited to attempt a rescue of Hambleton. On April 10, eight days after Bat 21 was shot down, Norris launched his rescue attempt, using a five-man team. The team moved some 2000 yards (1829 meters) into NVA-held territory and encountered a downed airman. It was not Hambleton, but one of the missing crewmen from the two OV-10s that had been shot down. Norris' team evaded to their forward operating base and returned the man to safety. On April 11, Norris and three others made two attempts to reach Hambleton, but on each occasion they found their path blocked and were forced to return to their base. Norris decided that a different approach was needed. The next day, he dressed as a Vietnamese peasant, and accompanied by a Vietnamese LDNN, Nguyen Van Kiet, paddled a sampan upriver to a pickup point to which Hambleton had been directed by rescue coordinators over the past few days. Norris and Nguyen found Hambleton and helped him into the sampan. They then covered him with banana leaves and slowly traveled downriver, taking care to avoid NVA patrols. Although Norris was using a primitive means of transportation, he had not neglected to take communications equipment with him. This came in useful on several occasions as Norris called in air strikes against NVA positions that lay in their path. After three hours of careful progress, Norris, Nguyen, and Hambleton were nearly at the forward base when they came under heavy fire. The rescue was not to be denied at this point and the air force appeared on scene in the manner of the 7th Cavalry in a western. The air support was effective and enabled the rescue party to regain friendly territory and to return Hambleton to safety. The epic rescue had been made possible by the tremendous determination of Norris and Nguyen. The SEAL was awarded a Medal of Honor, while Nguyen Van Kiet became the only Vietnamese serviceman to receive a Navy Cross. This was not the end of Tom Norris' war.

On October 31, Norris was part of a five-man team sent to capture an NVA prisoner. This, of course, was a standard SEAL mission with which Norris was familiar. Engineman 2nd Class Michael

Below: A UDT 13 team member makes final preparations before setting out on a mission. By 1971, when this picture was taken, the United States was withdrawing from South Vietnam, and the UDTs and SEALs would soon return home.

Thornton accompanied him, while the rest of the party was made up of LDNN personnel. Norris was unaware that he would shortly be taking part in an action that would make him unique in military history. The team landed in their operating area at about 0400 hours and patrolled inland for the next two hours. Just after dawn, the team received a signal that it had been inserted too far to the north and its exact position was unknown to supporting forces. This meant that the team would not be able to obtain naval gunfire support if required. Norris immediately turned the team back toward the beach so that it could contact the Vietnamese navy junk, which was serving as their floating base so as to obtain better navigational information. As the team reached the beach, two NVA soldiers spotted them and opened fire. The noise attracted another ten enemy soldiers and a fierce fight erupted while Norris endeavored to call in support. Norris' estimation of the team's position was accurate and naval gunfire was brought down in the nick of time. While the dozen NVA who had made the initial contact were all killed or wounded by the SEALs, the team was now confronted by the sight of at least 40 NVA soldiers approaching their position. For the next three-quarters of an hour, the small SEAL team, aided by naval gunfire, fought a desperate battle to hold the NVA off. One of the LDNN men was wounded and Thornton took shrapnel in both his legs. Norris recognized the need to withdraw and ordered his men to fall back. Norris and an LDNN stayed behind to provide covering fire while the three others ran to cover. Once they had done this, they would provide covering fire to allow Norris and the LDNN to withdraw and join them. The plan seemed to be working, but when the time came for Norris and the LDNN to head for the

Below: The SEALs won three Medals of Honor during the Vietnam War. This photograph shows Thomas Norris, twice-awarded the medal, (in center, in uniform) with family members. On the extreme left is another winner, Michael Thornton, who rescued Norris from the NVA.

Right: Men of UDT 13, who were still on active service in Vietnam in 1971 as the American effort was being wound down. Here the lieutenant briefs his men on an upcoming mission in the Delta.

rear position, only the LDNN appeared. He told Thornton that Norris had received a head wound as he had attempted to fire an anti-armor weapon at the NVA and this had proved fatal.

Thornton had no reason to doubt the word of the LDNN, but was determined not to breach the principle that no SEAL would be left for the enemy. Undaunted by the heavy fire from the NVA, he sprinted back to Norris' position arriving at the same time as two NVA soldiers. Thornton killed both of them before discovering that Norris was, in fact, seriously wounded but alive. He promptly picked the unconscious Norris up and slung him over his shoulder, then sprinted back to the LDNNs, who were still waiting for him. It was obvious that Thornton and the three LDNNs could not stay in among the sand dunes, so they took the only option available to them. Turning toward the beach, they ran hard, and evading the small-arms fire directed at them, plunged into the surf. Thornton swam with Norris over his back until they were out of range of the enemy gunfire. He paused to give first aid to the wounded SEAL officer, inflated their life jackets, and then began to swim out to sea, towing Norris as he went. At about 1130 hours, the junk that had deposited the team located them and picked them up. The five men were rushed to the USS *Newport News* for medical treatment. Doctors were unable to save Norris' eye and he required long and often painful medical treatment. Once this was over, Norris joined the FBI and began a second career. Thornton's wounds took less time to heal and he was awarded the third Medal of Honor given to a SEAL during the Vietnam War. This put Norris in the unique position of having been directly involved in the winning of two Medals of Honor in separate actions. Thornton remained with the SEALs and was commissioned some years later. The epic Medal of Honor action was the last fighting of the SEALs' war. It was almost the end for the remainder of U.S. forces, but there was one last round of fighting.

Turning toward the beach, they ran hard, and evading the small arms fire directed at them, plunged into the surf. Thornton swam with Norris over his back until they were out of range of the enemy gunfire.

Right: A UDT member calls for fire support while on a patrol in 1971. He is armed with a Colt XM177 Commando, a shortened version of the M16 rifle. The UDTs and SEALs became adept at calling in fire support, be it from ships, aircraft or artillery. This was not only used in defensive situations: when the need to bring in fire accurately arose, the use of a special forces controller meant that much greater precision could be achieved, a fact demonstrated even today in an era of precision-guided weapons.

While there may have been much wrong with some parts of the American armed services during the Vietnam War, it is impossible to level similar charges against the SEALs. The U.S. government may not have been able to enter peacetime with its honor intact but the SEALs certainly could.

The Final Assessment

Frustrated by the intransigence of the North Vietnamese, President Nixon launched Operation Linebacker II, the strategic bombing of key North Vietnamese targets, in December 1972. The eleven-day campaign had the desired effect: the North Vietnamese displayed a more pliant attitude at the next round of talks and in January 1973, American involvement in the Vietnam War ended with the signature of the Paris Peace Accords.

Nixon's description of the Paris Accords as being "peace with honor" was regarded with some cynicism almost at once—and certainly after the fall of Saigon to the NVA in 1975. However, the fact that the Vietnam War came to be seen as a defeat for the U.S. and a disaster for the armed forces is misleading. This is not to deny that there were serious difficulties and failings in certain elements of all the services during the course of the conflict, but these charges cannot be leveled against the SEALs. From their first involvement in combat, the SEALs forged a formidable reputation for themselves, inflicting serious casualties on the enemy and gathering much useful intelligence. While there may have been much wrong with some parts of the American armed services during the Vietnam War, it is impossible to level similar charges against the SEALs. The U.S. government may not have been able to enter peacetime with its honor intact but the SEALs certainly could.

Above: A SEAL moves carefully along the riverbank, his weapon ready for immediate action. Although SEALs have always been highly proficient with their weapons, many of their operations in Vietnam were carried out with the explicit intention of avoiding contact with the enemy. The SEALs emerged from the conflict with their reputation much enhanced by their record against the Viet Cong.

CHAPTER FOUR

FIGHTING THE COLD WAR

The 1960s and 1970s were not all about Vietnam for the SEALs—the threat of the Soviet Union meant that the specialists were kept busy elsewhere, performing covert missions around the globe.

Left: SEALs aboard a two-man swimmer delivery vehicle glide silently through the sea towards their destination.

Right: UDT men return to their boat after a training exercise. They are wearing early breathing apparatus, and the wetsuits date the picture to the early Cold War period. As the potential importance of the UDTs increased, they began to develop better equipment to meet their needs.

Although the Vietnam War represented the major action undertaken by the SEALs during the Cold War and the event for which most material is available to the historian, the SEALs were also involved in a variety of other small campaigns as the Cold War progressed. In addition, while Kennedy's decision to expand the special forces community was designed to ensure that the United States had a means of fighting communist insurgency, the SEALs were also forced to prepare for the possibility of full-scale conflict against the Soviet Union. Before the SEALs had been given much time to think about the way they would conduct their business, they were sent into action.

Cuban Escapade

On the night of the survey, the six men exited the submerged submarine and began swimming toward the beach. To their intense concern, they saw several Cuban patrol boats charging toward them.

On April 27, 1962, the SEALs from Team Two were given a daring mission: a reconnaissance of Cuban beaches as Kennedy considered a possible invasion of the island to remove Fidel Castro from power. Roy Boehm, who had reverted to the team executive officer on John Callaghan's arrival, was given command of the operation. Boehm took two SEALs and three UDT men to Key West, where they began training for a nighttime insertion from a submarine. The training progressed well, although there were moments when the participants worried that the noise created by the legs of six swimmers would attract sharks to the area. On the night of the survey, the six men exited the submerged submarine and began swimming toward the beach. To their intense concern, they saw several Cuban patrol boats charging toward them. To the relief of the SEAL team, however, the boats went on past. It is more than likely that the Cubans were not even looking for the swimmers, but simply patrolling against any American infiltration. If that is what they were doing, it is fair to say that they did not have a very good night. The swim team lined up in pairs and approached the beach. Just as Boehm was about to come ashore, he saw a man on horseback riding along the beach. Signaling to the others to stay low in the water, he made his way ashore, heading for the bushes. Boehm's idea was to remain in cover, well out of sight of the horseman. Unfortunately, shortly after Boehm reached the bushes, the horseman pulled up right next to him, stopped, and lit a cigarette. Boehm tensed, prepared to ambush the man if necessary—although exactly what he would have been able to do about the horse is open to conjecture. The wait was arduous. Boehm stayed as still as he could while the horseman stared out to sea, completely oblivious to the presence of an enemy commando a few feet away from him. Finally, the man finished his cigarette and carried on with his nocturnal ride.

The swim team then came ashore and conducted a survey along two miles (3.2 kilometers) of beach. Once this was complete, they swam out toward the pickup point. After waiting for half an hour, a nasty thought began to dawn in the minds of the men—had the submarine been forced to flee the area? Were they going to be left? Boehm was aware that the men were looking at him as their leader. They asked what they were going to do. Boehm then gave the memorable order that they would have to swim to the open sea and drown if necessary. While this was a sound order from the point of view of maintaining secrecy, the men did not see it as being sound in any other respect. Boehm led the team farther out to sea, and to everyone's relief, the periscope was sighted. The submarine had been waiting all along, hoping that the swimmers would realize that they were waiting above a coral reef,

Below: Two UDT men take depth readings on a training exercise. Although the means of taking depths is not particularly sophisticated, it is effective. In common with other special forces, the SEALs rate effectiveness above sophistication when it comes to equipment.

Left: Even in the years when military strategy was dominated by the threat of nuclear war, the need to carry on with amphibious training was not forgotten. Here, UDT members practice beach obstacle demolition as part of an amphibious exercise. This is exactly the sort of operation they might have performed if Cuba had been invaded during the Missile Crisis of 1962.

It became clear that the Soviet Union had stationed missiles on Cuba and the Kennedy administration was determined that they should not stay there.

Above: UDTs live up to the "demolition" in their title, despatching a number of obstacles with explosive while on a training exercise in the 1960s. In a real operation, the UDTs would have been unlikely to run up the beach in full view of the enemy.

which meant that it was impossible for the submarine to move in to get them.

By now, the team's breathing apparatus was not functioning correctly and it was important that they should be able to get aboard quickly. A further hitch occurred as Boehm and two others dived down to enter the submarine via the escape hatch, while the three remaining men stayed hanging on the periscope. After some confusion, Boehm—who was still in the lock-out chamber and using the intercom system to talk to the submarine's crew—managed to persuade the captain to surface partially, revealing a hatch through which the rest of his team could be recovered. As the submarine opened the hatch to allow the men in, patrol boats were spotted heading in its direction. The SEALs tumbled into the boat which then dived. As the SEALs breathed a sigh of relief, they could hear Boehm informing the captain that he was at risk of drowning his team if he didn't surface. The news that the team was in fact aboard was passed to Boehm, who then completed the procedure to reenter the submarine with his two companions in the escape chamber. On return to the United States, the team reported that the beach was far too steep to permit an amphibious landing.

Cuban Crisis

By the end of 1962, it was clear that the SEALs demonstrated the potential to be used effectively on intelligence gathering and sabotage missions as well as in counter-insurgency warfare and as advisors to the forces of allied nations. This was the theory—but before 1962 was over, the SEALs came very close to having to put their recent experimentation into practice. It became clear that the Soviet Union had stationed missiles on Cuba and the Kennedy administration was determined that they should not stay there.

As the crisis mounted, the SEALs were alerted to the possibility of their conducting operations in an invasion of Cuba. The first plan involved dropping SEAL Team One alongside a full-scale drop by an airborne division. David Del Giudice felt that this was not the best way to utilize his men and persuaded senior officers to abandon the idea. This was eminently sensible, since as Del Giudice noticed, landing the SEALs with thousands of paratroopers was pointless. The SEALs would be put to use in their clandestine role much better than as part of a completely overt arrival in Cuba.

As a result, the SEALs were called on to undertake another reconnaissance. Eight men led by Lieutenant William Cannon swam into the harbor at San Mariel, briefed to discover whether or not it would be possible for the SEALs to attack the boats moored there. Cannon's team swam carefully toward their target expecting to encounter a variety of

FOREIGN TRAINING MISSIONS

The SEALs undertook a number of training missions with NATO allies in the 1950s and 1960s. Elements from SEAL Team Two went to Greece and Turkey to see whether they could simulate sabotage missions. Seventeen SEALs went to Greece. As well as practicing raiding, they assisted in the training of Greek forces for similar duties. In Turkey, the SEALs worked with Turkish commandos, giving advice on infiltrating from submarines. A larger party (four officers and twenty enlisted men) went to Norway to spend two weeks at the local frogmen school in Bergen. They participated in a joint exercise in which they had to penetrate deep into "enemy" territory and then return to the safety of "friendly" areas. The mission went with few problems and was successfully completed.

obstacles. They found none. They swam into the harbor, counted the number of patrol boats, gained a good idea of the layout of the area, and swam back out to the submarine that had delivered them. Unsurprisingly, Cannon reported that he felt that there would be little difficulty in knocking out the patrol boats if the need arose. Although plans for the destruction of the Cuban boats were drawn up, the Soviets backed down before there was any chance of them being enacted. After their brief foray to Cuba, the SEALs returned to their bases; Team One made preparations to send men to Vietnam.

The commitment to Vietnam was, of course, to become the dominant consideration in what the SEALs did for the remainder of the 1960s, but they did not neglect working with other nations or training for a war in Europe. In 1963, the SEALs returned to Turkey to establish a training program alongside Turkish forces. Sadly, one of the SEALs died in a diving accident during the deployment. Other detachments worked on NATO exercises throughout the year, most notably in the Mediterranean area with the Greek and Italian forces. This established a pattern of exercises and training that continued for the rest of the Cold War and beyond.

Below: Two UDT members discuss the merits of breathing apparatus. The early breathing gear was unreliable, and there were several incidents in which users suffered oxygen poisoning. It took several years before an effective breathing set was available.

Dominica

On April 30, 1965, a small detachment drawn from Team Two went aboard the USS *La Salle* for deployment to the Dominican Republic. Sixteen days later, another detachment was ordered to Santo Domingo to undertake reconnaissance missions. This deployment came as a result of the increasingly fragile political situation in the country. The despotic Rafael Trujillo had ruled the Dominican Republic for nearly 30 years when he was assassinated by elements of the Dominican armed forces. His replacement, Juan Bosch, was deposed in a military coup in 1964 and this appeared to offer the prospect of some stability. However, the military split into two factions and at the beginning of April 1965 one of the factions attempted to overthrow the government. The

U.S. embassy signaled Washington that if the situation was not brought under control the risk of "Castro-type elements" taking power was considerable. President Johnson's response was to tell the American public that the threat of a communist takeover could not be ignored and that he would work with the Organization of American States (or, some critics claim, tell the OAS what it was going to do). Between them, the OAS and the U.S. would send 22,000 troops to the country. The SEALs were in the vanguard of the operation, with the second element being tasked to investigate reports that the rebels might be hiding arms and ammunition in caves in the Samona Bay area. The SEALs concluded that an overt search of the area would only encourage the rebels to move anything hidden in the caves and decided that they would conduct a very stealthy reconnaissance. The team dressed in civilian clothes and posed as a fishing party.

Had anyone been looking closely, they would have observed that the fishing party was not particularly interested in fish and spent a lot of time looking at the local scenery, particularly caves. The searches did not produce any weapons and it was concluded that the rebels must have moved the contents of the caves some time before—if, in fact, they ever had made use of them. The SEALs found the atmosphere in Santo Domingo somewhat livelier, running into several gunfights between the rebels and the government. They also had some difficulty with the high command, which generated a plan to use the SEALs to storm a radio station held by the rebels. The idea was not a good one. It would have involved sending the SEALs through an area totally controlled by the enemy with little cover. If the station really needed to be destroyed, one of the 60 or so U.S. Navy ships

Below: A picture dating from around the time of the formation of the SEALs shows warm water training for combat swimmers. In cold waters, wet or dry suits would be worn, since even a short time in the water would reduce the effectiveness of the swimmer. Even with wetsuits, extremities could become cold very swiftly.

Left: A SEAL practices entry to a submarine via the torpedo tube. The use of submarines for covert insertion of swimmers demanded considerable practice and was not for the claustrophobic. For operations demanding larger numbers of SEALs, the U.S. Navy made use of converted attack submarines, culminating with the development of a special pod to carry the necessary equipment and swimmer delivery vehicles to the target area.

sitting just off the shore could have done it with their guns. The SEALs were not slow in making their point and although the plan was overtaken by events—the rebels decided to surrender—it appeared to have been understood. Once again, it was a classic demonstration of an urge to use special forces when there were far more appropriate ways of achieving the desired result. This was not the first time that this had happened and it would not be the last.

The biggest threat to the SEALs in Dominica, therefore, remained the random gunfire from trigger-happy troops on both sides. Fortunately, none of the SEALs was injured, and the detachments returned to base by the end of May 1965. Once again the SEALs had done a good job. But Congress received news of the intervention in Dominica very badly. Journalists hunting the die-hard communists who had been thwarted in their bid for power discovered that the "Castro-type elements" that had so worried the embassy were in fact a group of around a dozen men. Of these, it might be observed that several of them had not quite grasped the nuances of Leninism, since they had made little effort to organize themselves into anything akin to a revolutionary movement. Congress felt that it had been deceived and its fury increased when the new regime proved utterly unable to prevent political violence. The vocal criticism of the president was not something that detained the SEALs for long, though, since they resumed their pattern of training and deploying to Vietnam.

SEAL Recovery Systems

As well as more conventional activities, the SEALs participated in a number of trials to find ways of deploying more effectively, and for that matter, exiting an area that had just been

Had anyone been looking closely, they would have observed that the fishing party was not particularly interested in fish and spent a lot of time looking the local scenery, particularly caves.

Right: SEALs practice swimmer recovery during the 1960s. Although this looks to be a simple technique, it requires much practice. A simple error such as not positioning the arm correctly can lead to injury, and carrying out the procedure at night, with the boat traveling at speed, is not for the faint-hearted.

subjected to their attentions. The Fulton Recovery System appeared to be a perfect extraction tool for the SEALs and UDTs and it was decided that trials of the system would be carried out near to the SEAL base at Little Creek. The trials held on June 24, 1964 to demonstrate Fulton's design were watched by an interested group of SEALs, who all seemed rather eager to be the guinea pigs to try out the system. Two were chosen and the first test went well: the system worked exactly as anticipated and the SEAL was winched aboard the aircraft. On the second run, though, something went wrong. As Photographer's Mate 3rd Class James Earl Fox was lifted skyward, and was on the verge of entering the aircraft, the line parted and he fell several hundred feet into the waters of Chesapeake Bay. Despite attempts to resuscitate him, Fox died. When Fulton examined the recovery rig, he discovered that the winch had not been turned off as Fox went into the belly of the plane. The winch had carried on turning and had snapped the line. The solution to the problem was to insert

THE FULTON RECOVERY SYSTEM

One of the first methods studied as a possible method for extracting SEALs from an operation was the highly dramatic Fulton Recovery System. Named after its inventor, Robert E. Fulton Jr., the system provided a means of literally snatching a man (or men) from the ground. The idea behind the device was simple, but rather difficult to put into practice. For the Fulton system to work, the person on the ground waiting to be recovered dons a special pair of overalls (and often a fur-lined jacket to protect him against the cold) before blowing up a small balloon with a can of helium. (The necessary equipment can be dropped by an aircraft beforehand). The balloon is attached to a strong nylon line and before it is released into the air, the person on the ground ensures that the line is firmly attached to the harness which has been built into the overalls he is wearing. The balloon is released and the nylon line extends vertically as the balloon rises into the air. At this point, an aircraft equipped with large V-shaped prongs on its nose extends the prongs and the pilot aims the recovery device just below the balloon (guided in by strobe lights attached to the top of the line). The prongs engage the line and, as the line goes taut, it lifts the man from the ground rather more gently than might be imagined. As the aircraft leaves the area, the man is pulled up and along by the aircraft. A winch mounted on the aircraft then winds in the line slowly, and the man is brought onboard by the aircraft crew once the line has shortened enough for them to reach him.

a device that shut the winch off automatically if the crewman failed to do so. Despite the tragedy, tests of the system continued. In October 1965, the trials expanded to include the lifting of a party of SEALs from small boats. Rather than a stand-alone trial of the recovery gear, this trial was included as part of an exercise. Four SEALs conducted a simulated attack on a target near to the naval base at Coronado, California, then swam out to rubber boats that had been dropped to them by aircraft. In the boats, the SEALs found the items they needed for the recovery. They put on the overalls and harnesses, inflated the balloons, and waited. Within a short space of time, the first two SEALs were whisked into the air. Once they were recovered, the second pair was extracted, although there was a long gap between the recoveries: the weight of two men on the line meant that it took over 20 minutes to reel the pairs into the aircraft. Shortly after this trial, it was concluded that although the system was perfectly viable, live training made little sense. The men on the ground only needed to be sufficiently competent to put on a pair of overalls, inflate a balloon, and make sure that the strobe lighting rig near the top end of the line was switched on. The skill in the pickup was needed on the part of the aircrew, who could practice to their heart's content with dummies. Since the Fulton system had evolved as a means of recovering equipment as well, the aircrew sometimes did not need to simulate recovery of humans at all. The training for the system passed into the hands of the air force, and live "flights" stopped.

Below: A SEAL glances at the photographer as he sets off aboard an SDV. The SDV in this picture derives from the "Chariot" or "Human Torpedo" vehicles employed in World War II, enabling swimmers to cover considerable distances to reach their objective.

147

Left: The USS *Grayback* began life as a missile submarine, carrying the Regulus surface to surface missile, one of which is seen here on deck. When the Regulus became obsolete, it was decided to use the *Grayback*'s hangars to carry SEALs and SDVs. Up to 67 men could be accommodated in the hangars, allowing a sizeable force to approach a hostile coast undetected.

While a swimmer in the ocean is a particularly difficult target for location, the ship from which the swimmers originate is not. For concealment, the SEALs and UDTs made considerable use of the converted missile submarine the USS Grayback.

Above: The USS *Grayback* entered service with the U.S. Navy in 1958 as a strategic missile submarine. The first patrol was carried out in 1959, but with the obsolescence of the Regulus I missile, the submarine was withdrawn in 1964. Conversion to a transport submarine then followed between 1967–69, and the *Grayback* remained in service supporting SEAL operations until 1984, when it was retired. *Grayback* was sunk as a target in a live fire exercise in 1986.

It is possible that we shall never know whether the system was used in anger to recover SEALs, other special forces, or interesting items of equipment. What we do know, however, is that the U.S. Air Force's fleet of MC-130 Hercules special operations aircraft were fitted with the "Fulton Yoke" (the V-shaped prongs) on their noses. Although the majority of the MC-130s have had the forks removed, some still retain them. Furthermore, the recovery gear was still being produced in the late 1980s, suggesting that the system may have seen use on the sort of operations on which thriller writers speculate and the government never comments.

Fulton also took part in the development of the system to recover a group of swimmers. The manner of doing this up until the 1960s was for the swimmer to thrust his arm through a loop held out to him by a crewmember of the recovery boat. This method works, but is slow since it only allows the recovery of one man at a time. Fulton came up with a new idea and, as with many of his ideas, the system was brilliantly simple. Two rubber sleds, linked by a line, would be dropped near the swimmers. The swimmers would clamber aboard the sleds, whereupon the recovery boat would charge for the point between the two sleds, snag the line, and winch the two sleds in. For some reason, the small number of sleds procured was dispersed among other navy units and it has been little used (as far as we know). The old-fashioned method of recovering swimmers is still used.

SDVs

As well as recovering SEALs from their mission, considerable thought went into getting them there as well. Parachuting, coming ashore in inflatable boats, or swimming provide obvious and simple ways of reaching an objective. The latter method, however, can be quite slow, particularly if the SEALs have to infiltrate from some distance away, for instance, from a U.S. Navy ship sitting in international waters off the coast of a potentially hostile nation. There was also the matter of approaching the target area stealthily. While a swimmer in the ocean is a particularly difficult target for location, the ship from which the swimmers originate is not.

For concealment, the SEALs and UDTs made considerable use of the converted missile submarine the USS *Grayback*. The *Grayback* was designed to carry the Regulus missile. Unlike the submarine-launched missiles of today, fired from silos in the submarine's hull, the Regulus was more like a small aircraft, carried in large hangars toward the bow of the vessel. When the time came for the missile to be fired, the *Grayback* would surface. The missile crew would run to the hangars; extract the Regulus; unfold the wings and empennage; elevate the missile to its firing position; and then retreat to a safe distance

Left: An SDV sets off on an exercise. While such craft can carry swimmers to their objectives more speedily than they could reach them under their own power, the crew are still exposed to the water and the cold. It takes a great deal of determination to overcome the discomfort, but the SEALs seem suited for this: doctors carrying out tests have discovered that SEALs seem able to operate in conditions that ought to disable them.

At the end of the war, the UDTs experimented with both Chariots and X-Craft, seeing their potential as delivery vehicles for their swimmers.

while the motors were fired and the missile went on its way. This was a cumbersome way to fire a missile and the Regulus soon fell from favor. With the *Grayback* likely to be retired, the SEALs appreciated that it might offer considerable advantages to them, thanks to the large hangars, which were custom-made to carry equipment. Although the *Grayback* was slow, its electric propulsion system (used when the submarine was underwater—it employed diesels when surfaced) meant that it was very quiet. The *Grayback* remained in service until the late 1980s. Although the large hangar capacity was lost with the boat's retirement, the SEALs had by then developed effective ways of deploying from nuclear-powered attack submarines.

The size of the *Grayback*'s hangars meant that it could be employed to carry one of the other solutions to reaching the objective—the swimmer delivery vehicle, or SDV. The SDV was not a new idea. During World War II, frogmen rode on what became known as a "chariot." The chariot looked like a large torpedo with seats on top and would carry two frogmen to their target, which was invariably an anchorage for enemy ships. The frogmen could quietly maneuver around the harbor on the chariot, placing limpet mines. In some cases, the nose of the chariot was detachable and contained a large explosive charge. This could be released beneath a ship and detonated by time fuse. These vehicles were used to particular effect by the Italian navy between 1940 and 1943 and the idea had caught on with other nations. The British made use of midget submarines known as "X-craft," as well as Chariots. Although the three- or four-man crew contained a diver, the idea was that the X-craft would quietly make its way beneath the target ship, release two huge explosive charges that were carried on the small craft's side, and then leave the area before they went off. This simple account of both methods does not reveal just how difficult and dangerous the work was. However, an evolution of these approaches appeared to offer a means of

Below: A two-man SEAL SDV in its element beneath the surface. The earlier two-man SDVs were followed into service by larger versions able to carry more men and equipment. The latest versions can be used to launch torpedoes against enemy targets using a special stand-off weapons assembly.

conveying swimmers close to a target. They could then swim to the objective and carry out their mission in a much quicker time.

At the end of the war, the UDTs experimented with both Chariots and X-Craft, seeing their potential as delivery vehicles for their swimmers. However, there were problems. The submarine service insisted that any craft that might be considered to be a submarine should be their property. In effect, this meant that if the delivery vehicle kept the occupants dry (like an X-Craft), it was a submarine, whereas if it was a submersible where the crew got wet (like the Chariot), it was not. This forced the UDTs to pursue the route of developing free-flooding submersibles. As a result the crew would be exposed to the cold as the SDV made its way toward the objective, with the associated degradation of their efficiency. The first SDV did at least have the side effect of keeping the swimmer a little warmer than he might have been through physical activity. The craft was a one-man vehicle propelled by the swimmer pedaling away with his arms at a crank, which turned a small propeller. This was succeeded later in the 1950s by the second SDV, which was rather different. The Mark 2 resembled a small aircraft, carrying two people. Powered by silver zinc batteries, the SDV used small thrusters to maneuver in various directions. Sadly, the little craft proved to be terribly unstable and had to be abandoned. In the interim, the SEALs made use of the Italian-designed "Seahorse," which was an evolution of the Chariot. Two men sat in tandem in an open front compartment, accompanied by another two swimmers sitting in a similar arrangement at the rear of the craft. Also, efforts were made to develop one-man propulsion systems whereby the swimmer wore a knapsack containing a battery-driven propulsion system. While the system caught the imagination of the scriptwriters for several

Above: SEALs congregate on the deck of USS *Grayback* during a goodwill visit to the Phillipines. When the *Grayback* was withdrawn from use, it was replaced by a number of specially developed Dry Deck Shelters that could be carried on the hulls of attack submarines.

Right: SEALs training with an SDV underwater. SEALs are expected to be proficient swimmers capable of traversing long distances, but the use of an SDV means a sharp reduction in fatigue levels.

The utility of the SDV to the SEALs was recognized when the term SDV was altered from "Swimmer Delivery Vehicle" to "SEAL Delivery Vehicle."

James Bond movies, it did not find similar acclaim from the U.S. Navy, which decided not to proceed with the program.

The first U.S.-designed SDV to be truly effective was arguably the Mark 7 SDV built by General Dynamics Convair. The four-man SDV was designed to travel at depths of up to 200 feet (61 meters) at a top speed of 4.5 knots. (As a comparison, a swimmer using muscle power travels at about one knot.) The Mark 7 could maintain this speed for up to eight hours and had a range of some 40 nautical miles. However, when considering the maximum range of all SDVs, consideration has to be given to the length of time that a SEAL, even wearing a dry suit, can be exposed to the cold without losing efficiency. The craft included a sliding canopy to protect the crew from the buffeting caused by the pressure of the water passing by them as they traveled. It also allowed the swimmers to hook up to a semi-closed breathing apparatus that dramatically reduced the quantity of bubbles that were produced as they inhaled and exhaled. The Mark 7 could carry around 50 pounds of equipment in addition to the swimmers.

The Mark 7 arrived in service in time to equip the first SEAL SDV platoon in 1969. Updated versions of the Mark 7 appeared in the 1970s, each adding slight improvements to the craft such as the use of nonferrous materials to reduce the SDV's acoustic and magnetic signature, thus reducing the risk of detection. The Mark 8, unsurprisingly, followed the Mark 7 into service. The Mark 8 carries four combat swimmers and has a crew of two to take them where they need to go. Powered by an electric system driven by rechargeable batteries, the Mark 8 also has a computerized Doppler navigation system to enable the crew to obtain great precision in navigating to the target area. There is also a specially designed obstacle avoidance system that gives automatic warning of anything in the way of the craft. Other improvements include an onboard breathing system for the crew and passengers and a free-voice communication system, which permits the six personnel aboard to talk to one another.

Finally, there is the Mark 9 SDV, which is designed to carry two swimmers, who also drive the SDV. As well as being able to carry out the normal tasks associated with the SDV, the Mark 9 can carry the Mk 32 Stand-off Weapons Assembly, which allows the SDV to launch torpedoes. The SDV can thus be employed as a means of attacking enemy ships from a considerable distance, obviating the need for the SEALs to swim up to the ships and place mines. Using the Mark 9 in this way provides an additional capability to the SDV force and increases the range of options that the SEALs have in operations against enemy shipping. The utility of the SDV to the SEALs was recognized when the term SDV was altered from "Swimmer Delivery Vehicle" to "SEAL Delivery Vehicle."

Although the SDVs are useful, they cannot, of course, deploy from the United States to a theater of operations under their own power. They have to be conveyed to the region

Below: A SEAL practices with a CH-46 Sea Knight helicopter on a training exercise. Helicopters are an integral part of SEAL team operations, being used both as a means of inserting and recovering swimmers from the water, and landing teams on objectives as diverse as buildings and ships.

While the SEALs have always been able to parachute in on an objective since their inception as a force, the Cold War saw the development of the helicopter from a rather unstable machine unable to lift a great deal into a machine that had immense versatility.

Right: A SEAL leaves an aircraft while carrying out jump training. The parachute is on a static line, and will open once the SEAL has fallen a certain distance from the aircraft. For covert insertion, SEALs will free-fall from high altitude, using steerable parachutes to glide in towards their targets. Modern parachutes allow special forces to cover considerable distances, allowing the aircraft dropping them to stand off from the target area, thus giving nothing away to enemy defenses.

Left: Although this photograph does not show SEALs, it is an excellent shot of one of the helicopter extraction methods that can be used. Here, infantrymen clamber up a rope ladder dropped from the rear of a CH-47. Use of this method means that troops can be recovered from areas where terrain or trees prevent helicopters from landing.

aboard ships or submarines. The latter method is preferable, since it allows missions using SDVs to be undertaken with much greater stealth than they can be when deployed from surface vessels. The U.S. Navy has not sought to obtain a ship that can deliver SDVs through a hatch in the underside, as the Italians did in World War II. The use of the *Grayback* was a simple solution to the question of where to store the SDVs, since the hangars served the purpose admirably. However, as the *Grayback* became increasingly obsolescent, the navy had to consider how it would go about replacing the load-carrying capacity offered by the Regulus hangers. The solution was to develop a Dry Deck Shelter (DDS), which was a large metal cylinder some nine feet (2.7 meters) in diameter. The DDS could be bolted to the deck of a submarine and connected to the interior of the submarine (where the SEALs lived on their way to and from the target) through a docking hatch that mated the lower hatch of the DDS to one of the submarine's hatches. The DDS was designed for attachment to the Poseidon missile boats *John Marshall* and *Samuel B Roberts* and these proved to be particularly effective in the role. As converted missile carriers, they were large enough to carry a platoon of SEALs and their equipment. In addition to the *Marshall* and the *Roberts*, five Sturgeon-class attack submarines were modified to carry the DDS, beginning in the early 1980s. The SEALs were not altogether happy with the Sturgeons, since they were notably smaller than the two ex-missile boats. The SEALs pointed out that the smaller boats could not readily accommodate large parties of SEALs and their associated equipment and there was some concern that operational effectiveness might be compromised if the Sturgeons were all that was on offer after the retirement of *Marshall* and *Roberts*. This concern did not go unnoticed, although it is possibly fair to say

The noise generated by a helicopter means that it is not the ideal tool for some missions that require great stealth, but the flexibility and versatility that they offer means that it is a highly effective way of conveying SEALs to their objective.

There were instances where Special Operations Forces parties under heavy fire from the Viet Cong were extracted by rope ladder, although the weight of fire was such that the helicopter pilots sometimes left the scene while the troops were still clambering up the ladder.

Right: A SEAL leaps enthusiastically into the surf on a training exercise in the late 1960s. The demands of the Vietnam War meant that the SEALs had to increase their numbers, and the training regime had to be expanded. Naturally enough, swim training was a key element of this.

SPIE RIG

As part of the development of heliborne operating techniques, the U.S. armed forces developed the Special Purpose Insertion and Extraction (SPIE) rig. SPIE operations (also known as Stabilized Tactical Airborne Body Operations or STABO) is a brutally simple method of removing a party of SEALs from the ground. A helicopter will approach trailing a long wire, onto which the SEALs attach themselves with the aid of a harness. The helicopter then lifts the SEALs off the ground and flies off, with the men still dangling beneath until they are out of danger. The ride is rather breezy and there is a degree of risk to the method. However, it is an effective means of recovering a party from enemy territory in a limited amount of time.

that the dictates of the Cold War meant that the issue was not given top priority. Indeed, the fact that the DDS was detachable meant that the submarines did not always carry them. Nonetheless, having seven SEAL-carrying submarines in the inventory was not unwelcome and it gave the SEALs an increased ability to deploy stealthily from submarines, even if not every submarine was available at the same time.

Helicopter Techniques

While the SEALs have always been able to parachute in on an objective since their inception as a force, the Cold War saw the development of the helicopter from a rather unstable machine unable to lift a great deal into a machine that had immense versatility. This meant that the Cold War era was marked by the development of techniques for heliborne insertion and extraction methods. The SEALs were not unique in doing this, but took considerable pains in training with helicopters since they were—and are—of such value to small forces seeking to enter or leave an area. The noise generated by a helicopter means that it is not the ideal tool for some missions that require great stealth, but the flexibility and versatility that they offer means that it is a highly effective way of conveying SEALs to their objective. The helicopter also provides a means of removing SEALs from an area with speed, as the SEALs discovered in Vietnam.

Other extraction methods developed with helicopters during the Cold War included the use of a simple rope ladder. This would be thrown out of the rear ramp of a transportation helicopter as it hovered above the surface of the sea (or any other water feature a SEAL team happened to be in). The SEALs would swim to the ladder and clamber

Below: A UDT member practices his demolition skills in the 1960s. It is notable how much remains the same since World War II: the wire, detonating box and helmet are little changed from the 1940s.

aboard and the helicopter would depart. The system remains in use, although with the H-60 Black Hawk family the ladder is hung out of the side door, since that particular helicopter does not have a rear loading ramp. The rope-ladder method was also employed in Vietnam for operations some distance away from the sea and is not exclusive to the SEALs. There were instances where Special Operations Forces parties under heavy fire from the Viet Cong were extracted by rope ladder, although the weight of fire was such that the helicopter pilots sometimes left the scene while the troops were still clambering up the ladder. There is, of course, one other method of entering a helicopter—the normal one, which simply involves climbing in while the aircraft is on the ground. While this seems an obvious statement to make, it is surprising how often casual observers forget that the more exciting-looking insertion and extraction methods associated with a helicopter are not employed for the adrenaline rush they can give to the SEAL or soldier employing them. They are methods of removing the man from the ground when the helicopter is unable to land because of the terrain or when the helicopter simply does not have the time to set down and pick the party up in conventional fashion.

Insertion by helicopter usually comes in two forms. The more conventional method takes place when the helicopter lands and the party of men aboard deplanes quickly, allowing the helicopter to spend the minimum amount of time on the ground. The other means is that of rappelling from the helicopter while it hovers. This seems to be a simple process, but there are actually a number of ways in which a SEAL may leave the helicopter. The preferred method is that of fast-roping, where a man controls his descent down the rope using just his hands (which are, of course, protected from friction burns by gloves).

Below: A recruitment advertisement from the 1970s aims to encourage would-be SEALs to join up. Such posters rarely revealed just how arduous the training would be. In the internet age, there is now an official SEALs recruitment website: while it hints that the training is rather rigorous, it leaves revealing the full details of the challenges faced by applicants to others.

Left: One of the last UDT courses in the late 1970s. While SEALs and UDTs were (and are) expected to display a certain degree of intelligence, this UDT instructor is taking no chances. The instructors show little tolerance for fools or the incompetent, since they are not prepared to compromise the quality of recruits simply to pass men out. On one occasion in the 1970s, an entire course failed to meet the required standards, and not one of the recruits joined the SEALs' ranks.

While this method is more dangerous than arriving with the rope running through a rappelling harness, it saves valuable time. There is no need to disentangle oneself from the harness at the end of the run, delaying the next man down (or, if the next man has not bothered to wait, collecting his boots in your face while still removing the encumbrance of the harness). The third, less usual means of leaving a helicopter developed during the Cold War was by parachute. The SEALs and U.S. Marine Corps seem particularly proficient at this means of approach and because the speed of the helicopter is less than that of a transportation aircraft, the parachute stick is less likely to be widely dispersed on landing. This said, the problem of making sure that the stick leaves the helicopter at exactly the right place to ensure landing on the intended drop zone remains. Insertion with the

THE END OF THE UDTs

One of the most significant developments in the SEAL story came in 1983. By this time, it was clear that the role of the UDTs and the SEALs was beginning to overlap. In fact, some of the actions undertaken by the UDTs in Korea and Vietnam modeled those planned for the SEALs. In 1983, the last eight UDTs were re-designated as SEAL teams or as SDV teams. The SEAL community thus expanded from Teams One and Two and Team Six, formed recently (discussed in Chapter Six of this book) to SEAL Teams One through Six. It marked the end of an era. At their peak, there had been 34 UDTs and they had made the major contribution to the development of American naval special warfare forces. Since the 1960s, they do not seem to have received the same level of regard as the SEALs, at least as far as public perception is concerned. However, this should not disguise the distinguished part the UDTs have played in recent American military history.

Right: A group of SEALs carries out physical training at the base at Coronado during the the 1970s. The SEALs are amongst the fittest members of any armed forces anywhere, with several being Olympic standard athletes. In this picture, they appear to be enjoying a relatively gentle run.

Below: The fatigue shows on the camouflaged face of a SEAL. Training is incredibly tough, and during the infamous "Hell Week" recruits get just a few hours' sleep in the course of seven days.

helicopter landing in or hovering above the desired landing area is a much surer way of inserting a special forces team exactly where they want to be (particularly with the now-widespread use of the Global Positioning System, known as GPS).

The SEALs and the Cold War

Historians do not agree on the exact date of the end of the Cold War. Some contend that it ended when East German citizens demolished the Berlin Wall in 1989, tearing it down when the Soviet president, Mikhail Gorbachev, made it clear that he could no longer support the repressive nature of the East German regime while he himself was promoting openness in the USSR. Others argue that the collapse of the USSR itself was the end point of the "war." Still others suggest that October 3, 1990, the day that Germany became one again was the day on which the Cold War passed into the history books. Most, though, agree that the Cold War was unique as a war, in that nobody died "fighting" it. Ironically, they are wrong. As well as the Vietnam War, which clearly originated in the ideological struggle against communism, the Cold War saw the deaths of several American airmen shot down on reconnaissance flights. The danger of death was always present for those conducting intelligence gathering operations. Information about what the submarine services of the United States and Great Britain did has, to some extent, filtered into the public domain. However, we know next to nothing about the role of the SEALs in this aspect of the Cold War. Given the reconnaissance missions in Cuba in 1962, it is not far-fetched to suggest that their skills must have been put to the test on occasion as the intelligence gathering contest between the Soviet and Western blocs went on. We may, of course, never know whether this supposition is accurate, but based on the skills and abilities the SEALs developed during the period, it seems to be a reasonable one.

The Cold War was a unique period in the history of the world and at its conclusion, there was a wholesale reorganization of armed forces around the world. Nuclear forces were reduced, as were tank regiments, infantry units, naval forces, air forces, and just about any other military force that was dedicated to stopping the feared Soviet onslaught. There were exceptions to this rule. Special forces, by virtue of their versatility remained very much intact and as the increased instability of the post-Cold War era became apparent, their relevance increased. For American special forces, this was no surprise, for they had demonstrated their abilities on several occasions when, in certain locations, the Cold War was remarkably warm: and the SEALs were in the forefront of almost all of them.

In certain locations, the Cold War was remarkably warm: and the SEALs were in the forefront of almost all of them.

Left: Two SEALs after an ocean swimming exercise. Both men are carrying special floatation boards that contain a compass. This is a simple device, but very effective. A trained diver can use the board to navigate with great precision, using the compass to maintain his course, while keeping track of the distance traveled by counting the number of kicks he has made.

CHAPTER FIVE

SAVAGE WARS OF PEACE

In the 1980s the SEALs were called upon to perform in two interventions in the United States' backyard. Grenada and Panama both provided new challenges for the SEALs to face.

Left: Two U.S. Army UH-60 Blackhawks come in to land during Operation Urgent Fury in Grenada.

There were certainly moments between 1945 and 1990 when the Cold War turned "hot" for the SEALs and other American forces. The causes for these outbreaks of fighting were not entirely down to superpower rivalry. While the Vietnam War resulted entirely from the ideological conflict between the U.S. and the U.S.S.R., the problems originating from the Middle East were not wholly a product of the Cold War. American support for Israel meant that the United States became a target for terrorists who had absolutely no thought of spreading world revolution and the communist system. American involvement with the Middle East was not just on ideological grounds, since the importance of the region as a source of energy resources also had to be considered among American vital national interests. Furthermore, the overthrow of the Shah of Iran added a new set of problems for American policy in the region, since the new regime in Tehran was violently hostile to the U.S. This was then combined with the Iran–Iraq war from 1981, when Saddam Hussein first indulged his penchant for sending his army uninvited across other people's borders. Other concerns that developed in the 1980s included dealing with some of the excesses of American allies who took their utility in the fight against communism as giving them *carte blanche* to behave as they wished. All of this was set in a context where the United States was scarred by the memory of Vietnam. By late 1983, the U.S. military had still not recovered in the eyes of the public. In 1980, the attempt to rescue American hostages held in Iran had failed, with several fatalities among the would-be rescuers after the infamous debacle at Desert One. Then, on October 23, 1983, 241 U.S. Marines had been killed in

Below: Fort Rupert in the Grenadian capital, St George's, where Maurice Bishop was first imprisoned and then later shot by elements of the PRA. This photograph taken after the U.S. intervention in 1983 shows the damage caused to the centuries-old structure.

Left: Inside the Fidel Castro barracks in Grenada. The presence of Cuban soldiers and workmen helped contribute to President Reagan's decision to intervene in Grenada, since he perceived a danger of Cuba gaining major influence over the island in the chaos following the murder of the Grenadian Prime Minister, Maurice Bishop.

Beirut when suicide bombers drove a truck packed with explosives into their base. American military prowess appeared to be at its lowest ebb. Within two days of the tragedy in Beirut, though, the U.S. military embarked on an operation. This began the process that would lead to the situation that pertained at the end of the twentieth century where no one seriously questioned American military proficiency. The SEALs were in the vanguard of this operation.

The setting for the start of the turnaround in fortunes was unlikely. It was a small island in the Caribbean that not many people had heard of and was an unlikely setting for military action: Grenada.

Operation Urgent Fury

Grenada is the southernmost of a chain of islands stretching for 400 miles (644 kilometers) from the east of Puerto Rico to off the coast of Venezuela. It was discovered by Columbus in 1498 and then colonized by the French in the seventeenth century. The Caribbean Native People on the island refused to surrender and were slaughtered by the colonists. More than a century of war and rebellion ensued, until, in 1803, Britain evicted the French and took Grenada as its own possession. By the 1960s, though, the pressure for independence was irresistible. Britain had announced that it was seeking to bring the imperial era to an end and allowed the governance of Grenada to pass to the locals. The leader of the Grenada Manual and Metal Workers Union, Eric Gairy, led the pro-independence movement with his Grenada United Labour Party (GULP). Gairy became chief minister in 1961, but a year later was removed from office by the British governor after it was discovered that much of the island's budget had been spent on

Gairy's control of the island was complete, but his control over reality was not. By 1979 he was convinced that UFOs posed a major threat to world security.

Right: Communist literature found by American troops while searching buildings on Grenada. The owner of the books must have been highly ideologically motivated, since the works of Kim Il Sung (the first North Korean communist leader) are not renowned for literary style or excitement for the reader.

building a splendid mansion for Gairy rather than being used for its intended purpose. Five years later, Gairy was allowed to return as chief minister after winning the 1967 elections. He then became an increasingly corrupt and autocratic leader, awarding himself an array of medals, honorary degrees, and self-created titles as the years passed by. As well as these baubles, he amassed a small fortune through corruption. All of this was protected by the vicious "Mongoose Gang," which used violence to control those who voiced opposition to Gairy's rule. By 1970, many Grenadians were thoroughly sick of their leader and their opposition found focus in the New Jewel Movement, a left-leaning party headed by Maurice Bishop. The British—unable to take any action for risk of being accused of colonialism—despaired as the island collapsed into mayhem and by 1974 they were delighted to grant the island its independence. The independence celebrations took place in the middle of a general strike and political violence. Gairy's control of the island was complete, but his control over reality was not. By 1979 he was convinced that UFOs posed a major threat to world security and left the island for New York, determined to demand a full debate by the UN general assembly on the subject of visitors from other worlds.

While on his mission, members of the New Jewel Movement launched a coup. Their task was easy. The island's Defence Force was not the most competent organization. The plotters seized their barracks easily, since the soldiery was sleeping peacefully when they arrived. This rather unusual coup brought to power a left-wing regime, the People's Revolutionary Government, which was as corrupt and brutal as its predecessor. Before long, it adopted an increasingly Marxist tone. Within three years of the coup, Bishop had turned Grenada into something resembling an armed camp. Bishop and the PRG turned to Cuba for assistance and Fidel Castro was prepared to provide it, albeit not to the extent that Bishop and his government hoped for. Three military agreements with Havana were

A COMMUNIST MONARCHY?

There were two notable oddities about Grenada. The first was the fact that, despite being communist, Grenada was part of the British Commonwealth and thus recognized the role of the British monarch, Queen Elizabeth II. It also made no effort to remove the British representative to the island. As a former colony Grenada had (and still has) a governor-general rather than just an ambassador. While both situations pertained, many Grenadians considered the British Queen to be the head of state rather than Bishop. This meant that Grenada was, in effect, a communist constitutional monarchy—a concept Karl Marx certainly never approved of.

signed, each of increasing size. Had they all been implemented, the equipment of the People's Revolutionary Army (the successor to the Defence Force) would have been sufficient to equip over 25 percent of the island's population.

The chaotic nature of government on Grenada meant that Bishop had enemies both among the population and within the communist party. The leading opponent was Bernard Coard, the Deputy Prime Minister, who felt that Bishop was not doing enough to create a truly Marxist state. By October 1983, Coard had gained sufficient support among the Grenadian politburo to attempt to overthrow Bishop. Bishop was arrested and taken to the military base at Fort Rupert, in the island's capital, St. George's.

Left: An aerial reconnaissance photograph of Port Salines airfield. The 10,000 foot (3048m) runway was a particular concern to the U.S. administration, who noted that no tourist jets would require such a length of concrete. It was feared that the airfield might be made available to Soviet reconnaissance aircraft, and this was a further factor influencing the decision to intervene.

STRATEGIC THREAT

There were fears in the U.S. that the PRG was becoming worryingly close to Cuba. In 1979, a contract had been signed between the PRG and Havana for the construction of an airfield on Grenada. The PRG justified this on the grounds that the airfield was needed for the tourist industry. Skeptics wondered why the airfield then needed a runway over 10,000 feet (3050 meters) in length, far longer than required for the average tourist jet. Cynics began to suggest that the "tourists" would be more likely to arrive wearing Russian uniforms, disembarking from aircraft such as the Tu-95 "Bear" long-range bomber and maritime reconnaissance aircraft. This consideration was not far from the minds of President Reagan and his advisors as the situation deteriorated.

As the turmoil unfolded, the American administration grew concerned about the safety of American nationals living in Grenada, particularly the students and faculty at the St. George's Medical School. The PRG had an odd relationship with the school, which brought in thousands of dollars to the island and was a vital part of the economy. The unease came from the fact that a communist state was heavily reliant on the United States of America. The financial benefits outweighed the ideological disadvantages, though, and Coard and the newly established Revolutionary Military Council were clear that they would do nothing that would lead to the school's departure from the island. The U.S. administration could not know it, but the idea of harming any of the Americans on the island was not in the plans of the RMC. They felt that any threat to an American citizen was a certain way of causing American intervention.

On October 19, many ordinary Grenadians made an attempt to free Bishop and to reinstall him as Prime Minister. Bishop was undeniably charismatic and this meant that

Right: The U.S. forces used the Bahamas as a base for the Grenada campaign. A slightly incongruous sight as a CH-46 and C-130 share the airfield ramp with two types of Soviet origin, an AN-2 and a member of the AN-26 family. The small hump on the C-130's fuselage shows it to be a special operations-capable aircraft.

many of the population tended to concentrate on this rather than the despotic nature of his regime. Bishop was freed from Fort Rupert, but as he was addressing a cheering crowd the PRA appeared and began firing into the crowd. Over 50 were killed. Bishop and several of his supporters who were imprisoned with him were recaptured and taken back to the fort. Coard realized that his coup would be in jeopardy as long as Bishop was alive and ordered the former Prime Minister and his companions shot. They were executed in the early afternoon of October 19. That evening, the Joint Chiefs of Staff sent a warning order to Commander-in-Chief Atlantic (CINC-LANT) to prepare to evacuate Americans from Grenada. This swiftly became a plan to invade Grenada and to remove the RMC as political considerations of the situation developed: the RMC was clearly pro-Cuba and unashamedly communist. This combination was anathema to President Reagan and the evacuation plan became something far larger. On October 23, 1983, as the U.S. was still reeling from the loss of the Marines in Beirut, President Reagan signed the order to launch what had now become known as Operation Urgent Fury with one word: "Go."

Above: The US assault on Grenada was notable for the operational parachute drop over Port Salines airport. The SEALs were tasked with placing navigation beacons for the airlifters bringing the paratroopers in, but as a result of poor weather were unable to do so, even after two attempts. The first attempt cost the lives of four SEALs, and the mission has been a source of controversy ever since.

SEAL Operations

Urgent Fury contained plans for the employment of SEAL Teams Four and Six as part of a strong special operations contingent that would also use the Army's secretive Delta Force, the Rangers, and the 1st Special Operations Wing of the U.S. Air Force. The SEALs were assigned a number of tasks in addition to their traditional beach reconnaissance role. There were three notable missions given to the SEALs. The first was an insertion near Point Salines airfield to reconnoiter the site and to support a small U.S. Air Force Combat Control Team (CCT) in placing navigation beacons to guide in transportation aircraft. Guided by the beacons, the transports would drop Rangers onto the airfield to seize it. The next task was to seize the radio station at Beausejour. This was a strange objective for special forces when the radio station was of almost no importance to the success of the campaign. Furthermore, using SEAL Team Six to take a radio station was hardly the best use of men trained in the art of hostage rescue and counter-terrorist operations. The radio station operation was not simply a case of employing specialist

Left: A C-130 taxis in at Port Salines in the aftermath of the fighting. Although designed in the 1950s, the C-130 remains in production and is a vital asset to the U.S. Air Force. SEALs have considerable experience of working with the U.S.A.F.'s C-130 fleet on operations, not least for parachute insertion.

It became clear that the United States was not in possession of up-to-date maps of the island and one writer later alleged that maps dating from the 1890s were used to back up a basic tourist map.

Right: This oblique angle view of Port Salines gives a good impression of the length of the runway and the sort of terrain with which the U.S. troops had to contend. The paratroops that dropped onto the airfield did so in the face of determined PRA opposition.

Below: A SEAL floats down towards the sea under a parachute. Parachuting into water is a hazardous task as the man beneath the canopy can be dragged along the surface or become entangled in rigging lines.

troops against an objective that could have been left to other forces, but against something that did not really need to be an objective at all. The third mission was far more appropriate for Team Six: securing the governor-general's residence and ensuring that the Governor-General (Sir Paul Scoon) and his family were safe. Once this was achieved, the SEALs would escort them to safety to permit their temporary evacuation from Grenada, to prevent the RMC from harming them.

There were complications even before the SEALs were deployed and not just with last minute changes of plan that changed the start time for the invasion and reduced the amount of time available for the SEALs and other special forces units to carry out their reconnaissance missions. It became clear that the United States was not in possession of up-to-date maps of the island and one writer later alleged that maps dating from the 1890s were used to back up a basic tourist map. He also claimed that much of the intelligence information obtained about Grenada came from listening to the British Broadcasting Corporation's World Service radio broadcasts. When the time for action came, matters rapidly became worse for the SEALs.

Early in the morning on October 24, the twelve SEALs and four members of the air force CCT making up the Port Salines team prepared to jump from two C-130 Hercules transportation aircraft. They were making one of the most difficult and potentially dangerous forms of parachute jumps—

into water at night. The plan was that the 16 men would rendezvous with the destroyer USS *Clifton Sprague*, which would take them closer to the target area, before the team went ashore in inflatable boats. The team would then make a reconnaissance of the airfield and employ directional beacons to guide in the transportation aircraft carrying the Rangers who would parachute in to take the airfield some 36 hours later. The plan was recognized as being risky and everything that could go wrong did. The weather was appalling and the wind made the state of the sea higher than would have been acceptable for a training jump. Furthermore, the relatively rushed nature of the mission meant that the aircrews carrying out the drop were not experienced in this sort of operation. The signal for the SEALs and the CCT to leave the aircraft was given when the aircraft were slightly farther away from the *Sprague* than was normal. This gave the sailors waiting to pick up the jumpers a more difficult task to find the parachutists and recover them. In addition, one of the aircraft dropped its stick of men wide of the ship. The end result was that the sailors manning the recovery boats could not find the jumpers to begin with and did not manage to locate four of them at all. The four men who were missing were all killed. This meant that 25 percent of the force was lost at the outset of the operation.

Since the SEALs are robust operators, they did not allow this tragedy to dissuade them. They continued toward the island in a Boston Whaler, but as they approached the coastline, they saw a Grenadian patrol boat. To reduce the risk of detection, they took the sensible precaution of cutting the engine. However, as the boat drifted silently toward the

Below: U.S. soldiers look on as a flight of Army UH-60s heads off on another operation during the Grenada campaign. As proven in Vietnam, helicopters offered unparalleled battlefield mobility, as well as serving in the casualty evacuation role. For the SEALs, the helicopter's ability to insert them with precision over enemy territory and to recover them quickly remain its prime advantages.

Questions have been asked ever since as to whether the parachute drop into the sea was the best way to deploy the SEAL/CCT unit, since it cost the lives of four valuable men and may not have been necessary.

Below: BTR-60 armored personnel carriers abandoned by the People's Revolutionary Army. Similar vehicles using the heavy machine guns mounted in the turret caused difficulties for the SEALs on more than one occasion during the Grenada operation.

shore, the choppy sea swamped the engine and it could not be restarted. The SEALs made several efforts to coax the engine into life, but were unsuccessful. When the engine finally responded to their attempts, it became clear that there was insufficient darkness left to complete the mission and the whole team returned to the *Sprague*.

This meant that the operation to seize Salines was put into doubt. The need for reconnaissance was undisputed and there were suggestions that the entire invasion of Grenada should be delayed by a day to allow another team to insert. This was overruled in Washington, but a compromise deal was reached, where another party of SEALs would be inserted that night, with less time to reconnoiter and place the navigation beacons. This decision meant that the time for starting the whole operation had to slip, since the SEALs and the CCT would need time to place the beacons accurately (and without being spotted). The new SEAL team jumped successfully on the night of October 24, but suffered the same fate with its Whaler as the first group. This meant that there were no navigation beacons on the airfield for the transportation aircraft—but there has been some debate as to whether the beacons were needed at all.

The airdrop force carrying the Rangers would include MC-130 Hercules, which are optimized for special operations, carrying extremely sophisticated navigational equipment. It was not beyond the bounds of possibility that the Hercules crews would be able to find the drop zone without the beacons. In fact it was quite probable and this is exactly what they did. Questions have been asked ever since as to whether the parachute drop into the sea was the best way to deploy the SEAL/CCT unit, since it cost the lives of four valuable men and may not have been necessary. If this is true (and there is some dissension), the fault for this cannot be laid at the door of the SEALs, who were very unfortunate indeed. The fault more likely lies with the planners who may not have fully appreciated the situation given the limited time that they had available for constructing the invasion plans.

The Radio Station

The next task for the SEALs was the seizure of the radio station. Lieutenant Donald "Kim" Erskine was selected to lead this group. They were inserted early on the morning of October 25 by UH-60 helicopters. The team was put down only a matter of yards from the building and they rushed forward and overpowered the small guard force. By 0630 hours, the station was under American control. Erskine had been told to hold the station until relieved later in the day, so placed his men in ambush positions alongside the road. Within a short while, an unfortunate PRA soldier appeared in a small van—he was captured with little difficulty and bundled into the radio station to join the other prisoners. The SEALs then saw a truck packed with militiamen heading down the road and opened fire on the vehicle. Five militia troops were killed and the others fled in disorder. All seemed to be going well for the SEALs, but at about 0800, the RMC ordered its troops to launch a counterattack against the radio station. Lieutenant Cecil Prime, closely linked to the RMC, was placed in charge of this mission. He obtained a BTR-60 armored personnel carrier (APC), a platoon of troops, and an 82mm (3.2-inch) mortar from units already in St. George's before heading off toward the radio station with the APC leading a convoy made up of an assortment of civilian vehicles pressed into service. At 0930, the SEALs spotted the approaching convoy and as it reached the bridge that crossed the river that lay between St. George's and the radio station, they opened fire. The Grenadian troops immediately found cover and opened fire with a squad machine-gun, while the APC started firing with the heavy machine-gun mounted in its turret. This presented the SEALs with a problem, since the radio station was not suited to withstand the 14.7mm (0.57-inch) machine-gun rounds. They did not have an anti-armor weapon to deal with the BTR-60 and were at a considerable disadvantage in terms of small arms—a sizeable proportion of the SEAL team

Above: Smoke rises as shellfire lands on a Grenadian position. It is not always appreciated that the SEALs are trained to call in fire support, be it from aircraft, artillery or naval ships lying offshore. This is just one of their many skills, and has proved its worth on countless occasions.

were carrying 9mm Heckler und Koch MP5 submachine guns, rather than assault rifles, which meant that their weapons were out-ranged. It became apparent to Erskine that he could not expect to hold the Grenadians off and ordered that his men begin to fight their way toward the sea. Erskine was wounded seriously just below the elbow (so seriously that doctors later wondered whether he would lose his arm), but carried on fighting. The SEALs successfully escaped and concealed themselves until they judged that it was safe to enter the sea. They then conducted a long swim out to the USS *Caron*, which picked them up. Erskine was awarded the Silver Star for his leadership and recovered from his wounds.

Once it became clear that the Grenadians had retaken the transmitter, senior officers ordered aircraft from the carrier *Independence* to destroy it. Despite several attacks, the tower remained intact, even though damage was inflicted on the radio station. Naval gunfire did no better, but the heavy fire perturbed the Grenadians. Once news filtered through to them of the landings that had been made by the Marine Corps, Prime and his men decided to leave the scene.

Above: The Governor General of Grenada, Sir Paul Scoon. Sir Paul was protected by members of SEAL Team Six during Operation Urgent Fury, and had to endure being besieged in his residence while the SEALs fought off repeated PRA assaults with the aid of AC-130 Specter gunships.

The Governor-General's Residence

The Team Six elements sent to recover Sir Paul Scoon had an equally fraught time. They arrived aboard Black Hawk helicopters at about 0615 and came under heavy ground fire. After being unable to make a landing on their first approach, the helicopters returned for a second attempt. Twenty-two SEALs fast-roped into the grounds of the governor-general's residence, Government House, and quickly captured the single policeman on duty, who was, in effect, keeping Sir Paul under house arrest. After entering the house, the SEAL officer in charge, Lieutenant Johnny Koenig, informed Sir Paul that he had come to ensure that he was safe. The intention was that the SEALs would protect the governor-general until other forces linked up with them later in the day. Sir Paul and his staff were asked to wait in the main dining room, which appeared to be the safest part of the house for them to stay. Shortly after this, things began to go wrong. The PRA launched a series of attacks on Government House and were driven back by the SEALs, with considerable help from an AC-130 Specter gunship, which prevented an APC from breaking through the main gate. Support from AC-130s remained important for the rest of the day and by the evening, the SEALs were still awaiting relief.

The situation was complicated by the fact that the information about what was going on at Government House was not altogether clear to the commanders of Urgent Fury, not

least since it was not all coming from the SEALs in the house. Vice Admiral Joseph Metcalf, the task force commander, ended up with the impression that the SEALs were running out of ammunition (which was true). He also believed they were taking casualties (which they weren't) and were in danger of being overrun (which was dependent on whether the Grenadians launched another assault when a Specter wasn't available).

More importantly, the Americans hoped that Sir Paul would publicly support their intervention—while he was trapped, he could not do this. Metcalf decided that the SEALs would have to be relieved as soon as possible and made a number of changes to the operational plan to achieve this. Finally, at 0730 on the morning of October 26, Marines linked up with the SEALs and discovered that the PRA forces had largely melted away during the night. Sir Paul Scoon was asked to sign a backdated document requesting U.S. intervention, which he did at 1600 that afternoon.

The Grenada campaign was over very swiftly and the administration, having made sure that reporters were not present during the critical hours of the invasion, declared that the operation had been an overwhelming victory. However, it was not long before questions began to be asked about a number of key aspects of the campaign, not least the employment of special forces. It became clear that some senior commanders had not understood the role of the SEALs and their fellow elite troops and had employed them in a fashion that did not make best use of their abilities. This, in turn, led to congressional demands for reform of the Special Operations community and the SEALs found themselves being incorporated into Special Operations Command—SOCOM. For the remainder of the 1980s, the SEALs

Above: One of the medical students from the St George's medical school kisses home soil after being rescued from Grenada. Although critics have claimed that the students provided a convenient excuse for the Reagan administration to intervene in Grenada as the Grenadian authorities had no intention of harming them, this was not clear when the decision to intervene was made by Reagan.

AWKWARD CALL

The importance of Governor-General Sir Paul Scoon's safety had been increased after Margaret Thatcher, the prime minister of Britain, had subjected President Reagan to an extremely long and awkward telephone call. She expressed anger at Reagan's decision to invade a British Commonwealth country (thus embarrassing the British Queen) without consultation (thus embarrassing the prime minister). She pointed out that this was no way to treat the only NATO government that had wholeheartedly embraced the need to deploy cruise missiles in its country in the face of public opposition. If anything had happened to the governor-general while he was in the care of the SEALs, the political repercussions might have been serious.

underwent an increase in size as the emphasis on special operations increased. Their first test under the auspices of the new command would be in Panama.

Operation Just Cause

Operation Just Cause was launched with the deliberate aim of removing the Panamanian dictator Manuel Noriega from power. Noriega had ruled the small nation since 1981, relying on a mixture of charisma and brutality. Although the U.S. had considerable influence in the country by virtue of the troops stationed there to protect the Panama Canal, the Reagan administration felt that it had to tolerate his behavior because of Noriega's support for the Nicaraguan Contra rebels and his involvement in the war on drugs. This tolerance drew to a close when it became clear that his participation in the war on drugs was to ensure that rival drug barons were arrested. He was also proven to be thoroughly corrupt by a Senate investigation. The final straw came when he stepped up the anti-American campaign that he had begun some years previously. This led to an

Right: After the intervention, graffiti such as this appeared across the island. The Grenadian regime was particularly unpleasant, making widespread use of fear and torture as weapons of control. Its departure was mourned by few.

attack on the U.S. embassy in 1987. The Panama Defense Force (PDF) stood by and watched and it culminated in a declaration of war on the United States by the Panamanian National People's Assembly on December 15, 1989. (This Assembly was dominated by Noriega's acolytes and deeply unrepresentative.) The next day, Panamanian troops shot and killed a U.S. Marine officer and then arrested another American officer and his wife who had witnessed the event. The officer and his wife were assaulted while in custody, being released after intervention by U.S. officials. President George Bush Snr decided

Panamanian troops shot and killed a U.S. Marine officer and then arrested another American officer and his wife who had witnessed the event. The officer and his wife were assaulted while in custody, being released after intervention by U.S. officials.

Left: U.S. Army military policemen guarding an Army hospital complex take cover during the Panama campaign as crowds gather to protest. The man in the foreground is armed with an M16 with an M203 grenade launcher mounted beneath the barrel.

Above: Graffiti demonstrates some of the problems facing the Americans in Panama. The dictator Manuel Noriega instigated a campaign of anti-Americanism that culminated in the murder of a U.S. Marine officer by Panamanian troops. This was the final straw for President George Bush Sr, and he ordered American troops in.

that this was enough and ordered the military to implement a plan to remove Noriega that had been drawn up some months before as the situation deteriorated. Bush gave authority for Operation Just Cause on December 17, 1989. The SEALs would be at the forefront of the action.

Paitilla Airfield

The first, and subsequently most controversial, task for the SEALs was to deny Noriega the use of his private Learjet to prevent him from escaping. At first glance, their mission seemed to be a relatively simple task. The Learjet was based at Paitilla airfield, a single runway field jutting from the southeastern coast of Panama. The location meant that the SEALs seemed a logical choice for the operation. Three platoons would insert from patrol boats near the airfield before moving slowly up the runway toward the hangar in which the Learjet was kept. This was where the plan stopped being simple. Trying to piece together exactly what the plan was after this point is equally complex, since there are at least three different published accounts of what the SEALs were meant to do. It appears that all accounts are agreed on the fact that the SEALs were not to destroy the aircraft, but to disable it. The confusion stems from what "disable" actually meant and when that instruction entered the planning process—at the beginning or as the SEALs approached the airfield. We do know for certain that the SEALs were told they could expect minimal opposition, so they were relatively lightly armed, but in significant contrast to the team that had secured Government House in Grenada, the party carried machine-guns, a mortar, and

Swedish-made AT-4 84mm (3.3-inch) anti-armor rocket launchers (also known as the Carl Gustav anti-tank "gun"). The team rehearsed the operation at Eglin Air Force Base, Florida on December 14, and it was judged to have been a success.

Some guesses about the plan can be made from combining the varying accounts. It appears that the idea of disabling the plane was around from the beginning. The term "disable" was relatively vague—simply, it meant that the SEALs were to make sure that the aircraft was not able to take off and that any means of achieving this short of destroying the Learjet were acceptable.

Initially, the SEALs considered surrounding the airfield and using sniping teams to ensure that no one could move about the airfield. They also mulled over employing the snipers to shoot out the tires on the Learjet. For added certainty, the teams would attempt to shoot holes in the fuel tanks. This was a sensible plan, although to guarantee that Noriega could not use the aircraft, an even more astute course of action would have been to have destroyed the Learjet, possibly by using an AC-130 rather than risking a SEAL team. Concerns over collateral damage meant that this was not possible and further complicated the plan. The SEALs would not be able to stand off and fire at the target from long range, but would have to go onto the airfield, getting closer in to the aircraft before they fired at it. The concerns then seem to have extended to preventing the teams from using snipers at all. Once the SEALs had moved into position, the new plan demanded that they would surround the hangar and disable the aircraft, either by slashing the tires, or by shooting them if necessary. While the sabotage party disabled the aircraft,

The SEALs would not be able to stand off and fire at the target from long range, but would have to go onto the airfield, getting closer in to the aircraft before they fired at it.

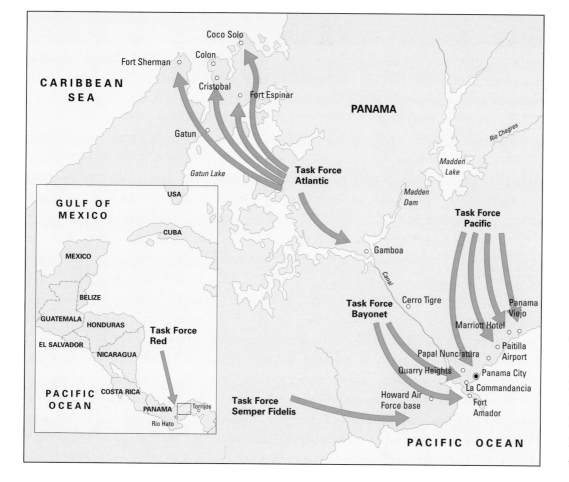

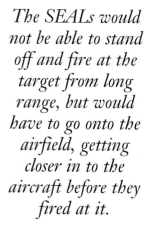

Left: The Panama campaign was aided enormously by the fact that U.S. troops were already based in the country thanks to the Panama Canal agreement. The SEAL operation at Paitilla Airport ranks as perhaps the most controversial in its history, as four men were killed and another nine were wounded.

Above: The Panama Canal does not look particularly spectacular, but is a vital strategic waterway. The SEALs were in their element operating around the canal and at Balboa Harbor in particular.

other members of the team would drag light planes onto the runway to prevent it from being used. This change in plan meant that the SEALs would not only have to go onto the airfield, but to enter the hangar, thus increasing the danger that they would encounter members of the PDF. This is not the controversial part of the plan. Rather, the controversy and confusion stems from when the plan changed, if in fact it changed at all. Several of the SEALs who participated in the mission are convinced that an order to disable the jet by slashing the tires arrived as the mission was in progress. We shall return to this question shortly.

The SEALs began their mission at sea, in their inflatable boats, awaiting H-hour, scheduled for 0100 hours. At about midnight, though, radio traffic increased and the SEALs heard the order that they were to disable the aircraft by entering the hangar and interfering with the tires. If this caused concern, reports that a helicopter had been seen taking off from the city of Colon created more: the reports gave rise to a fear that Noriega was heading for Paitilla and this prompted the SEALs to increase their pace. H-hour was moved forward by 15 minutes and they landed at 1245 hours. The platoons moved swiftly (but carefully) to the airfield. There, the platoons split into squads and Golf Platoon took the lead. As they did so, the sky over Panama erupted. Tracers shot skyward as the war began elsewhere. The SEALs reckoned that this would probably cost them the element of surprise and ahead of them they could see figures running. They could not tell if the figures were armed and held their fire. As Golf One and Golf Two

Left: A Medevac UH-60 leaves the ground, while the crew of a UH-1 prepare for flight. Although the Blackhawk family replaced many of the UH-1s in U.S. service, it did not replace all of them. The U.S. Marine Corps intends to use an upgraded Huey well into this century, which means that the aircraft is likely to be associated with the SEALs for some time to come as well.

came within sight of the hangar, they saw armed men—at which point all surprise was lost. The SEALs opened fire, but since they were quite closely bunched, they were vulnerable to return fire. Worse still, the Panamanians in the hangar had good cover, whereas the SEALs were out on the airfield with no cover at all. Two SEALs were killed instantly and others fell wounded. Lieutenant Tom Casey, leading Golf One, called out that he had taken casualties (by some miracle, he, alone from his squad was totally unscathed) and Golf Two, led by Lieutenant (Junior Grade) Mike Phillips immediately provided covering fire. This fire, though, was insufficient to allow Golf One to pull back:

As Golf One and Golf Two came within sight of the hangar, they saw armed men—at which point all surprise was lost.

without cover, a greater weight of suppressive fire was needed. Phillips radioed for help from Bravo Platoon, led by Lieutenant John Connors, who sprinted up to help out. As the platoon arrived, Connors received a minor wound, but carried on. It was quite clear that the original intention to use only their rifles had been overtaken by events and Connors and his platoon started to use the M203 40mm (1.57-inch) grenade launchers beneath their weapons. Connors got a single round away, but as he reloaded, he was hit by a burst of machine-gun fire and mortally wounded.

The remaining platoon, Delta, arrived on the scene and by this stage, the SEALs were employing all the weapons they had on hand. This represented a formidable amount of firepower and the Panamanian positions were quickly suppressed. At 0117, the enemy had stopped firing. The SEALs then formed a defensive perimeter and waited for helicopters to evacuate the injured. Regrettably, there was some confusion over the orders they received and they arrived an hour later. By this stage, one of the SEALs had succumbed to his wounds. This meant that four SEALs had been killed in the operation. As well as Connors, Chief Petty Officer Donald L. McFaul, and Petty Officers Christian Tilghman and Isaac G. Rodriguez had died, while another nine men had been wounded.

Below: U.S. troops occupy the airport in the aftermath of the bitter fight between the SEALs and members of the PDF. Although the SEALs suffered heavily, they succeeded in their aim of disabling Noreiga's jet, and preventing it being used as a means of escape.

Furthermore, questions were asked about the plan, the apparent changes to it, and the timing of those changes. There is no doubt that at least some of the SEALs were convinced that the plan was changed almost at the last moment and some have said so to the author Orr Kelly. By the same token, senior officers are mystified by this claim, pointing to the fact that the plans for Just Cause were in place well in advance and that there was no need to change them. Whether those plans included the need to slash the tires rather than shoot them out from range is not altogether clear. Histories of the operation have not helped by recounting markedly different stories. For example, some reports mention the involvement of armored cars, which do not appear to have existed. Armored cars were, however, mentioned in an official report by the House of Representatives. Some histories even disagree on the numbers of SEALs involved and the ranks of some of the personnel. It appears that this confusion was mirrored at the time of the operation and the question has not been clarified subsequently. All of this overshadows three key facts. Four SEALs were killed carrying out a difficult operation with their customary courage. The operation at the airfield was a success (the Learjet becoming decidedly worse for wear after being hit by grenades). Another dramatic SEAL operation was carried out at the same time, equally successfully, but without casualties.

Above: U.S. Rangers keep watch in Panama. The weapon obscured by the helmet is an M249 SAW (Squad Automatic Weapon) derived from the Belgian Minimi light machine gun. The weapon has found favour with special forces around the world, being popular as a result of its relatively light weight and high rate of fire.

Balboa Harbor

The other SEAL mission was to deal with the PDF's patrol boats based at Balboa harbor. As well as representing a potential threat to U.S. forces, there was a danger that Noriega

Right: A UH-60 sits in a field in Panama as excited children approach for a closer look. Just as the UH-1 was the subject of a multitude of photographs from Vietnam War, the UH-60 has found its way into numerous pictures of U.S. military operations since 1983.

might seek to leave the country aboard one of the vessels and this combination led to the decision that the boats should be attacked. Team Two was given responsibility for this task, under the guidance of Commander Norm Carley. Since, unlike Grenada, the planning for Just Cause began some months before the actual mission the SEALs were able to practice. One of the key difficulties they faced came from the fact that the patrol boats were aluminum hulled, which meant that limpet mines would not adhere to the surface. This forced the SEALs to old but effective technology, in the form of the World War II Hagensen pack. Four swimmers, each pair carrying a Hagensen pack, would swim into the harbor, attach the explosives to the struts mounting the propeller shafts, set the timers (specially adapted for this mission), and retire from the scene. The first the Panamanians would know of the operation would be the explosions under the two patrol boats.

The operation was set for the early hours of December 20, but when the team boarded its aircraft for the flight to Panama, it received the news that the harbor was empty of

LOSSES AT PAITILLA

The four casualties during the operation at Paitilla represented the heaviest loss that the SEALs had ever sustained since their creation and ensured that the mission was the source of much controversy. Questions were raised as to the validity of using SEALs for an operation that was possibly more suited to a larger force such as the Rangers. A counter-argument held that the task was perfectly suited to the SEALs, even if they were being employed in a larger group than was usual. It is perhaps worth recalling here the doubts about working in large numbers that were expressed on a number of occasions by the SEALs in Vietnam.

Left: A CH-47
demonstrates its lifting
capabilities as it carries a
heavy under-slung load in
the area of the
international airport in
Panama while the U.S.
forces consolidate. The
SEALs have become
closely acquainted with the
MH-47 Chinook models
now in use for support of
special operations.

patrol boats. By the time they arrived in Panama (which was not, strictly speaking, invaded, since the U.S. launched some of Just Cause from its bases in Panama), the news had changed: one of the boats, the *Presidente Porras* had returned and was tied up at Pier 18 of the harbor.

When the time to launch the mission arrived, Carley and his men set out toward the target in two rubber boats. Carley would command the mission from one of the rubber boats, while two swim teams would attack the boat. In addition to Carley and the four swimmers, the boats carried a coxswain each and a man armed with an M60 machine-gun to provide fire support if required. Carley led the boats to a mangrove swamp, where the swimmers disembarked and headed for their target. The swimmers—Lieutenant Edward Coughlin, Chief Electronics Technician Randy Beausoleil, Engineman 3rd Class Timothy K. Eppley, and Photographer's Mate 2nd Class Christopher Dye—swam to Pier 18, before

Just before they began to connect their explosives, the ship started its engines and the water reverberated to the sound of explosions from grenades dropping into the water.

Above: Facilities at Panama's main port burn in the aftermath of the raid by SEALs against PDF vessels based there. The SEAL's raid was a stunning example of the effect that could be achieved by a small group of swimmers using relatively low-technology equipment.

they rose almost to the surface so that they could locate their target. Having done this, they swam to the *Porras*. Just before they began to connect their explosives, the ship started its engines and the water reverberated to the sound of explosions from grenades dropping into the water. Undeterred, they attached the two packs of explosive, set the timers, and swam away. They surfaced by a nearby pier and worked their way out of the harbor, avoiding the grenades as they went. It transpired that the grenades were not being directed at them, but were coming from a fight between PDF units and American forces near to the harbor—the grenades had been badly aimed and were falling into the harbor rather than near their intended targets. After 45 minutes, the swimmers felt the blast as the explosives went off. They carried on toward the pickup point, having to dive underneath a passing ship as they went and swimming around a string of piers. Finally, they reached the pickup point and were hauled aboard by Carley and the other men in the rubber boats. The mission was a stunning success and ensured that the boat would not pose a threat to U.S. forces. It was also a demonstration of a classic SEAL mission—underwater sabotage by a small group of men. The tragic results at Paitilla meant that the raid does not always receive the attention that it deserves. Nonetheless, despite the losses at the airfield, the SEALs had a successful time during Just Cause. The missions at Paitilla and Balboa Harbor achieved their objective. Manuel Noriega had nowhere to run and made one last bid to keep his freedom by seeking sanctuary in the embassy of the Vatican. The nunciature was surrounded by American troops who played deafeningly loud rock music around the clock. Demonstrators also gathered there, eager to lynch their former leader. The Papal Nuncio, Monseigneur José Sebastián Laboa, persuaded Noriega that he could not hope to gain anything by staying there and said that he would order the former dictator out of the building if he did not leave voluntarily. Shortly after making this clear, the Nuncio persuaded the Americans to stop the music, which was driving him to distraction. Noriega realized that he had exhausted all his options and surrendered on January 3, 1990.

Assessment

Grenada and Panama offered two distinct challenges to American forces, not least to the SEALs. In both cases, the SEALs' operations carried distinct risks and questions were asked about the appropriateness of employing them in the manner in which they were used. In Grenada, the use of the SEALs at the radio station made little sense. It risked highly skilled operators for absolutely no meaningful return at that point in the mission. The parachute drop into the sea at night was extremely risky and with hindsight appears to have been unwise. The mission to protect the governor-general ended successfully, but was a very close run affair. While it was ideally suited to SEAL Team Six's method of operating, the SEALs perhaps ought to have taken heavier weapons with them; also, there appears to have been little consideration of what would happen if the forces supposed to link up with

Below: In a scene that could have been taken straight from the Vietnam War, SEALs work their way along the Panama Canal in a patrol craft. The vessel carries an M60 and a Mark 19 grenade launcher at the stern, offering a substantial amount of firepower for a small boat.

them were delayed, as they were. It might have been more appropriate for the SEALs to have heavier weapons (not least anti-armor rocket launchers) or to go in larger numbers. Given the potential scope of hostage rescue missions, Team Six had prepared to work in larger groups than SEALs normally do—they might have had less difficulty had they taken more men. The Grenadians eventually melted away after failing to storm Government House and after the attention of more than one AC-130: they might have decided to leave earlier if they were faced with a large number of SEALs.

In Panama, the two key SEAL missions were direct contrasts. One saw the use of a small team to achieve great effect, while the other saw the use of a large group and ran into difficulties. The events at Paitilla are still not clear and while the contention that the SEALs should not have been employed remains, there does not seem to be a clear-cut judgement as to whether the mission was appropriate or not: strong arguments can be made in support of both sides.

While it is important to assess the way in which operations are conducted, there is always a danger that historians will use the perfect vision provided by hindsight to come to unfair conclusions about the performance of personnel and those who send them into

Below: A U.S. Marine gives water to a captive taken during the fighting in Panama. The prisoners shown in this group have been restrained and blindfolded. This is most likely to prevent them from having any ideas of attempting escape while on their way to the prisoner holding area.

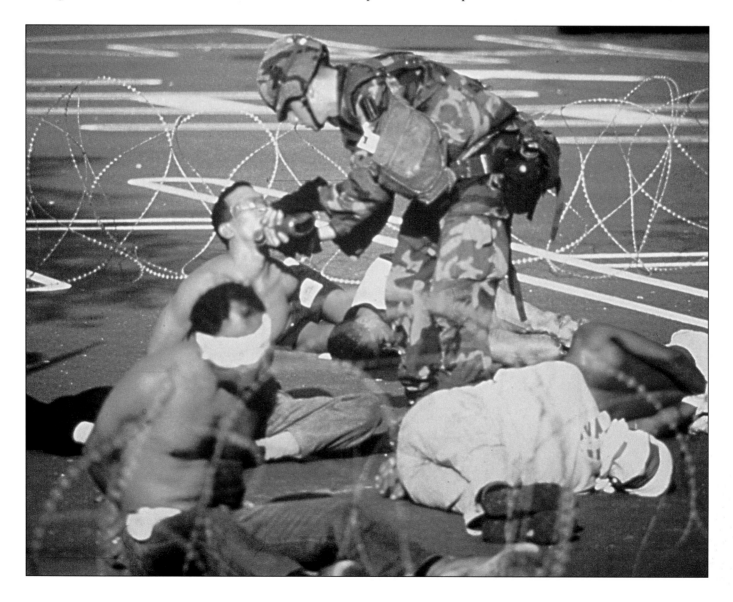

Left: Manuel Noriega, the former Panamanian dictator cuts a less-than impressive figure as his is hustled aboard a C-130 by Drug Enforcement agents. Noriega faced charges in the United States for drug running, and was handed a long prison sentence after he was convicted.

battle. There is also a problem in that arguing about the merits of an operation can obscure the performance of the men involved: in all cases in Grenada and Panama, there can be little doubt that the SEALs involved performed with flexibility, determination, and not a little courage. When assessing their role in both Urgent Fury and Just Cause, it is important not to forget this.

These were not the only combat challenges that the SEALs faced in the final years of the Cold War. On August 2, 1990, the last conflict of the Cold War—or the first conflict of the post-Cold War era, depending on your point of view—broke out when Saddam Hussein invaded Kuwait. This gave the SEALs an opportunity to renew operations in one of their old haunts: the Persian Gulf. It also gave a hint of the challenges that would be posed in the 1990s. Some said the decade marked the start of a new order in the world. In fact, it was part of what one commentator termed the new world disorder—and this disorder had started before Saddam's fatal decision to cross the Kuwaiti border. The SEALs were involved from the start.

In all cases in Grenada and Panama, there can be little doubt that the SEALs involved performed with flexibility, determination, and not a little courage.

CHAPTER SIX

NEW WORLD DISORDER

Since the 1980s the SEALs have been regularly called to arms to help keep the peace and eliminate the threat of terrorism, notably in the Former Yugoslavia, Afghanistan and Iraq.

Left: A SEAL pauses for breath while on exercise. He is carrying the team's radio along with an M4 carbine with an M203 Grenade launcher.

Right: Iranian prisoners taken by SEALs during Operation Praying Mantis are escorted aboard a US Navy LPH. The guards carry an interesting assortment of MP5 sub-machine guns and what appears to be an M14 rifle. The prisoners were returned to Iran once the operation was complete.

The end of the Cold War marked a dramatic change in the patterns of global security. Although two years passed between the fall of the Berlin Wall and the dissolution of the Soviet Union, the superpower status enjoyed by the communist state ebbed away as the realities of market forces permeated the eastern bloc. A worrying number of Russian soldiers sold their weapons and equipment to the highest bidder so as to supplement their wages. While there is debate over the exact end point of the Cold War, it is not unfair to say that by the middle of 1990 it was clear that the war was ending if it had not passed into history. Commentators began debating how the international security environment would develop in the post-Cold War world. Governments seized on the opportunity to capitalize on what became known as the "peace dividend," cutting back their armed forces on the assumption that any future threat would not demand such large numbers of troops, ships, and aircraft. Although there was considerable dispute as to the nature of the possible future threat, there was general agreement that terrorism would become a more prominent phenomenon. As a consequence of this, special forces such as the SEALs were not under such great threat of cutbacks as conventional units. But before anyone had the opportunity to develop thinking on the new world order, Saddam Hussein invaded Kuwait.

The Gulf

The invasion of Kuwait on August 2, 1990 demonstrated that Saddam Hussein regarded the invasion of neighboring countries as a perfectly acceptable means of enacting his policy and stemmed almost directly from the invasion of Iran in 1980 that provoked the Iran–Iraq war. While Saddam had been the aggressor in the war, he was fortunate that Iran's behavior

Left: An Iranian oil platform burns after being destroyed during Operation Praying Mantis. The Iranians were using such platforms as a base for armed speedboats that were employed for attacking oil tanker traffic. Two Iranian oil platforms were destroyed: one by U.S. naval gunfire and another by SEALs using explosive charges.

in the aftermath of the 1979 revolution had led to near-pariah status. It might be an exaggeration to say that western support for Saddam was wildly enthusiastic, but a number of governments—notably including that of the United States—took the view that Saddam was the lesser of two evils and ensured that weapons and weapon-making technology found their way to Iraq. Although Saddam enjoyed a technological advantage over the Iranians, his prosecution of the war did not mark him out as a great strategic genius. By 1982 the war had become bogged down. There had been over 100,000 casualties and the cost of the fighting had spiraled to over $1 billion per month. Even though the two combatants were oil-rich nations, this was a crippling figure. It soon became obvious to both sides that expanding attacks on their opponent's oil industry might provide a route to victory. Both sides had suffered heavy blows against their oil industry from the outset, but now turned to attack oil exports. This, inevitably, meant attacking neutral merchant shipping in the Gulf.

While Saddam had been the aggressor in the war, he was fortunate that Iran's behavior in the aftermath of the 1979 revolution had led to near-pariah status.

From March 1984, Iraq began to increase the tempo of operations in the Gulf. It had ordered Dassault Mirage F1 fighter/attack aircraft from France, along with Exocet anti-shipping missiles; while waiting for delivery, the French obligingly loaned Iraq a handful of Super Etendard attack aircraft, which were also capable of carrying the Exocet. This enabled the Iraqis to increase attacks on neutral shipping dramatically and it was not long before the Iranians retaliated.

This situation was deeply worrying for Kuwait, since it found itself in the unenviable position where its tankers were being attacked while it was increasingly dangerous for would-be buyers of Kuwaiti oil to obtain it. Consequently, the Emir of Kuwait appealed for international protection of its shipping. The U.S.S.R. led the way, chartering several vessels to the Kuwaitis. This encouraged the United States—anxious to avoid increased Soviet influence in the Gulf—to follow suit. On March 11, 1987, Washington offered to re-flag eleven Kuwaiti tankers, providing them with U.S. Navy protection. This move seemed to work well, but the attacks continued.

Right: SEALs disentangle themselves after fast-roping to the beach from a UH-1. The SEALs make great use of this technique to insert into an operating area. On this occasion, they are practicing their skills in the Persian Gulf.

USS STARK

On May 17, 1987, one of Iraq's recently arrived Mirage F1s fired two Exocets at a target that turned out to be the USS *Stark*. There is still debate as to whether the attack was deliberate or whether the Iraqi claim of pilot error was truthful. Thirty-seven sailors died in the attack and another 21 were injured. This marked a major escalation in the tanker war. Although it was Iraq that had attacked the *Stark*, the U.S. administration took the view that Iran represented a greater threat to Gulf shipping. This view was not totally without foundation: while the

Iranians took care not to directly target the U.S.-flagged tankers and escort vessels, it adopted a form of maritime guerrilla warfare instead. The Iranians employed small patrol boats, extensive mining, and stop-and-search operations as a means of interfering with traffic. This represented more than just an irritation and U.S. naval forces increased their presence in the Gulf under the auspices of Operation Earnest Will. While the U.S. Navy's ships were of great use, the nature of the tanker war meant that there was a part to be played by the SEALs.

Left: SEALs fast rope onto a ship from a CH-46 (affectionately known as a "Frog,") training for boarding operations. These played an important part in Operation Earnest Will, and have been in near-constant use ever since as the U.S. Navy has contributed to enforcing sanctions and arms embargoes against Iraq and the Former Yugoslavia.

Operation Earnest Will

The threat posed by mines and small patrol craft prompted the instigation of Operation Earnest Will in the early summer of 1987. On the first escort mission, in July, the re-flagged tanker *Bridgeton* was hit by a mine. By the end of the month, two more tankers had been damaged. The sheer size of the tankers meant that they proved very difficult to sink, but the threat could not be underestimated. The use of fast attack craft—some of which were little more than speedboats carrying machine-guns and anti-armor weapons—meant that the Iranians could carry out hit-and-run attacks against tankers not directly escorted by the Americans. To deal with these attacks, it was clear that patrol forces were required in the northern Persian Gulf. This called for the use of special operations forces (SOF), which included Army assets as well as the SEALs and their associated Special Boat Units. The SEALs and army special operations forces had the advantage of great experience of nighttime operations, which was when the Iranians tended to carry out their attacks. Between them, the Army and the SEALs offered important capabilities: the Army's special operations helicopters were difficult for the Iranians to locate with radar and had a relatively low acoustic signature. This meant that they were able to close in on any targets and deliver an attack. As well as providing night surveillance and direct action capabilities, the SEALs' use of their patrol boats was useful for reconnoitering waters that had not been swept for mines—the shallow draft of the patrol craft meant that they were most unlikely to set off any mines before detection. Two SEAL platoons and half a dozen Mark III Patrol Boats deployed in August 1987 and it was not long before they were in action.

On the evening of September 21, three AH-6 Little Bird army SOF helicopters took off from the frigate USS *Jarett*, with orders to follow an Iranian ship, the *Iran Ajr*, which was behaving suspiciously. It did not take long for the force to find the *Iran Ajr*, which, almost on cue, extinguished its lights. Since the Little Birds were equipped with night-vision gear, this was a fairly pointless exercise. Within minutes, the *Iran Ajr* begin laying mines. The helicopter crews requested permission to engage the ship. Once this was given, they

The use of fast attack craft—some of which were little more than speedboats carrying machine-guns and anti-armor weapons—meant that the Iranians could carry out hit-and-run attacks against tankers not directly escorted by the Americans.

Right: The Persian Gulf had been an unstable region since Iraq invaded Iran in 1980. Shortly after the end of the Iran–Iraq war, Iraq invaded Kuwait, leading to a coalition of forces against Saddam Hussein. The SEALs moved to the Persian Gulf in readiness for the liberation of Kuwait. This map shows the various routes used by Coalition aircraft during the airstrikes before the land campaign began.

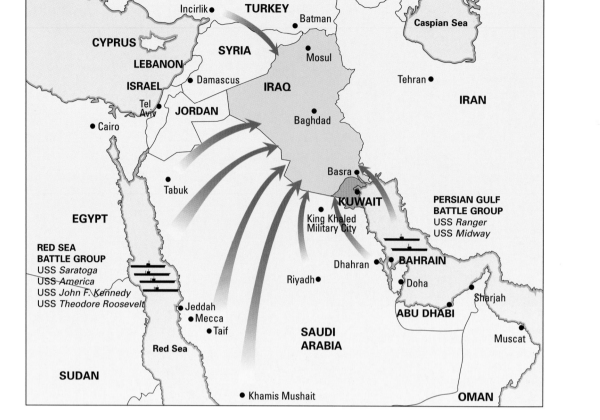

The Iranians had been administratively efficient and had kept records of where they had laid mines. This was deeply embarrassing for Tehran, since the documents suggested that the Iranians were conducting mining operations in international waters.

attacked with a mixture of guns and rockets. The *Iran Ajr* was badly damaged and was stopped. Either because of a determination to cause as much difficulty as possible or from a desire to pretend that they had been doing nothing wrong, the *Iran Ajr*'s crew began to push the mines over the side of their vessel. At this point, the helicopters resumed firing until the crew abandoned ship.

Rear Admiral Harold J. Bernsen, the commander of the Middle East Force, then ordered a SEAL platoon aboard the USS *Guadalcanal* to board the *Iran Ajr*. Shortly after first light, the SEALs boarded the ship. A search revealed that the Iranians had not been able to dispose of all their mines; nine were found, along with fuzing mechanisms. The patrol boats—sent to provide cover should the Iranians try to make a fight of things—rescued 10 Iranian crewmen from a lifeboat and found another 13 in life jackets floating nearby. The SEALs also found some useful paperwork: the Iranians had been administratively efficient and had kept records of where they had laid mines. This was deeply embarrassing for Tehran, since the documents suggested that the Iranians were conducting mining operations in international waters. Once the search had been carried out, the *Iran Ajr* was sunk in deep water on September 26. Despite the international criticism of the Iranians for laying mines outside territorial waters, the *Iran Ajr* incident did not bring an end to work for the SEALs.

On October 16, the Iranians fired a shore-based Silkworm anti-shipping missile at a tanker, the *Sea Isle City*. The missile hit the tanker, injuring 18 of the crew. This prompted a response from U.S. forces. On October 19, Operation Nimble Archer saw an attack by four destroyers on two of the Iranian oil platforms in the Rostam oil field (the platforms served a dual role—as well as oil production, they were bases for Iranian patrol craft). After

OPERATION PRAYING MANTIS

On April 14, while steaming some 60 nautical miles east of Bahrain, the frigate USS *Samuel Roberts* hit a mine. Ten members of the crew were injured and a large hole was torn into the hull. Washington's patience with the Iranians had worn thin and the Americans responded by launching Operation Praying Mantis. U.S. Navy aircraft engaged a number of Iranian ships, causing carnage with a mixture of missiles and laser-guided bombs. American warships bombarded oil platforms in the Sirri and Sassan oil fields. The platforms in the Sirri field were targeted for demolition by the SEALs, but this plan did not quite survive contact with friendly forces. The warships employed incendiary shells against the platforms, which meant that when the SEALs tried to board them they found that it was impossible. This hardly mattered, since the platforms were destroyed.

the destroyers had shelled the platform, SEALs went aboard one of the platforms and demolished it with explosives. They searched a third platform and various documents and items of equipment were seized.

By this time, the SEALs and Army SOF were employing two converted oil barges, the *Hercules* and the *Wimbrown VII*, as operating platforms. These were extremely useful in that they obviated the need for land bases (which were vulnerable to attack) and gave a degree of operational security to missions. Since access to the barges was strictly controlled, it reduced the possibility of Iranian sympathizers transmitting details of patrols. The two barges saw much activity as the SEALs and the Army helicopters undertook regular patrols. The barges became something of a regular feature in the lives of the SEALs, since they were rotated to and from the theater regularly. By 1988, some personnel had "enjoyed" two or even three tours. The presence of the U.S. forces did much to reduce the threat to international shipping in 1987, but 1988 marked the climax of events.

Left: A SEAL instructor walks his charges through ship assault training on board a U.S. Navy vessel somewhere in the Persian Gulf. As well as the SEALs, the U.S. Marines undertake boarding operations, and the two organizations co-operate very closely in such work.

Right: A SEAL armed with an MP5 sub machine gun charges up a set of stairs aboard a ship. The thick gloves hanging from his belt clip are those used to protect the hands while fast-roping to the deck.

As well as the destruction of the oil platforms, the American forces inflicted a massive blow against the Iranian navy. Two ships were sunk and five others were damaged. Although the Iranians tried to retaliate by launching two Silkworm missiles at the mobile barges, the missiles were decoyed by chaff fired by USS *Gary*. A further attempt to attack the barges by Iranian fighter aircraft and patrol boats was thwarted when the *Gary* warned the aircraft off by locking its missile systems onto them. Praying Mantis marked a turning point. It was clear to the Iranian leadership that they would not be able to win the tanker war and there is little doubt that war-weariness had set in. Attacks on neutral shipping

declined and on July 18, 1988, Iran announced that it would accept the terms of the United Nations cease-fire that had been proposed (and rejected) some time before. The Iran–Iraq War ended on August 20. Saddam Hussein surveyed the damage to his country and declared that he had won a famous victory, demonstrating that his definition of success was substantially different to that of the rest of the world. Analysts agreed that no one could be said to have won the war and noted that if Iran had been humbled as completely as Saddam claimed it would not have been demanding reparations from Iraq. Although the war was over, the SEALs remained deployed: the *Hercules* remained as their base until June 1989, when the SEAL teams returned to the United States. No one quite appreciated that they would be returning in little more than a year.

Shield and Storm

By the summer of 1990, Saddam realized that he was facing potentially serious difficulties as a result of the Iran–Iraq war. Iraq was heavily in debt and Saddam feared unrest among the population. He also felt a sense of grievance toward Kuwait, claiming that the Emirate was taking oil from under Iraqi territory. Saddam decided to resort to bullying in an attempt to gain financial assistance, but by July 1990 was making threatening noises about seizing territory. In another piece of spectacular misjudgment, Saddam interpreted the diplomatic platitudes of the American ambassador as being a sign that the United States would not intervene if he attacked Kuwait. Although President George Bush Snr sent signals that this was not the case, Saddam attacked anyway. In only 24 hours, Kuwait had fallen and Iraq had acquired a new enemy.

Within hours of the invasion, the Bush administration orchestrated the first of a series of United Nations Security Council resolutions condemning Iraqi action. This was soon followed by the decision to send forces to Saudi Arabia to protect the kingdom should Saddam try to invade it, under the codename of Desert Shield. The rationale for Desert

By the summer of 1990, Saddam realized that he was facing potentially serious difficulties as a result of the Iran–Iraq war. Iraq was heavily in debt and Saddam feared unrest among the population.

Right: SEALs stride ashore on beach reconnaissance training—training they were able to use to good effect in the Gulf War. Both men carry M16A1 rifles, dating this photograph to the 1980s. They wear closed breathing apparatus, which does not give off air bubbles, thus making it harder to detect their presence in the water.

On November 29, 1990, the UN passed Resolution 678 authorizing the employment of "all necessary means" to evict Iraqi forces from Kuwait.

Shield now seems to be less convincing than it seemed at the time: it would appear that Saddam had no intention of commandeering the Saudi oil fields as another stage toward dominating the Persian Gulf. However, in the tense atmosphere of August 1990, anything seemed possible and American forces began arriving in large numbers to ensure that Saudi Arabia was safe. On August 11, 105 SEALs and associated support personnel were setting up their base near the city of Dhahran in southern Saudi Arabia. Once American and British forces were in Saudi Arabia in sufficient strength to guarantee that an invasion would be prohibitively costly, the SEALs began to take part in the planning process for any action that would lead to the liberation of Kuwait. Diplomacy appeared increasingly unlikely to succeed and the United Nations passed a further series of resolutions demanding that Iraq withdraw from occupied territory. Militarily, the United States set about assembling a strong coalition of 38 nations that would, if necessary, seek to eject Iraqi forces from Kuwait. Eventually, it was clear that Saddam had no intention of leaving Kuwait of his own volition. On November 29, 1990, the UN passed Resolution 678 authorizing the employment of "all necessary means" to evict Iraqi forces from Kuwait. It also gave Saddam a clear choice: vacate Kuwait by January 15, 1991 or face war. Saddam stayed.

War

The resultant operation to remove Saddam Hussein has entered history as the "100-hour war." This is something of a misnomer, since the majority of the war was conducted in the air during a massive sustained bombardment of key Iraqi targets that began on the night of January 17, 1991 and continued for over a month before the ground offensive commenced. The general story of the war is well known and runs along the following lines: after the air campaign achieved tremendous success, ground units inflicted a crushing defeat on the Iraqis. Iraq's attempts to bring Israel into the war by firing Scud missiles at Tel Aviv and other major cities were unsuccessful, although the attacks led to what became known as "The Great Scud Hunt," diverting some of the air effort from its intended targets. Also, as part of the Scud hunt, special forces, notably the U.S. Army's Delta Force and the British Special Air Service, conducted daring raids behind enemy lines, sowing confusion and destruction among Iraqi forces. The Iraqis were evicted from Kuwait and the war ended with their forces in disarray. But this was still not enough to prevent Saddam from proclaiming that he had won another famous victory. While this generic summary of Desert Storm is accurate, it omits a number of key activities; also, while special forces were very active, the SEALs were not employed in the Scud hunt and behind enemy lines. Instead, they conducted a series of important tasks that have not received the same level of attention as those of their army counterparts, not least

Below: A SEAL walks along a shallow trench somewhere in Kuwait during the Gulf War of 1991. The trench shows no sign of permanent occupation, and is probably a defensive fire position for use in an emergency. It also serves as a walkway guaranteed to be clear of enemy mines.

Right: SEALs practice with CH-53 Stallion helicopters as they return from a training mission. The rope ladder hanging from the rear ramp of the helicopter is notable. The CH-53 is one of the most powerful helicopters in the world, and is capable of carrying over 50 fully-equipped troops. When supporting the SEALs, however, they are likely to carry far fewer men.

since they did not involve much direct combat with the enemy. Despite this, the SEALs were far from underemployed and made a notable contribution to the progress of the war.

SEALS at War

The earliest SEAL missions took place even before the first bombs were falling on Iraqi targets. UN resolutions imposed an embargo on Iraq and the SEALs participated in boarding parties inspecting ships that might have been attempting to breach the blockade. Ironically, the only time that weapons were employed during the interception missions was when an Iraqi ship carrying more than 200 peace activists attempted to breach the cordon. A substantial boarding party made up of Marines and SEALs from USS *Trenton* and USS *Shreeveport* was joined by U.S. and Australian personnel from three accompanying destroyers. Once aboard

BEACH RECONNAISSANCE

Groups of SEALs began reconnoitering Kuwaiti beaches on January 16, closing in on the target beaches in inflatable boats before swimming the last few hundred yards to the beaches. Their reports on the suitability of the beaches for an amphibious operation were far from encouraging. The Iraqis enjoyed commanding fields of fire over many of the beaches and had set up an array of beach obstacles to prevent an easy time for would-be invaders. In addition, a survey of the hydrography of some of the beaches revealed that they were totally unsuitable for a landing. One beach, at Ash Shuaybah, did prove to be acceptable in terms of the hydrography, but the beach was overlooked by high-rise buildings, most of

which had been fortified. As well as the threat of heavy fire from the buildings, a nearby natural gas plant was a further concern, since it could have been blown up by the Iraqis as forces came ashore. The U.S. Marine Corps concluded that the buildings and the gas plant would have to be destroyed by a preparatory bombardment before the landings. However, General Norman Schwarzkopf, the commander of the coalition forces, was extremely reluctant to inflict such huge destruction on Kuwait, particularly if it was not essential to stage an amphibious landing. Schwarkopf's thoughts were already turning to the idea of a massive thrust into Iraq itself and the amphibious option became increasingly less attractive to him.

Left: SEALs prepare to jump from the rear of a helicopter (probably a CH-46) on a training mission. Their gear is stowed in an Inflatable Boat, Small (IBS), which will be pushed out of the helicopter before the SEALs drop into the water. The helicopter must be at the correct altitude and travelling slowly, since dropping into water from too great a height and too great a speed is akin to falling onto solid concrete: fatalities have been caused when errors in speed or altitude have been made.

the ship, the activists proved less peaceful than might have been expected. They obstructed the boarding party (which had every right to be there as a result of the UN resolutions) and some of the activists were unwise enough to make a grab for the boarding party's weapons. This led to several warning shots being fired, the use of disorientation munitions, and a robust search, which uncovered contraband material. The peace activists received far less publicity than they had hoped for and were escorted to a port in Oman. The interception missions continued for the remainder of the conflict and were a resounding success.

Ironically, the only time that weapons were employed during the interception missions was when an Iraqi ship carrying more than 200 peace activists attempted to breach the cordon.

Above: SEALs aboard a container ship while enforcing the arms embargo against the warring parties in the Former Yugoslavia. The SEALs would inspect throughout the vessel to ensure that no banned goods were being sent into the country. Ships that were not in breach of the embargo were allowed to continue, while those carrying illegal items would be compelled to pull into port for the authorities to take action.

While debates over the final plan for the land campaign were being conducted, the SEALs were carrying out a series of small operations. An attempt was made to provide radios to the Kuwaiti resistance: SEALs used their inflatable boats to take a number of Kuwaiti commandos up to the shore south of Kuwait City. The idea was for the Kuwaitis to smuggle the radios in, but the plan had to be abandoned when an Iraqi patrol was spotted. The Kuwaitis assessed that slipping past the patrol without being spotted would be extremely difficult and decided not to take the risk. On January 24, the SEALs participated in the recapture of the first piece of Kuwaiti territory, Qurah Island. U.S. Navy A-6 Intruder attack aircraft had surprised a small group of Iraqi ships and sank a patrol boat and two mine warfare vessels. The rout was completed when another minelayer, making desperate efforts to evade the A-6s, ran straight over one of its own mines and sank itself. Helicopters from the frigate USS *Curts* went to recover the survivors, but were fired on from Qurah Island as they did so. The helicopters returned fire, calling on the ship for assistance. *Curts* moved in closer to the shore and began to bombard the Iraqi positions. After some six hours, the Iraqis decided that they had suffered enough and indicated their intention to capitulate. SEALs based on the destroyer *Leftwich* were ferried to the island by the ship's helicopters and took the surrender. Five days later, another group of SEALs, acting as forward observers, found itself entangled in the Iraqi invasion of Saudi Arabia, when the town of Al-Khafji was briefly taken, before the Iraqis were driven back. In addition to this direct involvement with the war, the SEALs provided a search-and-rescue service, operating from U.S. Navy helicopters. There were not many of these operations, not least since the few allied aircraft lost were forced down over Iraq, which was in the operating area of the U.S. Air Force rather than the Navy. Nonetheless, the SEALs saved at least one flier, recovering the pilot of an F-16 who had been forced to eject over the Gulf.

The SEALs were faced with the problem that several of their specialized skills and their preferred mode of operations did not necessarily fit in with the campaign against Iraq. Saddam was convinced that the coalition would invade Kuwait from the sea and had stationed up to 60,000 men in approximately 25 miles (40 kilometers) of coastline. In these circumstances, direct action operations by small groups of men made no sense whatsoever and would have represented an unnecessary level of risk. Moving the SEALs from their normal operating environment to conduct direct action missions in the Iraqi desert did not make a great deal of sense either, since the SOF from the U.S. Army and British forces were already there in considerable numbers. The simple fact was that although the SEALs were eager to participate directly, their specialization in the maritime environment meant that they were not able to engage in combat in the same way that their predecessors had in Vietnam. This did not mean that their role was unimportant. The commander of the Naval

Left: Special forces troops practice their abseiling skills from a UH-60 during the mid-1990s. The Blackhawk will remain the mainstay of U.S. helicopter forces for many years to come, with as yet no requirement for a replacement. The U.S. Navy is taking delivery of new models of the maritime version (the Seahawk) for use in a variety of roles, including SEAL support missions.

Unlike in Vietnam, Grenada, and Panama, the SEALs were fighting as part of a huge joint force and this meant that their contributions were often best made in an environment where there was little fighting.

Right: A SEAL in full swimming gear floats gently down to the sea. The alarming "holes" visible in the parachute canopy are meant to be there, since they enable the SEAL to steer his parachute very precisely so that he can land in exactly the right place.

Special Warfare Task Group in the Gulf, Captain Ray Smith, had laid down five concepts of employment, number four being to contribute to the overall effort of coalition forces. Unlike in Vietnam, Grenada, and Panama, the SEALs were fighting as part of a huge joint force and this meant that their contributions were often best made in an environment where there was little fighting. This makes some of the contributions hard to quantify, but there is little difficulty in judging the importance of one SEAL mission—the operation to support the invasion that never was.

Deception

The final plan for the ground war did not include an amphibious operation, but General Schwarzkopf was naturally eager to keep the Iraqis guessing. An amphibious landing would have been hazardous, but there was little doubt that it would have been the source of major difficulties for the Iraqis. As a result, an amphibious force was kept relatively close to Kuwait to worry them. The media was invited to cover the rehearsals for a landing. While the press was obtaining a great deal of material, the SEALs—fully aware that a landing was not going to occur—were busy planning a deception operation that would be small in scale but massive in effect. An elegant plan was worked out by a platoon commanded by Lieutenant Tom Dietz and put it into action on the night of February 23, 1991.

For several days before the SEALs' mission, the supposed invasion beach had been subjected to heavy naval gunfire, as would be expected before a landing. The gunfire stopped on the night of the operation and the SEALs approached the beach in their

Above: A SEAL is recovered from the water by a CH-46 as it swoops low over the sea. Such extraction methods are dramatic and not without danger. In the face of the enemy, however, such an approach negates the need for the helicopter to hover and winch men aboard, thus exposing itself to a tremendous level of risk from ground fire.

Right: The liberation of Kuwait by Coalition forces in February 1991. The SEALs conducted operations to test the suitability for an amphibious landing, but it was deemed too dangerous to proceed.

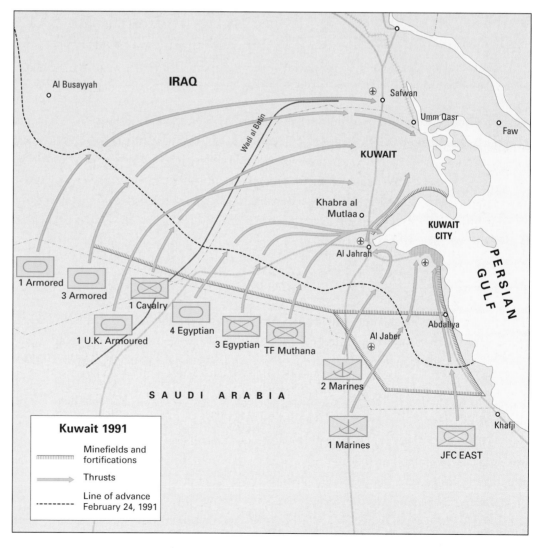

Al Busayyah

IRAQ

Safwan

Umm Qasr

Faw

Wadi al Batin

KUWAIT

Khabra al Mutlaa

KUWAIT CITY

Al Jahrah

PERSIAN GULF

1 Armored

3 Armored

1 Cavalry

4 Egyptian

Abdaliya

1 U.K. Armoured

3 Egyptian

TF Muthana

Al Jaber

2 Marines

SAUDI ARABIA

1 Marines

Khafji

JFC EAST

Kuwait 1991

|||||||||| Minefields and fortifications

→ Thrusts

- - - Line of advance February 24, 1991

inflatable boats until they were some 500 yards (460 meters) from the shore. Dietz and five of his men then slipped over the side of the boats and swam in toward their target. The six men stopped when they could touch the bottom with their flippers and broke out the 20 pounds (9 kilograms) of explosives that each was carrying. They carefully laid their charges, pulled the timers, and swam out to their inflatable boats. They then returned to the patrol boats that had brought them into the area, which were lying about seven miles (11 kilometers) offshore. Two more patrol boats were waiting a little closer to the shore and at 0030 hours they raced toward the shore and opened fire on the beach with all their armament. The Iraqis found themselves under fire from machine-guns, mortars, and grenade launchers. After making a great deal of noise for about ten minutes, the patrol boats sped away, hauling more explosive packages overboard, just as the first of the explosive charges laid by Dietz's team went off. The charges were not set to go off together, but at intervals—just as they would if a team of men were seeking to demolish underwater obstacles in preparation for an amphibious assault. These explosions were then followed by the detonation of the packs tossed over the side of the patrol boats, adding to the confusion ashore. The patrol boats then sped back to base where the SEALs debriefed. Dietz later recalled that the team was happy that the mission was successful, but did not regard it as being particularly exciting. While it may not have been exciting for the SEALs, it certainly excited the Iraqis, who were convinced that an amphibious assault was in the offing. Elements of two Iraqi divisions headed toward the beach to try to fend off the attack—only to find that the attack had arrived in the form of a massive thrust to the west of Iraq, miles away from where they could have any effect. The mission was the perfect demonstration of

Left: This photograph of a SEAL, who has just come ashore on beach reconnaissance training, provides an excellent view of the latest equipment, particularly his wetsuit and fins. These contrast with those seen earlier in this book, being made out of more advanced materials, offering improved performance and endurance in the water.

Left: A SEAL fire team comes ashore. The team is large enough to conduct ambush operations and reconnaissance tasks, yet small enough to evade detection by the enemy if lying up in a hide, and able to move quickly through the enemy lines. All are armed with weapons from the M16 family.

The threat from terrorist groups did not seem to merit the highest priority, although it had been clear that the United States was a tempting target for over a decade. These priorities were totally overturned on September 11, 2001 the date of the attacks launched by Al-Qa'eda against the World Trade Center and the Pentagon.

Right: A SEAL shows off his personal kit. He is wearing desert BDUs and nomex gloves, from which he has removed the fingers to provide greater sensitivity of touch. His personal weapon is the M4 Carbine with M203 grenade launcher slung beneath, along with five magazines, giving him around 130–140 rounds of ammunition. Although the magazines can contain up to 30 rounds, they are rarely filled to capacity to avoid over-straining the spring and causing feed problems (which are guaranteed to occur at the most inopportune time).

the effect that can be achieved by using a small group of specialists to achieve a particular outcome. While the SEALs may not have felt that they had an "interesting" Gulf War, there can be little doubt that they had a highly effective one.

Although there were occasional worries about Saddam Hussein and the possible need for further intervention against Iraq, the 1990s seemed to point the way forward for military operations for some time to come: they would be associated with peace-keeping and, where necessary, peace enforcement. There was an additional concern in the form of terrorism. The threat from terrorist groups did not seem to merit the highest priority, although it had been clear that the United States was a tempting target for over a decade. These priorities were totally overturned on September 11, 2001, the date of the attacks launched by Al-Qa'eda against the World Trade Center and the Pentagon. The need to counter terrorism and those who would support it could not have been demonstrated any

SOMALIA

The end of the Gulf War did not mean that the SEALs found less to do. In fact, they took part in a series of operations during the remainder of the 1990s. The SEALs participated in the humanitarian intervention in Somalia, although their involvement was far more highly publicized than they would have liked. As they landed on the Somali beaches, they were met not by hostile troops but a barrage of photographers and cameramen. The Somalia mission ended after the loss of 18 U.S. servicemen in the events immortalized in the book and motion picture *Black Hawk Down*. Although the book and movie rightly concentrate on the Rangers and Delta personnel engaged in these operations, a small number of SEALs also participated in the brutal fighting.

more clearly. The military means of addressing the terrorist threat were long established in the form of special operations forces and the SEALs have been at the forefront of the response. It would be wrong, however, to see this as being a new duty for the SEALs—in truth, they have been practicing the counter-terrorist role for years.

Dealing with "Old-style" Terrorism

The threat posed to states by terrorist groups is centuries old, but it is arguable that the level of the threat increased dramatically during the latter half of the twentieth century. Perhaps the first terrorist organization of note that operated beyond national frontiers was the Palestine Liberation Organization (PLO) and its assorted offshoots, which came to prominence in the late 1960s. The first significant action was the hijacking of three airliners in 1970. These were flown to the old Royal Air Force base at Dawson's Field in Jordan, where the hostages were released. The terrorists gained much publicity, not least since they destroyed the three airliners while the world's media looked on from a safe distance. Two years later, terrorists struck against Israeli athletes at the Munich Olympics. The German authorities were unprepared for such an attack and their attempts to free the hostages were unsuccessful. The terrorists were told that they would be allowed to leave Germany and were taken to the airfield at Fürstenfeldbruck by helicopter where they were to board an aircraft to Cairo. In fact, the German police intended to launch a rescue mission, but this went disastrously wrong. A gun battle broke out and all of the hostages were killed.

The events at Munich caused considerable concern among European governments, who simply did not have the means to deal with hostage incidents. The West German authorities established Grenzschützgruppe 9 (GSG 9), a specialist counter-terrorist group from the border police; the French created the Groupement d'Intervention de la Gendarmarie Nationale (GIGN) while the British turned to the 22nd Special Air Service Regiment. The United States, however, appeared initially unconcerned, even though the

Below: A SEAL aims his M60A3 machine gun. In contrast with the Vietnam-era M60, this model is lighter and equipped with a foregrip to allow it to be fired from the hip or the shoulder with improved accuracy (although accuracy is always sacrificed when firing from the hip).

terrorists would soon begin targeting its citizens. The massive amounts of aid provided to Israel during the 1973 Yom Kippur War made America a legitimate target in the eyes of many radical Arab groups seeking to destroy the Israeli state. In addition, a number of left-wing terrorist groups appeared in Europe, most notably the Red Army Faction, or RAF (also known as the Baader–Meinhof Gang) in Germany. As well as killing the German industrialists who represented the capitalist system they wished to overthrow, the RAF also began to attack American military targets. Perhaps their most notable effort was the failed attempt to kill General Alexander Haig as he drove to work.

While these events gave credence to the insistence of a number of officers within the U.S. services that America required specialist forces to meet the terrorist threat, little was done until the mid-1970s. In 1976, the Israelis were faced with a crisis when Palestinian terrorists hijacked an Air France airliner carrying a large number of Israeli citizens. The hijackers ordered the crew to fly it to Entebbe in Uganda, where it became obvious that the country's dictator, Idi Amin, intended to cooperate with the terrorists. The Israelis responded by sending a commando team to Entebbe, which killed the terrorists and a number of Ugandan troops and, to prevent pursuit of their transportation aircraft, destroyed the Ugandan air force on the ground. A year later, a Lufthansa jet was hijacked by Palestinians operating on behalf of the Red Army Faction. After the terrorists shot the pilot, the German government deployed GSG 9. The anti-terrorist group followed the aircraft to Mogadishu, where they stormed the aircraft. The assault was an outstanding success—the hostages were rescued and three of the four terrorists died; the fourth survived despite being severely wounded. It also demonstrated the validity of having specially trained and equipped units to deal with terrorist incidents. This finally led authorization for the creation of the first U.S. unit in 1977. Special Operations Force

Below: Special operations forces such as the SEALs have made increasing use of light vehicles in recent years, such as this Desert Patrol Vehicle (DPV—also known as a fast attack vehicle). A development of civilian dune-racing buggies, a variety of DPVs have been procured. On average, they carry teams of three men, and can be armed with a mixture of machine guns, anti-tank missiles and even cannon of up to 30mm (1.18-inch) caliber. Such vehicles provide excellent cross-country mobility, although the ride on the earliest types was incredibly hard, as they had no suspension.

Left: A SEAL stands guard, armed with an MP5. He is presumably in close proximity to the observation post that he is manning, since he is not carrying a rucksack containing personal gear. SEALs must be prepared to go anywhere in the hunt for terrorists.

Detachment DELTA (or Delta Force) was established under the command of Colonel Charles A. Beckwith. After some bureaucratic rivalry and infighting (at one stage, a rival but near-identical outfit to Delta known as "Blue Light" was in existence), Delta took its place in the order of battle.

Operation Eagle Claw

Delta's first test came with Operation Eagle Claw, the attempt on April 24–25, 1980 to rescue the hostages held in Tehran. The mission was daring, but failed in tragic fashion. The plan demanded that the Delta operatives be ferried to Tehran in RH-53D Sea Stallion helicopters, but when lack of serviceableness reduced the number of helicopters below the minimum required, Colonel Beckwith (quite correctly) canceled the operation. The helicopters needed refueling, but as one of them was repositioned, it crashed into an MC-130 Hercules transportation aircraft. Eight Americans died in the resulting inferno and the hostages were not to be released until 1981. Although the operation and its disastrous end resulted in controversy, the need for special forces to counter terrorists was not questioned: if there was any doubt, it disappeared within days of Eagle Claw. Six Iraqi-sponsored terrorists seized the Iranian embassy in London. Six days later, the terrorists shot one of their hostages. After his body had been dumped outside the

Although the operation and its disastrous end resulted in controversy, the need for special forces to counter terrorists was not questioned: if there was any doubt, it disappeared within days of Eagle Claw.

Right: SEALs leave a
CH-46 by parachute.
Parachuting from
helicopters on operations
is normally only carried
out by special operations
forces. This is yet another
role where the versatility
of the helicopter is
extremely useful.

embassy, the terrorists threatened to start executing all of their captives; then, more shots
were heard. The British authorities concluded that a second hostage was dead (in fact,
this was not the case) and turned the matter to the SAS. The SAS assaulted the building
live on national television. The embassy was left a burnt-out wreck, but all but one of the
hostages was rescued. Five of the six terrorists were killed and the sixth (who had the
good sense to act completely passively when the SAS appeared) was given a 30-year
prison sentence.

SEAL TEAM SIX

Command of the new team was given to Commander Richard Marcinko, a determined and charismatic officer with a distinguished record in Vietnam, but not without his critics. The saying "You can love him, you can hate him, but you certainly can't ignore him," might have been coined for Marcinko. At the time of his appointment, views about him were already polarized and his tenure in command did nothing to bring the opposing camps together. Those who disliked Marcinko argued that what his admirers saw as enormous self-confidence was actually overbearing arrogance. The controversy relating to Marcinko reached its peak when, in 1990, he was tried for a variety of criminal offences relating to alleged misappropriation of funds and sentenced to 21 months in jail. Marcinko then published a series of books relating to Team Six. These debates about Marcinko overshadow the fact that he drew on the experience of Mob Six members and built on it to create one of the most highly trained, best equipped, and most effective anti-terrorist groups in the world within six months of taking charge.

SEAL Six

In these circumstances, the U.S. Joint Chiefs of Staff decided to create hostage-rescue forces that would be able to respond instantly around the world. Rather than have the rescue teams rely on a slightly ad hoc support mechanism (as Delta had been forced to do), it was decreed that the U.S. Air Force and Army would ensure that there would be specially equipped aircraft and helicopters to support the special forces. The U.S. Navy, as well as

Left: A SEAL comes ashore, his MP5 at the ready. He wears a bulky dry suit, while the lack of breathing apparatus suggests that he has approached the shore by swimming close to the surface. Despite common perception, it is not always necessary for combat swimmers to wear breathing gear: it is worn only when the parameters of a mission dictate that it will be necessary for lengthy underwater work.

Below: A classic pose from a special forces operator as he practices his patrol techniques. He is armed with a Colt Commando, the large flash-hider of which is shown to advantage here. The shortened barrel length degraded long-range accuracy, but this was less of an issue for the SEALs, who were likely to engage the enemy at relatively close range.

providing ships, would provide its own hostage rescue force, designed for operations in a maritime environment. It was an obvious step that this unit would be drawn from the SEALs, not least since there had already been some work on the formation of an anti-terrorist capability, particularly within Team Two.

In February 1978, the operations officer of Team Two, the then-Lieutenant Norm Carley, gathered together around twenty of the more experienced men in the team to consider how to deal with the terrorist threat. This group became known as "Mob Six," as a reference to the fact that its existence could be considered to mark the formation of a sixth platoon in Team Two (although the number of men in the team did not increase). Mob Six provided security services at the NATO symposium held at Annapolis in 1978. Their performance was highly professional and was not forgotten by senior naval officers. In late 1980, as part of the development of the anti-terrorist capabilities desired by the Joint Chiefs of Staff, a new SEAL Team was created. The new team was designated SEAL Team Six, even though there were only two other SEAL teams extant at the time. There is some dispute as to the origin of the name. Some sources claim that the intention was to mislead Soviet intelligence and others that it was simply an outgrowth of Mob Six.

Operations

With the exception of those incidents played out on television, special forces operations against terrorists are shrouded in secrecy. As a result, details about the work Team Six undertakes in this field are relatively limited. Their most publicized activities concern the mission to protect Sir Paul Scoon during Urgent Fury and involvement in Panama as part of the forces trying to track down Manuel Noriega. They are known to have participated in an attempt to capture the Colombian drug lord Pablo Escobar in 1990, although the mission failed as the result of a lack of intelligence information. In 1991, the team is reported to have recovered the deposed Haitian leader Jean-Bertrande Aristide after the army refused to recognize his election victory and deposed him. The other notable operation conducted by Team Six followed the hijacking of the Italian cruise ship the *Achille Lauro* in October 1985. The ship was carrying a large number of American passengers and the terrorists killed one of them, the wheelchair-bound Leon Klinghoffer. This brutal act made the U.S. administration determined to bring the terrorists to justice and the SEALs were ordered to prepare an assault on the ship.

Before the SEALs had the chance to launch their mission to rescue the hostages, the *Achille Lauro* put in to Alexandria, Egypt. The PLO persuaded the Egyptian authorities to agree to allow the terrorists to leave the ship and to fly to the PLO's stronghold in Tunisia. When the U.S. government inquired as to the

Left: A close up of one of the crew of a Desert Patrol Vehicle (DPV). He is wearing commercially-made goggles to protect his eyes; the crash helmet is very necessary, given the risk of being thrown about as the DPV makes its way over rough terrain. The machine gun is a venerable M2 0.5-in (12.7mm) Browning with a large ring sight mounted.

whereabouts of the terrorists, the Egyptians replied that they had left the country. Signals intelligence revealed that this was not true and an operation to intercept the terrorists was quickly put in place. As the Egyptian airliner carrying the terrorists was over the Mediterranean, it was intercepted by F-14 fighters from the USS *Saratoga* and forced to land at the U.S. naval base at Sigonella in Italy. The airliner was followed onto the runway by a C-141 transport carrying elements of Team Six. The SEALs left the aircraft and surrounded the airliner, but before they could remove the terrorists, Italian forces appeared and surrounded the SEALs. The Italians, who had not been told of the operation, were considerably irritated by this and determined that they would take responsibility for the capture of the hijackers, not least since they had taken over an Italian ship. While the Italian

DEVGRU

Although SEAL Team Six may not have conducted a great number of operations officially admitted, there was no doubt that it was one of the leading counter-terrorist teams in the world by the 1990s. Despite this, the U.S. Navy decided that the bad publicity that the Team had accrued as a result of the Marcinko affair was enough to merit a change in direction. Team Six disappeared from the SEALs' order of battle and a shadowy organization known as the Naval Special Warfare Development Group (or DEVGRU) appeared. The U.S. Navy has been able to maintain greater operational security about the work of DEVGRU than its predecessor, although there is little doubt that it is in fact a continuation of Team Six with a similar anti-terrorist brief.

and U.S. governments negotiated, a tense standoff between two groups of heavily-armed NATO allies ensued. One of the SEAL officers was reported to have been overheard at one point debating whether or not he should order his men to open fire on the Italians. The question was almost certainly not serious, but demonstrated the farcical situation that had arisen. Eventually, after the U.S. administration had secured a promise from the Italian government that it would take strong action against the hijackers, the SEALs were called off. The Italians fulfilled their side of the agreement by prosecuting the hijackers, but inexplicably failed to realize that the man who planned the hijack was also aboard the plane. By the time that the Italians had established his identity, he had been allowed to leave the country and had disappeared.

9/11

Below: Two SEALs take up firing positions on a beach during at night exercise. The man on the left is one of the fire team's machine gunners: there may be another M60 and one or two M249s rounding out the weaponry in use.

The attacks by Al-Qa'eda on September 11, 2001 led to a new development in counter-terrorism, since the response by the United States saw the deployment of ground forces against both the terrorists and the forces of the government that chose to host them. Rather than use conventional troops, the United States turned to its special forces. Although Afghanistan is not a maritime environment, the SEALs were sent alongside their U.S. Army counterparts. The nature of the conflict in Afghanistan was also rather different to previous anti-terrorist campaigns in that the soldiers on the ground were able to call on a range of military capabilities not normally seen in anti-terrorist operations, most notably air power and artillery. The United States has placed considerable reliance on air power in recent years, but the difficulties presented by the Afghan terrain demanded that ground forces be used. While air support proved to be immensely useful, the Taliban and Al-Qa'eda forces made use

of the rocky and cavernous landscape to make targeting difficult and to escape the effect of some of the bombs used. In addition, the network of caves known to be employed by Al-Qa'eda could not be inspected from the air. The solution came in the form of ground troops.

The task in Afghanistan was potentially difficult. It has to be understood that although special forces played a key role in the fighting, the small size of elite units means that they cannot do everything. This demanded the use of larger units, drawn from specialist raiding

Rather than use conventional troops, the United States turned to its special forces. Although Afghanistan is not a maritime environment, the SEALs were sent alongside their U.S. Army counterparts.

Left: A SEAL stops for a break while on a training exercise. The photograph shows the collapsible stock on the M4 Carbine to advantage. The stock is notably firmer that sliding stocks on other weapons, and can be set in more than one position so that it suits the firer's stature. Some of the latest models have up to six positions.

Right: A SEAL with an M4A1 Carbine goes to ground in Afghanistan. The M4A1 is notable for the number of items that can be attached to the gun, such as optical sights and laser pointers. This particular M4A1 has a reflex sight in place of the carrying handle more usually found above the receiver; a foregrip to aid handling and a small but powerful tactical light.

Below: Although Afghanistan is a landlocked country, the SEALs played an active part in the campaign.

forces such as the Rangers and Marines (and later the British Royal Marines). An additional feature of the war against the Taliban was the use of local troops. Since the Soviet invasion in 1979, the Afghan population had been at war—first with the Russians, then with each other. While the Taliban had established itself as the government in Kabul, opposition forces controlled significant areas of the countryside. It was evident that working with these local forces was a very sensible idea, not least since many of the troops detested Al-Qa'eda.

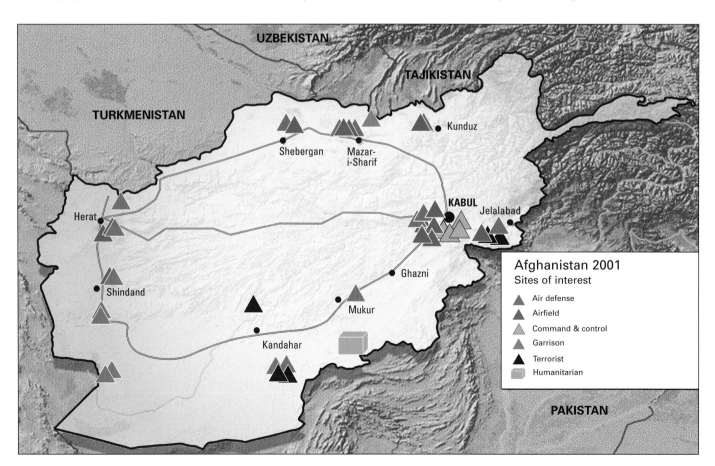

Afghanistan 2001
Sites of interest

▲ Air defense
▲ Airfield
▲ Command & control
▲ Garrison
▲ Terrorist
▬ Humanitarian

As the SEALs had demonstrated in Vietnam, working with indigenous troops is a task to which they are ideally suited and they were put to work advising local Afghan commanders.

Despite the fact that the area of operations was 400 miles (644 kilometers) from the sea, SEALs played a prominent part in running and fighting the war. The special operations effort was divided into two task forces—Task Force Dagger in the North and Task Force K-Bar (TF K-Bar) in the South. Both entities came under the overall command of Rear Admiral Albert Calland III, while Captain Robert S. Haward led Task Force K-Bar. Haward's command was multinational. As well as SEALs, he had special forces from Australia, Denmark, Germany, New Zealand, Norway, and Turkey under his control.

The SEALs were put to work immediately, reconnoitering landing areas for the Marines and providing security for the operation that seized the ground on which Camp Rhino at Khandahar was to be built. While these operations did not demand contact with the enemy, others did. On one occasion SEALs were seen on horseback leading local forces into battle, causing raised eyebrows around the world. The SEALs saw nothing unusual in this. As one of them later remarked, "It's our job to be unconventional." The SEALs also operated without the accompaniment of local forces, making use of Desert Patrol Vehicles (DPVs) in the process. In fact, the use of DPVs by the SEALs perhaps above all else demonstrated that the skills of the SEALs extend beyond strictly maritime missions. It has been shown that special operations forces can be inherently versatile because of the skills and flexibility of their personnel. The caves were raided by the SEALs and TF K-Bar. Several of these raids turned into large-scale firefights, with the SEALs inflicting casualties on the Taliban and Al-Qa'eda forces. By the end of December 2001, operations to deal with the enemy forces in Tora Bora Mountains were drawing to an end and attention turned to a suspected network of caves in the Zawar Killi area. A SEAL platoon was sent to locate the caves and was briefed for a 12-hour mission. The platoon arrived and discovered a complex that was awe-inspiring in its size and complexity. The SEALs found 70 caves and

Left: Two SEALs look out over the inhospitable terrain of Afghanistan, while on a reconnaissance mission. The campaign against Al-Qa'eda and the Taliban was conducted in poor terrain, difficult climatic conditions and against a fanatical enemy: an environment in which the SEALs excelled.

By the end of February 2002, the SEALs and their fellow TF K-Bar members had killed at least 115 enemy fighters and had taken 107 prisoners.

approximately 60 buildings as the search progressed. The mission lasted for nine days, rather than the anticipated matter of hours, as the SEALs came across huge weapons caches and piles of documents that were sent off for intelligence assessment. The SEALs also discovered an abandoned dog tied up in one of the terrorist's houses. They freed him, expecting him to run off, but after the mongrel persisted in following them around, they adopted him as the seventeenth member of the platoon. The team then called in air strikes to demolish various structures and blew up a number of the caves themselves.

Other operations included a raid on Hazar Gadam, which followed some unsuccessful efforts at inserting reconnaissance teams in the area. This meant that the raid went in with virtually no information on enemy dispositions and it ran into a large number of enemy fighters. The SEALs dealt with this problem in their traditional style, killing 16 men and taking another 27 captive. It transpired that the area contained three separate enemy compounds, which were searched and rendered unusable as the mission progressed.

By the end of February 2002, the SEALs and their fellow TF K-Bar members had killed at least 115 enemy fighters and had taken 107 prisoners. They achieved this for the loss of one of their number, a member of the Australian SAS, killed when his patrol vehicle had struck a mine. The SEALs were not to escape unscathed, however. In March 2002, the war in Afghanistan shifted from a largely unconventional conflict to one on more conventional lines. The reason for this was the launch of a major operation against the Taliban and Al-Qa'eda forces located in the Shar-i-Khot region to the south of the Afghan city of Gardez.

Operation Anaconda

Operation Anaconda was designed to seal the escape routes available to the Taliban and Al-Qa'eda from the Shah-i-Khot valley. The exact number of enemy fighters in the area was not known, but it was certain that there were at least several hundred of them. The

Right: A SEAL looks on as an arms cache is destroyed in the mountains of Afghanistan in February 2002. He carries another variation on the theme of the M4 Carbine: a variety of interesting fixtures appear to be attached to the Rail Attachment System (RAS), including a tactical light.

Left: The enemy—a poster praising Osama Bin Laden, discovered in a former Al-Qa'eda position in Afghanistan. The actions of the international coalition against Al-Qa'eda drove Bin Laden into hiding: at time of writing, there is still speculation as to whether or not he was killed during operations in the Tora Bora mountains.

operation was to involve over 2000 men drawn from the U.S. Army, special forces of several nations, and local fighters. Anaconda began on March 1, 2002, but almost immediately ran into problems. Afghan forces commanded by Zia Lodin were meant to capture a three-mile (5-kilometer) long ridgeline that was later christened "the Whale" because of its appearance from the air. As the first forces moved in, they came under fire from enemy mortars. Several men were killed, including a Special Forces advisor, Chief Warrant Officer Stanley L. Harriman. Zia Lodin's men were forced to withdraw. At the northern end of the valley, bad weather prevented the men of the U.S. Army's 101st Airborne Division from arriving to seal the valley. The combination of these two factors meant that escape routes were left open for the enemy, although the fighting that followed suggested that many of them did not take them. Heavy fighting ensued, with perhaps the most intense combat coming on March 4.

AFGHAN SUCCESS

Perhaps the most-reported SEAL operation in Afghanistan was the capture of Mullah Khairullah Kahijhawa. "Mullah K," as the members of TF K-Bar seem to have preferred to call him, was a high-ranking member of Al-Qa'eda and managed to elude capture for several weeks after the outbreak of war. Finally, an unmanned U.S. Predator reconnaissance drone located him. Captain Haward and his planning team secured the services of a number of Army AH-64 attack helicopters and briefed an assorted group of SEALs and TF K-Bar commandos. The teams were lifted into the area by helicopter and seized Mullah Khairullah and the supposedly safe house in which he was staying. The Mullah was removed from the area and began his journey to the prisoner compound established at Guantanamo Bay, Cuba, courtesy of the SEALs.

Right: A SEAL stretches
his arms to provide scale
to the cave network that
his patrol is investigating.
This particular cave was
discovered in the Zhawar
Kili area of Eastern
Afghanistan on 14
January 2002.

Right: A SEAL stretches his arms to provide scale to the cave network that his patrol is investigating. This particular cave was discovered in the Zhawar Kili area of Eastern Afghanistan on 14 January 2002.

During the fighting, SEALs were heavily involved, as efforts to take The Whale and to secure the Ginger Valley continued in the face of well dug-in opposition. On March 4, a special operations MH-47 Chinook helicopter carrying SEALs was attempting to land when it came under fire. Three rocket-propelled grenades hit the helicopter, but none of them detonated. One entered the passenger compartment and cut a hydraulic line, spraying fluid throughout the fuselage. At this point, one of the aircrew in the back of the helicopter lost his footing and fell out. While frightening, the aircrew are equipped for such an eventuality, being provided with long straps attached to the helicopter that enable them to walk around in the rear of the airframe with the loading ramp open. If they fall out, the strap leaves them dangling in midair, but they can be pulled back in by other crewmen. After the man fell out, one of the SEALs, Petty Officer 1st Class Neil Roberts, removed his harness and ran to assist. He pulled the man back in, but slipped on the hydraulic fluid and fell out himself. Roberts fell some ten feet (3 meters), but as he landed, the helicopter took off again, the pilots unaware of the fact that they had left a man on the ground as they struggled to regain control of their aircraft. They somehow managed to fly the helicopter for about half a mile (one kilometer), and crash-landed.

Neil Roberts, now alone on the ground and armed only with a pistol and some grenades, crawled some 200 feet (61 meters) to hide in a crevice. He turned on his rescue beacon and waited. Shortly, a second helicopter appeared, but the Taliban forces had not left the area. As it came in to land, the Taliban opened fire with a machine-gun. Despite the fact that he was lightly armed, carrying only a pistol, Roberts opened fire. He killed the machine-gun crew and began engaging the other enemy troops firing and maneuvering as he did so. The odds, however, were too great. Roberts was hit several times and mortally wounded. The Taliban dragged his body away, but before they had gone very far, the forces from the next helicopter had surrounded them. The details as to what happened next are sketchy, but it appears that the Taliban forces were very severely mauled during the course of the fight, losing their cohesion and running as their casualties increased.

The fighting on March 4 was the most intense of Operation Anaconda. Over the course of the next five days, the allied forces gained control of the Ginger Valley and secured positions overlooking The Whale. This enabled air controllers and special forces (including SEALs) to call in heavy air strikes that further undermined the Taliban's grasp on the area. Finally, on March 12, The Whale fell to Zia's forces. Follow-up operations revealed yet more complexes in the caves, which contained weapons and documentation. The lack of intelligence available prior to the operation meant that it was impossible to tell how many Al-Qa'eda and Taliban forces had been in the area. This made it was difficult to gauge how many casualties had been caused to the enemy, although American commanders suggested that they probably ran into the "several hundreds."

The fighting in Afghanistan concluded with the collapse of the Taliban regime and was followed by the difficult task of creating a representative government and building stability in a nation that has known little other than inter-factional fighting and instability for much of its existence. At the time of writing, the country appears to be progressing well, but it is perhaps too early to say how matters will conclude. What is clear is that the efforts and sacrifices made by the allied troops during the intervention in Afghanistan removed the Taliban and inflicted serious damage on Al-Qa'eda's operations. That said, the terrorists remain a threat, since it was clear that Osama Bin Laden and his subordinates recognized that they were losing their operating base at an early point in the fighting and made efforts to relocate their operations elsewhere. Subsequent attacks by groups affiliated to Al-Qa'eda have not been as spectacular as those against New York, but demonstrate that the fight is far from over. It is difficult to speculate as to how the war on terrorism will develop, but it is equally clear that the SEALs will be at the forefront of the fight.

It is difficult to speculate as to how the war on terrorism will develop, but it is equally clear that the SEALs will be at the forefront of the fight.

THE SECOND GULF WAR

On Thursday March 20, 2003 the second Gulf War began with the Coalition forces aiming to rid Iraq of Saddam Hussein's regime and ensure the decommissioning of any weapons of mass destruction. The SEALs were tasked with the role of seizing Iraq's two oil terminals in the Persian Gulf, Mina al Bakr and Khawr al Amaya. Four fast boats, each carrying a SEAL platoon, took part, two boats to each platform. The Iraqi guards were caught by surprise and offered no resistance to the SEALS. For security, four Mark 5 patrol boats were stationed around the terminals during the operation, while helicopters circling overhead carried snipers with night vision equipment. More than 40 Iraqi prisoners were taken without casualties to either side.

It will be some time before the full details of SEALs operations in Iraq become known. It is clear that the SEALs were also involved with the amphibious landing on the Al-Faw peninsula at Iraq's southern tip, probably checking the proposed landing beach for obstacles and guiding in the Coalition forces.

However one SEALs operation grabbed the headlines worldwide—the rescue of Private Jessica Lynch. The 19-year-old Lynch had been captured near Nasiriyah when her convoy from the 507th Ordnance Maintenance Company was ambushed by Iraqi forces on March 23. Badly injured, she was kept in hospital, where a sympathetic Iraqi spotted her and told the U.S. forces outside the city. A rescue operation was quickly mounted, with the U.S. Marines used to provide a diverting attack elsewhere in the city to draw away any Iraqi forces.

On entering the hospital, the rescue team were also told of the location of some bodies which might be American. The rescuers called out, "Jessica Lynch, we're United States soldiers and we're here to protect you and take you home." Lynch and the bodies were safely evacuated back to Ramstein AFB in Germany.

CHAPTER SEVEN

SELECTION, TRAINING, AND EQUIPMENT

Joining the U.S. Navy SEALs is no easy task—but if you make it through the tough selection process, you will serve in an elite force that has the best possible equipment to do the job.

Left: Two would-be SEALs struggle across a rope on an assault course—a small fraction of the physical effort required to be a SEAL.

Right: A BUD/S trainee takes a brief rest (the instructors will guarantee the brevity), covered in mud and thoroughly fatigued. Mud played a major part in SEAL training until a number of BUD/S candidates fell victim to a debilitating virus caused by bacteria that lived in the mud. Health and safety concerns dictated less mud. The instructors, adaptable as ever, simply ensured their charges became covered in wet sand instead.

So You Want to Be a SEAL?

It should be apparent from preceding chapters that SEALs are a particularly determined and efficient group. But what does it take to become a member of this elite organization? The high level of regard in which the SEALs are held means that they are unlikely to be short of recruits. So the SEALs are in a position to implement an extremely tough selection process, which goes under the apparently benign acronym of BUD/S. BUD/S, or the Basic Underwater Demolition/SEAL course is legendary for its rigor, pushing candidates to their limits. The selection process is so strenuous that the majority of volunteers do not pass the course and on one occasion, an entire class failed to make it to the end of the process. The course demands tremendous physical conditioning, but volunteers do not need to have the physique of Arnold Schwarzenegger to succeed. It is far more important that they have considerable mental toughness—this is what will carry them through the trials and tribulations of training.

BUD/S begins with a strict physical examination and an expectation that the candidate will pass the basic fitness test with a very high score. Once through this obstacle, the volunteer will head for the base at Coronado. Although Coronado is attractive to tourists, the prospective SEALs will almost certainly come to detest the place. The first phase of the course at Coronado consists of the basic conditioning program of ten weeks' duration. Despite the label "basic," the program is not for the faint-hearted. Students find themselves running along the beach or swimming in the surf. When they are not doing this, they are rolling around in the mud, getting coated in sand, running around in teams carrying logs and other assorted heavy, awkward objects, and attempting to control rubber boats. Although running on the beach may sound like a pleasant activity, anyone attempting a long run on soft, shifting sand or hard, wet sand will beg to differ, particularly when wearing boots. Likewise, the swims are hardly pleasurable activities and candidates have been seen to leave the water shivering with cold—and then carry on shivering with cold for some time afterward. In addition to the physical pressures, the instructors constantly harry their charges, demanding ever-greater effort and never failing to point out the candidates' inadequacies. As the course progresses, men are removed or voluntarily depart. Until 1990, anyone wishing to quit could march smartly over to a large brass bell that stood in the courtyard at Coronado and ring it three times to signify that he had endured enough. This bell, however, was removed after growing concerns about the effect that it had on trainees. Ringing the bell took place in the full view of everyone else and there were fears that some

Below: Although swimming and water work plays a major part in training and selection, traditional tests such as the obstacle course are still important in maintain the physical condition of the trainees.

Above: SEAL recruits collapse exhausted into the mud after performing yet another arduous physical exercise routine during "Hell Week." In this time the individual trainees will discover exactly how much physical punishment their bodies can bear.

candidates, regarding the process as a humiliation, would go on with the course and risk severe injury attempting to achieve a task that he was not capable of. Now, anyone wishing to drop out goes through a more formal process where they are counseled by the instructing staff. Some former SEALs have decried this as a drop in standards. But this argument is countered with the reasoning that some men who would otherwise have left have been persuaded to stay with the course and have turned into outstanding SEALs once through the pain of the selection process.

Despite the sheer vileness of Hell Week, the instructors have balanced these tough tests of endurance with concerns for their charges. Rolling around in the mud of the Tijuana River ended when it became clear that many of the students were contracting deeply unpleasant diseases as a result. On occasion, the illnesses proved so severe that students were permanently disabled by them. Swimming in the freezing seas has also been monitored more closely after the death of a student during a five-mile (8-kilometer) swim.

The survivors of Hell Week are given a few days respite before commencing the last three weeks of phase one, in which they begin to learn the basic skills of a combat diver. The next phase of selection and training then introduces the candidate to a variety of skills, including demolitions, reconnaissance, patrolling, and weapons handling. Although the handling of weapons is important, the instructors take care to stress that small parties, no matter how well armed, should avoid shooting and giving away their location if they hear enemy fire. Before returning fire, the SEALs are taught to work out where the enemy fire is coming from before simply shooting back and revealing their presence. Instructors also take pains to point out that teams on reconnaissance missions should try to avoid exchanging fire with the enemy unless it is absolutely essential. These missions are designed to garner intelligence rather than inflict damage or casualties on the opposition. Revealing your presence tells the enemy that somebody was looking for (or at) something and may prompt them to change their dispositions, rendering any information that has been gathered useless. Once the would-be SEALs have begun to master the weapons and tactics that they will need, they move onto the final phase, which concentrates on underwater work. The trainees spend much of their time in a 50-foot (15-meter) tall diving tower, working with breathing gear and making free ascents to the surface. This sounds easy, but it is not. The students have to master the necessary breathing techniques, become aware of the risks of oxygen poisoning, and learn the techniques required in leaving a submerged submarine. The tank is equipped with a lock-out chamber similar to those found on fleet submarines. Trainees soon discover whether they have any latent claustrophobia as they undertake this part of the course. Once they complete tank training, the students are then

HELL WEEK

Although the first weeks of BUD/S are tough, the candidates discover that they are nothing compared to the famed "Hell Week." This name is not inappropriate. The week begins on the morning of Sunday of sixth week. Being precise in their terminology, the instructors normally consider sixth week to begin shortly after midnight on Sunday. They rouse their tired students with the gentle sound of machine-gun fire (blank rounds), artillery simulators, or something equally pleasant. The instructors appear next to the beds of the candidates, bombarding the students with shouted encouragement to get out of their beds. Hell Week is deliberately designed to deprive the students of sleep—many get just over half an hour a night if they are lucky. The theory is that this will push the students to their limits and beyond. Within two days, all the students are desperate for sleep, but they are not given the chance to drift off. Many of them report that they begin to hallucinate as they go through a seemingly endless round of drills, runs, swims, log races, and boat races. These pleasures are interspersed with rolling around in the sand—becoming coated with the stuff in the process—or gamboling through thick, glutinous mud, all at the whim of the instructors.

Even after a year of selection and training, it is possible for SEALs to be filtered out during their probationary period. It is rare, but can still happen.

taken to the ocean to perfect their swimming and navigation skills. Some of the training involves swimming into harbors and simulating attacks on shipping with limpet mines.

After six months at Coronado, the trainees may seem close to their goal of becoming SEALs, but are still some way away. Having completed BUD/S, they then move to the Army's Airborne School at Fort Benning, Georgia, where they learn to parachute. This course lasts three weeks and begins relatively effortlessly for the SEALs. The first week involves physical conditioning and the SEAL trainees tend to find this easy, generally being much fitter than their Army counterparts as a result of the six months of BUD/S that they have just endured. By the third week, the trainees are ready to jump from an airplane for real, conducting a total of five jumps. At the end of week three, with all the jumps completed, the trainees are awarded their parachutist's wings. This is still not the end of selection for the SEALs, though. Despite having passed through the demands of BUD/S and having won their parachute qualification, the students are still not fully qualified SEALs. They have ceased to be trainees at this point, but are still probationary SEALs. They spend six months with a SEAL Team or a SDV team, aware of the fact that their performance is being closely monitored. Even after a year of selection and training, it is possible for SEALs to be filtered out during their probationary period. It is rare, but can still happen. Finally, at the end of these six months, the SEALs are presented with the large gold badge that signifies membership of the naval special warfare community.

SEAL TRAINING AND SELECTION

The training and selection process for the SEALs is as rigorous as any to be found for any special forces unit in the world and some argue that it is the toughest. It takes a year to become a fully-fledged member of the SEALs' community. A candidate will have endured aching muscles, injury (ranging from the minor to the severe), the risk of hypothermia, sleep deprivation, the risk of injury from gunfire and explosives, and the delights of survival, escape, and resistance-to-capture training (an unpleasant process indeed). They are fully exposed to any fears and phobias they may have and the risk of death (wryly described by a former member of Britain's SAS as "nature's way of telling you you've failed selection"). This may sound daunting enough on paper, but encountering it for real is another matter entirely. SEAL

Teams have special requirements and need a particularly determined individual to meet them. The BUD/S regime ensures that the SEALs obtain exactly the sort of person that they require for their tasks, resulting in a formidable fighting force.

Weapons and Equipment

Once graduated, SEALs are likely to use a range of equipment as their career develops. Most of this is not quite as exotic as moviemakers would have us believe and much of a SEAL's personal equipment is standard government issue. However, in common with other special forces, the SEALs will use nonstandard equipment if it is particularly reliable and will enable them to perform their task efficiently. What follows is far from exhaustive, but is intended to give some insight into what the SEALs have used (and still use) to carry out their work.

Pistols

The SEALs have made use of a variety of handguns since their inception. The famed Colt M1911 0.45-inch pistol and derivatives have been employed, not least since the gun was (and is) reliable and hard-hitting. It was the standard U.S. service handgun for more than seventy years. The current Beretta M9 is also used as a result of its employment as the standard pistol of the American forces, even though some consider it sacrilege to move from the 0.45 round to the smaller and less hard-hitting 9mm (0.35-inch) caliber. The SEALs do not seem to have been too concerned with this debate, since they have made use of a number of 9mm handguns. In Vietnam, the Smith and Wesson Model 39 was used, although it proved susceptible to the mud and dirt found in the Mekong Delta and had to

Above: BUD/S candidates run along the beach carrying inflatable boats above their head. They will perform this exercise numerous times, harried all the way by the instructors as they seek the maximum effort from their trainees.

Left: Two SEALs lie in front of their boat, practicing fire support drills on landing. The man on the right is carrying an M4 Carbine, while his colleague shows off the M60E3. The foregrip is slightly obscured by the bipod. The bipod was originally positioned on the barrel, making it impossible to change barrels without a struggle. While the lighter M60E3 is not perfect for the sustained fire role, it is ideal for the SEALs, who value its ability to lay down heavy fire. SEAL squads tend to have two M60s apiece.

In Vietnam, the Smith and Wesson Model 39 was used, although it proved susceptible to the mud and dirt found in the Mekong Delta and had to be treated carefully.

be treated carefully. The gun was perhaps most important for being the basis of the famed Model 22 Mk 0 "Hush Puppy," a silenced weapon that was only used by the SEALs. Some 9mm Browning HP35s were also procured for use in Vietnam and these were highly prized by the SEALs who were able to obtain them. More recently, the sophisticated Heckler und Koch P9S saw use and the SIG-Sauer P220 series of pistols have found favor. The P226, with its large-capacity magazine, seems to be popular with SEALs at the moment. Despite this proliferation of 9mm weapons, the old 0.45-inch cartridge has made a re-appearance, courtesy of the Heckler und Koch Model 23 pistol, also known as the SOCOM pistol. This is a remarkable weapon stemming from a requirement generated by Special Operations Command (SOCOM) that demanded an Offensive Handgun Weapon System rather than just a simple pistol. As well as the pistol itself, the requirement called for the weapon to come with a laser-aiming module (LAM) and a sound-and-flash suppressor. The criteria for the pistol were very demanding and only Colt and Heckler und Koch submitted entries. The design by Heckler und Koch won, entering service from May 1996. The Mk 23 has a large magazine, containing twelve rounds. If there is a disadvantage to the pistol, it is that the gun is quite hefty.

Below: A SEAL emerges from the water with his MP5. The MP5 is probably the finest sub machine gun ever built, and is in widespread use with special forces around the world. The SEALs have used them since the early 1980s.

Left: A cutaway of an MP5. Firing from a closed bolt, the MP5 is extremely accurate in the hands of a skilled operator, making it an ideal weapon for hostage rescue operations.

Submachine Guns

While pistols are useful weapons, they are generally employed as secondary armament. This is because they have a comparatively low rate of fire and are not particularly accurate, even in the hands of a skilled shooter, over any great distance. As an alternative, the submachine gun (SMG) has found favor for close-range work, originating in World War I when the Germans were looking for a weapon that could be used in the confines of the trenches and which had a high rate of fire. The resulting MP18 Bergmann was probably the first submachine gun to be used on a wide scale, although the famed Thompson submachine gun (the Tommy gun) was the first to obtain widespread acclaim. Although the Thompson was superbly made, it was difficult to mass-produce. This led to the introduction of the M3, popularly known as the "Grease Gun" because of its appearance. The M3 was much less popular with the troops, but the SEALs made some use of it even though the design was 20 years old when they were formed. Although crude, the M3 was effective and its low rate of fire (for an SMG) meant that it was possible to achieve good accuracy. Both the Thompson and the M3 were 0.45-inch weapons, but this caliber largely fell from fashion after World War II and the 9mm round took over.

The SEALs employed two interesting SMGs in Vietnam—the Swedish M45 "Carl Gustav" and the very similar Smith and Wesson M76. These weapons had quite large magazines (36 or 50 rounds of ammunition) and could be equipped with silencers, making them well suited to covert operations. The Swedes cut off the supply of weapons in protest against the Vietnam War, but Smith and Wesson's M76 filled the gap, not least since it was based on the Swedish design. The guns may not have been sophisticated, but they were robust and effective, remaining available for use until the early 1980s. In addition, the SEALs made use of a small number of Walther MP-L and MP-K SMGs, which differed only in the length of their barrels. These weapons deserved to sell more successfully than they did, since they were well made and accurate. However, they only attracted a small amount of interest, being preferred by special forces. As well as the SEALs, Delta Force used the MP-L and MP-K, but the gun was superseded by the SMG that has become the standard submachine gun for special forces around the world: the Heckler und Koch MP5 series.

The gun was superseded by the SMG that has become the standard submachine gun for special forces around the world: the Heckler und Koch MP5 series.

The SEALs were among the original users of the carbine M16s, notably the XM177 Colt Commando. The gun was popular, but by the 1980s was wearing out.

Right: The XM177 Colt Commando was a Vietnam-era weapon and was notable for the revised hand guard, collapsible butt, and the large flash-hider required as a result of the shortened barrel.

The MP5 is a superbly made and accurate weapon but it requires a good maintenance routine to ensure that its sophisticated mechanism remains functioning. This is of little concern to the SEALs, however. For them, good weapons care is second nature. The MP5 fires from a closed bolt (that is to say that it does not reciprocate every time a round is fired). The subsequent lack of movement in the gun makes it much easier to achieve accuracy. The MP5 first appeared in the later 1960s, but only really found fame when used by the British SAS when they ended the siege at the Iranian embassy in London in May 1980. While this gave the gun a wide audience, it was already popular with special forces. The MP5 comes in a near-bewildering variety of models. As well as the commonly seen sliding-stock model, the MP5 can be fitted with a fixed stock or simply a butt-plate to aid concealment. Some models come with a three-round burst facility in addition to the standard single-shot and fully automatic fire selections, although it seems that some operators consider this an unnecessary addition as a skilled user can control the number of rounds in a burst from the MP5 anyway. The MP5SD series is fitted with a silencer and comes with the usual range of stocks. While the MP5K is still recognizably an MP5, it is much shortened to allow concealed carriage of the weapon. The MP5K does not normally have a butt-stock but it is provided with a vertical handgrip to give the user more control. All of these weapons have been used by the SEALs, notably in Grenada, Panama, and the Gulf, in addition to their employment as the standard weapon of counter-terrorist teams.

Rifles

The SEALs have predominantly used the M16 series of rifles as their main battle weapon. Although the gun had serious difficulties at the start of its service, it has matured considerably and is one of the best rifles available. The SEALs have used the original M16 and the improved M16A1 and M16A2 versions, although they now make great use of the M4 carbine version of the gun. The SEALs were among the original users of the carbine M16s, notably the XM177 Colt Commando. The XM177 was a Vietnam-era weapon and was notable for the revised hand guard, collapsible butt, and the large flash-hider required as a result of the shortened barrel. The gun was popular, but by the 1980s was wearing out. This led to the development of the M4, which can be considered a carbine version of the M16A2. The M4 has a longer barrel than the XM177 and does not require the large flash-hider, but it retains the collapsible stock. In addition, the barrel is specially configured to allow the M203 grenade launcher to be added to the gun. The latest versions of the M4 come with a rail interface system. This means that the carrying handle

Below: The 7.62mm (0.3-inch) cartridge remains standard in sniping rifles and the SEALs use the M21 version of the M14 rifle. However the M21 fires semi-automatically, which purists regard as being less than perfect for a sniper's weapon.

Many SEALs appreciate the fact that the 7.62mm (0.3-inch) round is famed for its ability to drop an opponent with the first shot, while 5.56mm (0.22-inch) rounds have proved to have less stopping power.

can be removed and replaced with an optical sight, while other rail attachments around the barrel permit the carriage of tactical lights, laser aiming, projectors, and a vertical hand guard. Yet even with all these features the M203 remains a portable weapon. The M4 is now the standard special-forces rifle and was issued en masse in Afghanistan, although there were complaints that the slightly shorter range of the M4 in comparison to the M16A2 was a disadvantage for regular troops trying to engage the enemy over a longer range. The M16 series will remain the standard equipment of the SEALs for some time to come.

This does not mean that other rifles have not been used. The standard service rifle before the M16, the M14 has also seen use. The M14 suffers in comparison with the M16 from being heavier and more difficult to control on automatic fire, since the gun uses the much more powerful 7.62mm (.308 inch) round rather than the M16's standard 5.56mm cartridge. In fact, most M14's had the fire selector locked to prevent selection of automatic fire. However, many SEALs appreciate the fact that the 7.62mm (0.3-inch) round is famed for its ability to drop an opponent with the first shot, while 5.56mm (0.22-inch) rounds have proved to have less stopping power. The benefits of the additional firepower of the 7.62mm weapon mean that the SEALs still make much use of the M14. During the Vietnam War, they also employed the Heckler und Koch G3 in the same caliber and there have been rumors that examples of the De Soto Arms version of the FN FAL rifle have found their way into the SEALs' inventory.

The 7.62mm cartridge remains standard in sniping rifles and the SEALs use the M21 version of the M14, along with the G3/SG1 model of the Heckler und Koch G3. Both

Right: A SEAL nearly smiles for the camera while carrying an M14. This particular M14 is one of the light machine gun models (although it has probably been modified for semi-auto fire only) since it clearly has a pistol grip, unlike the standard M14 rifle version.

Left: Hidden in the long grass, a sniper takes aim with the massive Barrett 0.5-inch (12.7mm) sniping rifle. This weapon is used in the anti-materiel role, providing special forces with a precise means of dealing with items such as radar dishes and vehicles without the need to get too close to the target.

these weapons fire semi-automatically, which purists regard as being a less than perfect solution for a sniping weapon. The G3/SG1 model, indeed, can fire fully automatically, but it is most unlikely that this function is ever used, since firing a 7.62mm rifle on full automatic means that it is almost impossible to control. The SEALs also employ bolt-action 7.62mm weapons for sniping, notably the M40 rifle. They have also indulged in "big caliber sniping" using 0.5-inch (12.7mm) rifles such as the Barrett M82 and the MacMillan in the same caliber. These weapons are not just intended for use against individual personnel, but against targets such as radar dishes and aircraft, where a well-placed 0.5-inch round will disable the target.

AK47

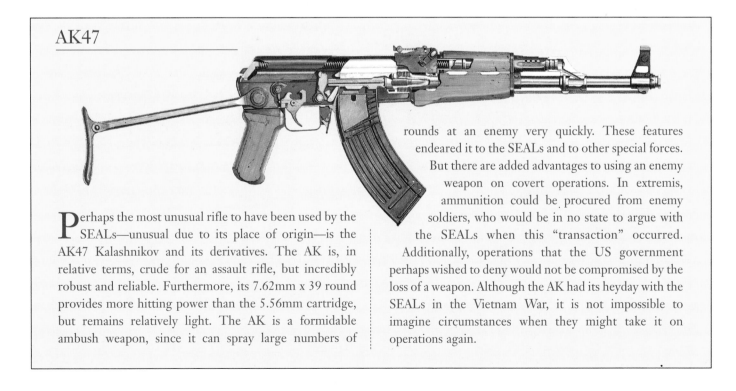

Perhaps the most unusual rifle to have been used by the SEALs—unusual due to its place of origin—is the AK47 Kalashnikov and its derivatives. The AK is, in relative terms, crude for an assault rifle, but incredibly robust and reliable. Furthermore, its 7.62mm x 39 round provides more hitting power than the 5.56mm cartridge, but remains relatively light. The AK is a formidable ambush weapon, since it can spray large numbers of rounds at an enemy very quickly. These features endeared it to the SEALs and to other special forces. But there are added advantages to using an enemy weapon on covert operations. In extremis, ammunition could be procured from enemy soldiers, who would be in no state to argue with the SEALs when this "transaction" occurred. Additionally, operations that the US government perhaps wished to deny would not be compromised by the loss of a weapon. Although the AK had its heyday with the SEALs in the Vietnam War, it is not impossible to imagine circumstances when they might take it on operations again.

Right: Knee deep in water, a SEAL aims his M60. Having two of these weapons in an eight-man squad gives the SEALs prodigious firepower, and provides a useful means of keeping the enemy at bay when conducting a fighting withdrawal.

Machine-guns

At first glance, a list of the SEAL's chosen machine-guns would not suggest that they have deviated from the standard-issue weapons. They have used the M60 and the more recent M249 Squad Automatic Weapon (SAW), in 7.62mm and 5.56mm respectively. However, the M60 did not have a particularly stellar opening to its service career. It was dogged by the fact that it was perhaps a little too heavy, earning it the nickname of "The Pig." It also

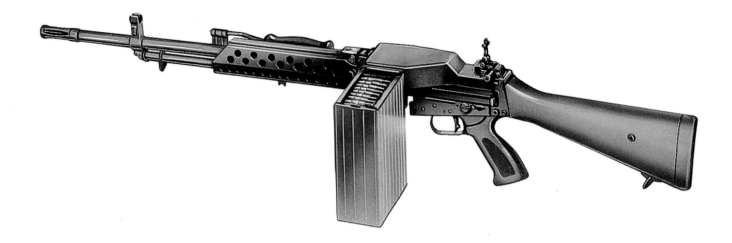

had some design faults, not the least of which was the way that the bipod was attached to the barrel. This did not present a problem until it came to changing the barrel (necessary on a machine-gun undertaking heavy volumes of fire), which left the gun without any means of holding it up. This meant that the gunner had to clasp the weapon between his knees while his number two changed the barrel over. The SEALs chose to use the M60 in a different way, with one man carrying it. To lighten it, they were partial to sawing lengths off the barrel and this does not seem to have had any adverse effects on the SEALs using the gun. The M60 provided massive amounts of firepower, however. Later versions, particularly the M60E2 with the bipod relocated to the receiver (so that barrel changing is much easier) and a forward handgrip are highly valued for their ability to lay down massive volumes of fire, either in an ambush situation or a withdrawal.

The SEALs also made use of the one weapon that can truly be said to be the classic choice for a SEAL, namely the Stoner 63. It is difficult to know how to categorize the Stoner, since it was a weapons system rather than just a simple gun. Designer Eugene Stoner (responsible for the M16) created a modular gun, which, by using a variety of different barrels and receiver parts could be configured as an assault rifle, a folding-stock carbine, or a light machine-gun. The light machine-gun could have a box magazine feeding from the top of the weapon (like the British World War II Bren gun) or from a belt. The belt could be accommodated in a drum magazine or a box. The Stoner was not a universally popular weapon, since it required a great deal of cleaning and had an unfortunate tendency to fire fully automatic unbidden. However, the relative lightness of weight of the Stoner in the machine-gun role meant that the SEALs made great use of it. The SEALs were finally forced to stop using the Stoner when the guns started to wear out and there were no more spare parts for them as production of the weapon had ceased many years previously.

Shotguns

The SEALs have also been proponents of the combat shotgun, since this provides the user with massive short-range firepower. A variety of guns have been used, most notably the Ithaca Model 37, the Remington 870, and the Mossberg 500. The shotgun would not be employed on missions where engagement with the enemy over any distance would be anticipated. However, for jungle fighting or the defense of a covert observation post, the

Above: The Stoner M63 was a popular weapon of the SEALs, but found little favor elsewhere. It was too sensitive for general issue, but the light weight of the gun in the machine gun role meant that the SEALs were partial to taking it along on operations. The model shown here has the side-mounted belt-box, as opposed to the 150-round drum magazine alternative.

Right: A SEAL takes aim with his pump-action shotgun. For close quarters fighting, the shotgun is hard to beat as a weapon. It proved its worth in the Vietnam, and remains a useful tool, despite its relatively low ammunition capacity and short range. People rarely argue with a levelled shotgun, and this makes it a useful means of persuasion when it is employed on missions such as ship boarding.

shotgun is an ideal choice. The U.S. forces have recently procured a version of the Benelli M4 shotgun, the M1014, and the SEALs are likely to make use of this if the need arises. It should also be recalled that the shotgun is useful in hostage-rescue scenarios, since it can fire a variety of loads, including those to take doors off their hinges, or even CS gas pellets to disable opponents.

The SEALs are able to choose from a wide range of weapons. However, it is the skill of the men who employ them rather than the items of equipment themselves that earn the SEALs their fearsome reputation. They are dedicated professionals capable of incredible feats of endurance and military skill. Throughout their existence, these qualities have been accompanied by enormous amounts of courage. The value of the SEALs to the United States is shown in the fact that they are in increasing demand. The SEAL community was expanded at the end of 2002, with the creation of two more teams, Team Seven and Team Ten. These teams did not mean that the number of SEALs increased, since the new teams were made up by reorganizing the structure of the existing units to ensure that enough SEALs are available for deployment. At the start of the SEALs' life, senior officers and officials were not certain what they could use such special forces for. Forty years on, they have little doubt. The SEALs, as part of America's elite forces, are firmly at "the tip of the spear." In conventional warfare and unconventional conflicts, they have proved their inestimable value time and again. They are a vital component in the defense of the United States and will undoubtedly remain so.

The SEALs, as part of America's elite forces, are firmly at "the tip of the spear." In conventional warfare and unconventional conflicts, they have proved their inestimable value time and again. They are a vital component in the defense of the United States and will undoubtedly remain so.

Left: Silhouetted in the setting sun, a SEAL displays his M4/M203 combination. When it is recalled that an eight-man SEAL squad goes out equipped with two M60s, at least one M249 and several M4/M203s in its arsenal, it is hardly surprising that enemy reports of encounters with SEALs talk of the heavy weight of fire brought against them.

CHRONOLOGY

1941

7 December – Japanese attack on Pearl Harbor. Navy diving specialists participate in rescue and salvage operations.

1942

Mid-year – first party of Scouts and Raiders established.

8 November – first Scouts and Raiders mission as part of Operation Torch. Scouts sent to cut cable blocking Wadi Sebou. Mission compromised and aborted.

10 November – Scouts and Raiders repeat mission to cut cable in Wadi Sebou. Succeed despite appalling conditions and heavy enemy fire.

1943

6 May – Admiral Ernest J. King, Chief of Naval Operations, orders formation of units trained in clearance of beach obstacles. First postings of men for Naval Combat Demolition Unit follow.

10 July – Invasion of Sicily. Scouts and Raiders guide landing craft to shore. CDU present not required to support invasion, but employed on obstacle clearance tasks subsequent to disembarkation.

November – Scouts and Raiders teams start arriving in United Kingdom to prepare for invasion of France.

20 November – Invasion of Tarawa. Problems encountered during assault lead to reconsideration of role and size of NCDUs. Decision that NCDUs need to be larger and have capability to carry out beach reconnaissance duties leads to

formation of Underwater Demolition Teams (NCDU training school remains extant).

1944

31 January – UDTs see first action at Kwajalein Island. Ensign Lewis F. Luehrs and Chief Bill Acheson carry out first combat swimming operation by UDT, swimming in for close reconnaissance of target beach.

May onwards– UDTs carry out beach reconnaissance and demolition duties as U.S. forces capture islands en route to Japan.

30 May - UDTs 5, 6 and 7 leave Hawaii to join force for invasion of Saipan.

6 June – D-Day. Scouts and Raiders assist in leading invasion fleet into the American beaches (Omaha and Utah). NCDU teams carry out combat demolition of beach obstacles. 52 per cent of NCDU team-members killed or wounded on first day.

1945

UDTs continue to support amphibious landings as US forces close in on Japan.

14 August – Japan surrenders after atomic bomb attacks on Hiroshima and Nagasaki.

1947

UDT 1 experiments with dry suits when working in arctic waters while exercising with submarine USS *Perch*.

1950

28 June – North Korean forces invade South Korea, starting Korean War.

July – UDTs begin to carry out series of raids on transportation targets in North Korean territory, including operations with British Royal Marine Commandos. Raids and reconnaissances continue to end of Korean War.

1953

27 July – Armistice signed with North Korea.

1956

UDT 13 disestablished.

1961

25 May – President Kennedy announces decision to expand United States' special warfare capabilities. U.S. Navy planners meet directive with suggestion for commando unit to complement UDTs: Sea Air Land teams (SEALs).

December – Authorization for SEAL teams granted.

1962

January – SEAL Teams One and Two commissioned. SEAL Team One commanded by Lieutenant David Del Giudice; SEAL Team Two assigned Lieutenant John Callaghan as commanding officer; Lieutenant Roy Boehm assumes temporary command while Lieutenant Callaghan completes duties in current post.

10 March – Members of SEAL Team One arrive in Republic of Vietnam to provide training to South Vietnamese commando units.

27 April– SEALs carry out reconnaissance missions on Cuba to provide information necessary for an invasion of the island to remove Fidel Castro from power. Further reconnaissance mission carried out by team led by Lieutenant William Cannon during autumn as part of American response to crisis caused by revelation that Soviet missiles have been based on the island.

1963

January – UDTs carry out beach reconnaissance missions in South Vietnam.

12 March – UDTs reconnoitring beach at Vinh Chau come under heavy fire. Although no casualties sustained, U.S. Navy decides that risks to UDTs now outweigh benefits of continuing beach surveys as most information required has been obtained.

1964

January – President Johnson authorises "OP-34 Alpha" missions in which SEALs will support South Vietnamese commando raids on the North.

16 February – first OP-34A mission takes place.

1965

8 March – U.S. Marines land at Da Nang, supported by UDTs. UDTs carry out series of survey missions for remainder of year, in support of amphibious raids by Marines against suspected Viet Cong targets.

28 April – First UDT casualty when Commander Robert J. Fay (serving as an advisor to the South Vietnamese) is killed when his jeep is hit by mortar fire.

30 April – SEALs sent to Dominican Republic as part of U.S. and Organization of American States operation to restore stability after a coup and increased violence in the country.

1966

18 February – First SEALs arrive in Vietnam to carry out direct action missions. Operations start almost immediately, predominantly in the form of small unit direct action missions, or with reconnaissance patrols. These continue for the remainder of American involvement in the Vietnam War.

26 March–7 April – SEALs and UDTs operate in conjunction with U.S. Marines during Operation Jackstay.

19 August – Petty Officer Billy W. Machen killed during ambush by Viet Cong, the first SEAL to die as a result of enemy action.

1967

SEALs begin to place more emphasis on ambush operations, increasing the number of such missions in relation to reconnaissance-only patrols.

1968

22 January – SEAL patrols kill regular North Vietnamese soldiers in ambush carried out alongside Australian Special Air Service Regiment. This is amongst the first signs that North Vietnamese troops are in South Vietnam in some numbers for an as-yet unknown reason.

31 January – North Vietnamese and Viet Cong launch Tet Offensive. SEALs heavily engaged in defence of a number of locations.

September – Admiral Elmo R. Zumwalt Jr. launches SEALORDS plan for interdiction of Viet Cong supplies arriving by boat and sampan. SEALs expand intelligence-related operations as part of this plan.

November – Richard M. Nixon elected President of United States.

1969

14 March – SEAL patrol led by Lieutenant (JG) Joseph Kerrey attack VC unit on Ham Tam Island. Kerrey awarded Medal of Honor for his part in the operation, in which he is seriously wounded.

8 June – President Nixon announces that 25,000 US troops are to be withdrawn from South Vietnam as part of "Vietnamization" process.

1970

Easter – First moves to reduce number of SEALs in Vietnam theater begin.

1972

2 April–12 April – EB-66 Destroyer electronic warfare aircraft call-sign "Bat 21" with Lieutenant Colonel Iceal Hambleton among crew is shot down. Prolonged rescue operation concludes with recovery of Hambleton by SEAL Lieutenant Tom Norris and South Vietnamese LDNN Nguyen Van Kiet. Norris is awarded Medal of Honor for his efforts; Nguyen becomes only Vietnamese serviceman to be awarded US Navy Cross.

31 October – SEAL team led by Tom Norris sent to capture a North Vietnamese army officer compromised on landing. Fierce

exchange of fire for three-quarters of an hour, aided by U.S. Naval gunfire support. During attempt to exfiltrate, Norris is hit and left for dead by LDNN accompanying SEAL Team. Engineman 2nd Class Michael Thornton returns to recover Norris' body, but discovers that his officer is still alive. Thornton carries Norris to beach, and then swims out to sea with him on his back. Team recovered by supporting vessel. Thornton awarded Medal of Honor.

1973
January – Paris Peace accords signed, bringing U.S. involvement in Vietnam to an end.

1978
Elements of SEAL Team Two begin planning and training for counter-terrorist role, becoming known as "Mob Six." This forms initial element of SEAL counter-terror capability.

1980
SEAL counter-terrorist team formed under Commander Richard Marcinko, designated as SEAL Team Six.

1983
UDTs disestablished or reorganized into SEAL Teams.

23 October – President Reagan launches Operation Urgent Fury, the invasion of Grenada following serious instability on the island after the murder of the former Prime Minister and several of his followers by the faction supporting the new premier.

24 October – Mission by SEALs and USAF Combat Control Team to reconnoitre Port Salines area ends in disaster when parachute

drop into the sea goes wrong in poor conditions. Four SEALs die. Second attempt at paradrop also fails, but without casualties.

25 October – SEALs seize Grenadian Radio station, but are forced to carry out fighting withdraw when large force of Grenadian People's Revolutionary Army arrives with armored personnel carriers. Radio station destroyed by an air strike from USS *Independence*.

25 October – Members of SEAL Team Six arrive at Governor-General's mansion to ensure safety of Sir Paul Scoon. Team trapped in residence for twenty-four hours until relieved by U.S. Marines.

1985
October – SEALs placed on alert when terrorists seize Italian liner *Achille Lauro*. Terrorists disembark before SEALs can assault ship, but SEALs involved in capture of the terrorists when the airliner carrying them out of Egypt is intercepted by U.S. Navy F-14s and forced to land in Italy.

1987
SEALs support Operation Earnest Will in Persian Gulf, as part of U.S. forces protecting oil tankers from attack by warring parties in Iran–Iraq War.

21 August – Iranian mine-layer *Iran Ajr* disabled by U.S. helicopters; crew captured by SEALs.

19 October – Operation Nimble Archer launched in response to attack by Iranian missile battery on tanker *Sea Isle City*. SEALs destroy one Iranian oil platform being used as a base for operations by Iranian

Revolutionary Guards, and seize documents from another.

1988
14 April – USS *Samuel Roberts* hits a mine. U.S. Navy launches Operation Praying Mantis, in which air and sea attacks on Iranian naval targets are carried out. SEALs are tasked with boarding Iranian oil platforms, but damage inflicted by gunfire from supporting US destroyers makes this task impossible.

1989
June – last SEALs depart from Persian Gulf.

17 December – U.S. launches Operation Just Cause to remove Panamanian Dictator General Manuel Noriega from power. SEALs carry out first mission of the operation, disabling Noriega's private jet at Paitilla airfield. Controversy follows the death of four SEALs and the wounding of nine others, with some commentators later averring that the mission is not one appropriate for the SEALs to carry out.

20 December – SEALs sink patrol boat at Balboa Harbor, knocking out 50 per cent of Panama's naval capability.

1990
2 August – Iraqi forces invade Kuwait. International outrage leads to sanctions against Iraq. SEALs involved in enforcement, boarding vessels suspected of carrying contraband cargo to Iraq.

1991
16 January – SEALs carry out reconnaissances of Kuwaiti beaches to provide information for projected amphibious assault.

Information obtained dissuades General Schwarkopf from allowing Marines to attack as it suggests that any landing attempt would be fraught with difficulty.

24 January – SEALs participate in capture of Qurah Island, first piece of Kuwaiti territory to be liberated.

23 February – SEAL team led by Lieutenant Tom Dietz carries out diversionary operation to confuse Iraqis into believing that an amphibious assault on the Kuwaiti coast is imminent.

2001

11 September – Al-Qa'eda terrorists attack World Trade Center and Pentagon with hijacked aircraft, killing over 3,000 people. U.S. demands to Taliban government in Afghanistan for extradition of Osama bin Laden go unheeded.

7 October – US Forces launch Operation Enduring Freedom against Al-Qa'eda and Taliban forces. SEALs participate in direct action missions and strategic reconnaissance tasks into 2002.

2003

19 March – Operation Iraqi Freedom launched against Saddam Hussein and Iraqi regime. SEALs secure oil platforms in Gulf to prevent environmental terrorism as U.K. Royal Marines and U.S. Marines land on Al Faw peninsula.

1 April – A SEAL team (supported by Army Rangers and USAF Special Operations forces) rescues Private Jessica Lynch from Iraqi captivity.

NAVAL SPECIAL WARFARE COMMAND ORGANIZATION

SEAL Teams are part of Naval Special Warfare Command, which is responsible for all elements of naval special operations. It includes the SEAL teams, SDV teams and Special Boat Units. The commander of Naval Special Warfare Command (COMNAVSPECWARCOM) is an admiral. Special Warfare Groups are commanded by a captain, as is DEVGRU. SEAL Teams are headed by a commander—a far cry from the early days when the Teams were led by lieutenants.

A reorganisation of SEAL Teams took place in 2001/2002 under plan NSW 21. This created two new SEAL Teams (Teams Seven and Ten), although this was accomplished by reassignment of personnel rather than an expansion in numbers. SEAL Teams have moved from a previous structure of eight 16-man platoons to one of six 16-man platoons.

Naval Special Warfare Group 1 (NSWG 1) – Coronado, California
SEAL Team One
SEAL Team Three
SEAL Team Five
SEAL Team Seven
SEAL Delivery Vehicle
   Team One
Special Boat Squadron One –
   Special Boat Units 11, 12 & 13
Combat Service Support Team

Naval Special Warfare Group 2 (NSWG 2) – Little Creek, Virginia
SEAL Team Two
SEAL Team Four
SEAL Team Eight
SEAL Team Ten
SEAL Delivery Vehicle
   Team Two
Special Boat Squadron Two –
   Special Boat Units 20, 22, 24
   & 26
Combat Service Support Team

Naval Special Warfare Center – Coronado, California
NSWC is the training center for Naval Special Warfare Command.

Naval Special Warfare Development Group (DEVGRU) – Dam Neck, Virginia
As its name suggests, DEVGRU is responsible for the development of naval special warfare techniques and equipment. There is evidence to suggest that it is the successor to SEAL Team Six, and thus responsible for specialized counter-terrorist operations.

INDEX

PICTURE CREDITS

Aerospace Publishing: 13t, 148, 198, 224b, 245b;

Amber Books: 13b, 15, 16t, 30, 34, 35t, 39, 48, 52, 61b, 83, 105, 169, 181;

De Agostini UK Ltd: 35(b), 51, 111, 220, 241, 243, 247;

TRH: 8-9, 10, 11, 14, 16b, 17, 18, 19, 20, 23(both), 24-25, 26, 27(both), 28, 29, 31, 32-33, 43, 44-45, 49, 61(t), 62, 63, 64, 65(b), 66(both), 67, 68, 69, 70, 71, 72-73, 74, 76, 77, 78, 79, 81(U.S. Navy), 84(b), 86-87(U.S. Navy), 88, 89(U.S.Navy), 90-91(U.S. Navy), 92 (U.S.Navy), 93 (U.S.D.oD), 96, 97, 98, 107, 108, 113, 116, 120, 121 (U.S. D.oD), 122, 133 (TRH/U.S. Navy), 137, 138-139, 140, 142, 146-147 (U.S.Navy), 149, 150 (U.S. Navy), 155 (U.S. Army), 157 (U.S. D.oD), 161, 162-163, 164, 165, 166, 167 (U.S. Air Force),168 (U.S.D.oD), 170-171 (U.S.D.oD), 172t (U.S.D.oD), 172b (U.S. Navy), 173 (U.S.D.oD), 174, 175, 176 (U.S.D.oD), 177 (U.S.D.oD), 178 (U.S. Army), 179 (U.S.D.oD), 180, 182 (U.S. Navy), 183 (U.S.D.o.D/U.S. Air Force), 184, 185 (U.S.D.oD/U.S. Air Force), 186, 187 (U.S.D.oD/U.S. Air Force), 188 (U.S.D.oD), 189 (U.S.D.o.D/U.S. Air Force), 190 (U.S. Navy), 191 (U.S. Air Force), 192-193 (U.S. Navy), 195 (U.S. Air Force), 196, 197 (U.S. Navy), 199 (U.S. Navy), 200 (U.S. Navy), 201 (U.S. Navy), 203 (U.S.D.o.D/U.S. Air Force), 204 (U.S. Navy), 205 (U.S. Air Force), 206 (U.S. Navy), 207, 208 (U.S. Navy), 209 (U.S.D.oD), 210 (U.S. Navy), 210-211 (U.S. Navy), 233 (U.S. Navy), 234, 235 (U.S.D.oD), 236 (U.S. Navy), 237, 242 (U.S. Navy);

TRH/U.S. National Archives: 21, 85, 136, 194;

U.S. National Archives: 22, 36(both), 37, 38, 40, 41(both), 42, 46, 47, 50, 53, 54, 55, 56, 57, 58, 59, 60, 65(t), 75, 80, 82, 84t, 94, 95, 99, 100, 101, 102, 103, 104, 106, 109 (both), 110, 112, 114-115, 117, 118, 119, 123, 124, 125, 126-127, 128, 129, 130, 131, 132, 134-135, 141, 143, 144, 145, 151, 152, 153, 154, 156, 158, 159, 160 (both), 202, 232;

U.S. Department of Defense: 224t, 225, 226, 227, 228, 229;

Robert Genat: 211, 212-213, 214, 215, 216, 217, 218, 219, 221, 222, 223, 238-239, 240, 244, 245t, 246, 248, 249;